Cascadia

FIELD GUIDE

Cascadia

FIELD GUIDE

ART | ECOLOGY | POETRY

edited by
Elizabeth Bradfield,
CMarie Fuhrman,
and Derek Sheffield

MOUNTAINEERS
BOOKS

MOUNTAINEERS BOOKS is dedicated to the exploration, preservation, and enjoyment of outdoor and wilderness areas.

1001 SW Klickitat Way, Suite 201, Seattle, WA 98134
800-553-4453, www.mountaineersbooks.org

Printed in Canada
Distributed in the United Kingdom by Cordee, www.cordee.co.uk

27 26 25 24   3 4 5 6 7

Copyeditor: Jennifer Kepler
Design and layout: Jen Grable
Cartographer: Martha Bostwick
Front cover illustration: *Eastern River Cluster* by Justin Gibbens; back cover illustration: *Chum Salmon* by Chloey Cavanaugh; spine illustration: *Western Redcedar* by Sarah Van Sanden
Artwork on page 360: Joe Feddersen, *Echo 03, 2019*. Photo Credit: Mario Gallucci
Illustration on page 400: *Ten-lined June Beetle* by Xena Lunsford

This project was supported, in part, by a grant from 4Culture.

Library of Congress Cataloging-in-Publication data is on file for this title at https://lccn.loc.gov/2022038595

Mountaineers Books titles may be purchased for corporate, educational, or other promotional sales, and our authors are available for a wide range of events. For information on special discounts or booking an author, contact our customer service at 800-553-4453 or mbooks@mountaineersbooks.org.

Printed on FSC-certified materials

ISBN (paperback): 978-1-68051-622-7

An independent nonprofit publisher since 1960

This book is for fellow beings—for those who leap,
flap, walk, root, crawl, swim, and slither.
It is for a region we love and would love to care for more fully.
And it is for you, dear reader, for your own wonder and engagement
with the terrifically diverse and ever-changing place we call Cascadia.

Contents

Tidewater Glacier 22

Muskeg 46

Pine Forest 176

Eastern Rivers 204

Shrub-Steppe 232

Montane 254

Cascadia Cento

If I were water, I'd catch in the cup of you,
a charm against entropy.
How to fight the insuperable pain of unbelonging
roosting (safely) below my caged window?
Reach, brace, resist, avoid, deflect, split, notch, rustle, shake,
    bend and shimmy.
The racket of sandhill cranes and the peep-whistles geese make—
waves of awakening air vibrated above the stillness of melting
    snow.
The animals and the plants. They care nothing for our likes.
Which of us is animal, compromising root systems as we forage?
Who could resist touching the moon, if it came down, in its
    thousand little bodies?
Imagine a land breathing and rolling with blue
through the firedamp of grey air and the final smudge of scarlet
    that was the sun.
Even now, I cannot detail each way I perceived you—
Wet-sticky-salty-gritty—alive.

A cento is a poetic form composed entirely of lines from existing poems. Here, the lines come from this anthology, one from each community. Only punctuation has been changed.

ALASKA

Copper R.

YUKON

•Valdez

Mt. St. Elias
/Yaas'éit'aa Shaa ▲

•Yakutat

Mt. Fairweather ▲
/Tanaku

R   •Juneau

O   C   K   Y

Dixon Entrance

Queen Charlotte Sound

C o a s t

Haida
Gwaii

Cascadia

N

P a c i f i c   O c e a n

0   100   200   400

Miles

CANADA

UNITED STATES

ALBERTA

BRITISH
COLUMBIA

Columbia R.

M O U N T A I N S

MONTANA

Mountains

▲ Mt. Waddington

Vancouver .

**Bitterroot
Mountains**

Columbia R.

Spokane

Cascade

**Columbia
Plateau**

WYOMING

Salmon R.

Salish Sea

Seattle .

WASHINGTON

Olympic
Mountains

▲ **Mt. Rainier/Tahoma**

**Sawtooth
Range**

▲ **Mt. St.-Helens/Loowit**

IDAHO

Astoria .

. **Portland**
**Willamette
Valley**

. **Boise**

Snake R.

Willamette R.

OREGON

UTAH

Mountains

. *Crater Lake*

Klamath R.

**Mt. Shasta
/Ako-Yet**

NEVADA

Eel R.

CALIFORNIA

Introduction:

Welcome to Cascadia

Welcome to rugged mountains, lush temperate rainforest, icefields, rolling plains, high desert, fertile lowlands, and hundreds of miles of shoreline, highway, and trail that span international boundaries and homelands.

Welcome to the home of Madrona, Geoduck, Giant Palouse Earthworm, and Cassia Crossbill. Welcome to a distinctive place beloved by current residents, many Ancestors, and visitors. And welcome to a new way of seeing: where poetry, art, and ecology might work together to envision not just a place, but a rich engagement with place.

Upon first hearing the word Cascadia, some might focus on the Cascade Range, but its roots actually lie in the waters of our region. Cascadia is defined, according to the Sightline Institute, by "the watersheds of rivers that flow into the Pacific Ocean through North America's temperate rainforest zone." That's a big zone!

Cascadia stretches from Alaska's Prince William Sound in the north to Northern California's Eel River in the south, from the Pacific coast to the Continental Divide. Alaska's panhandle, British Columbia, Washington, Oregon, Idaho, Northern California, and even edges of Montana and Wyoming are held in Cascadia.

WHY BLEND ART AND SCIENCE? TURNING STEM INTO STEAM

Most traditional field guides help people identify plants and animals by describing their appearance, sounds, range, behavior, and, in some cases, relationships with people. In this guide, we honor that important information in the stories included with each being, and we counterbalance and amplify it with more subjective engagements: art and poems.

A drawing or poem might not tell you the average life span of Steller's Jay, but it tells you how you might feel to have Jay on a branch by your shoulder. A painting might not offer the identifying field marks of Eulachon, but it may give you a sense of what it means to shimmer up a river.

So much of twenty-first-century education has prioritized STEM (science, technology, engineering, and mathematics), but for all that STEM provides, it does not offer a way to ethically engage the heart. Through art, we can connect more fully with the non-Human world. In *A Child's Christmas in Wales*, Dylan Thomas's list of dreadful "Useful Presents" includes "books that told me everything about the wasp, except why." Well, in *Cascadia*, the *why* matters, and art and literature are wonderful ways to express love, wonder, and meaning.

CASCADIA'S ORIGINS

Cascadia holds glaciers, plains, rivers, volcanoes, tidelands, and many, many people. From Tlingit and Haida of coastal Cascadia to Nimiipuu of the interior, from westward-moving colonial settlers to Norwegian and Cambodian immigrants to Mexican and Chinese migrant workers whose children came to call this place home: we are Cascadia.

The word Cascadia was first used in 1892 when the community of Cascadia, Oregon, was established fourteen miles east of the current city of Sweet Home. It was Bates McKee who first used the word Cascadia to define a region in his 1972 book, *Cascadia: The Geologic Evolution of the Pacific Northwest*. David McCloskey, a Seattle University bioregionalist, then used the term in 1993 to describe and map a "land of falling waters" defined by "a true matrix in which things are naturally woven together."

Since that time, Cascadia has been used as a unifying term for many people in the Pacific Northwest, particularly those who are interested more in watersheds than arbitrary political boundaries.

BIOREGIONALISM AND CASCADIA

A bioregion is defined by the characteristics of the natural environment rather than by Human-made divisions—essentially, a "life place." The term *bioregion* helps describe our understanding of Cascadia. Bioregionalists know that Humans and our cultures are part of nature, not apart from it, and we should focus our efforts on building sustainable relationships within our sociological and ecological environments.

This special field guide grows out of our own bioregional sense of place. We know Cascadia as "a communion of subjects, not a collection of objects," as cultural historian and self-described "geologian" Thomas Berry states and as many First People have always believed. In this book, we have done our best to honor the wisdom of the First People. If we have failed, that is our own failing. Traditional Ecological Knowledge (TEK) is the evolving knowledge acquired by First People over thousands of years through direct contact with a bioregion and its beings. Influenced by the lore and practices found in TEK, we want to transcend sustainability and honor Cascadia in a way that expresses reciprocity. This essential relationality has given us an array of phenomenal gifts. Shouldn't we be wondering how we can give back?

ANOTHER/OTHER: ORIGIN AND VISION WITH SOME NOTES ON NAMING

In addition to bioregionalism and some key ecological thinking, *Cascadia* has also been influenced by a new phenomenon: the literary field guide. We are glad to acknowledge the other editors, artists, and writers who guided us: *The Sonoran Desert: A Literary Field Guide* and *A Literary Field Guide to Southern Appalachia* were inspirations for us, and *Cascadia* shares much with these other beautiful collections.

It was important to us that our field guide embody our vision of our region as much as words, images, and paper can. Instead of *species*, we like the term *being* to refer to our neighbors. Whereas *species* feels dry, dusty, and objectifying, *being* feels vital and full of agency. We are Human beings living among Bird beings and Plant beings and so forth.

Our vision is also expressed in our choices of grammar and capitalization. In the ecological stories we have written for each being, we've capitalized names in order to honor them (Brown Bear browses on Salmonberry). In that same spirit, Devil's Club is not *it* but *they*. This decision was inspired by *Braiding Sweetgrass* author and founder of the Center for Native Peoples and the Environment, Robin Wall Kimmerer. Her embrace of *ki* as a pronoun and the work of many others guide us to acknowledge the agency and animacy of non-Human beings.

HOLDING THIMBLEBERRIES: SOME NOTES ON ORGANIZATION

This is not a comprehensive guide but an introduction, a starting point favoring depth over breadth. Instead of using traditional taxonomic divisions (mammals with mammals, birds with birds, etc.), we've done something else. To better reveal the many cohesions that make up Cascadia, we selected and organized 128 iconic and endemic beings, such as Mountain Goat, Redcedar, Canada Jay, and Rocky Mountain Snail, into thirteen communities, some of which include Temperate Rainforest, Urban Shore, Eastern Rivers, and Pine Forest. Our thirteen communities might be thought of as life zones. They overlap and represent much but certainly not all of Cascadia. Our guide takes readers generally from north to south, with a jaunt here or there east and west.

Loosely describes our sense of organization. If you've ever had the pleasure of picking Thimbleberries, you know that only a loose grasp will allow the berries to retain their integrity. Squeeze too tight, and they'll go to mush. Likewise, it is our hope that a loose grasp of these communities and beings will allow readers to have the most complete sense of the diversity, wonder, and connection that is Cascadia.

In these communities, beings are tied to each other as habitat (a tree hosts a bird's nest), as sustenance (one eats another), and in looser, more mysterious ways (Elk bugling echoes the air over Pearly Everlasting). The temporal nature of place, it should be noted, is highlighted in two communities of Cascadia: Tidewater Glacier and Loowit–Mount St. Helens. Time is a clear and present part of place and ecology in these two communities.

GETTING TO KNOW CASCADIA

How do you get to know any being? Observe, smell, listen, dream, share stories, research, imagine. To really get to know *anyone* takes time. It takes mind, heart, and memory. To pay attention, to attend, is a sensual, devotional, and intellectual act. Through curiosity, we can discover the wildness and wonder in the beings we walk among every day: Salal, Raven, Coyote, Red-osier Dogwood.

This guide encourages a wide-ranging spirit of engagement. We want to celebrate both knowing and wondering. In our being stories, we have included many examples of our own sensory interactions. But don't take our words for it! Please find your own sun-warmed duff, your own Ponderosa Pine. Lean in, touch, and smell.

Take this collection into the field, by foot or by ferry. Open it as a Chinook wind blows through grasses, riffling the pages; let rain patter down on it from overhanging Garry Oak; set your morning mug of coffee on Oregon Junco's page, holding it open as you watch birds hop through a Snowberry patch. Stand in a Pine Forest and read Bill Yake's "The Tree as Verb." Let those words in your voice enter into the consciousness of those lives. It is our hope, and our experience, that your senses will work in combination with your imagination to make pure Cascadian magic!

Tools for Exploring Cascadia

Your best tools for enjoying Cascadia, in addition to this special guide, are time and attention. That said, a few simple items can enhance your experiences.

- **Binoculars:** Good binoculars are no longer a break-the-bank purchase. Look for 8x40 or 10x42 binoculars. The first number is the magnification; the second number is the diameter of the objective lens in millimeters (a larger lens lets in more light). Birders mostly prefer 8-power binoculars. The editors particularly appreciate waterproof, warrantied, barrel-shape binoculars (we are clumsy, and we drop things and hike in the rain). Image-stabilized binoculars are cool, but if you can do without, you won't worry about running out of batteries.
- **Hand lens:** A small loupe like a jeweler uses is helpful for looking closely at plants, lichens, and rocks. Seek a sturdy 10x lens and put it on a string. You can wear it around your neck as you walk.
- **Notepad and pen:** So old school! But it's true. Anything will do, from a Rite in the Rain notepad (founded in Tacoma, Washington) to a stapled set of scrap paper. A pencil never freezes, and the Fisher Space Pen is able to write upside down as well as in freezing temperatures. Taking notes, making lists, and sketching can help focus your attention. A smartphone is a good tool too.

VOICES OF CASCADIA

All of the voices here, from the editors to the poets to the artists, have resonant ties to Cascadia. They either grew up in Cascadia or spent significant time here. In assembling this book, we wanted voices that would speak to, from, and for Cascadia out of deep connections.

We wanted voices and visions that have been shaped by this place, and we wanted diverse voices that reflect the rich cultures within Cascadia—urban and rural, Native and settler, Canadian and American—and diversities of gender, race, sexuality, and more. As we gathered literature and commissioned people to create new work, we were newly amazed by the vast talent Cascadia has nurtured.

When we began seeking writing for this guide, we turned first to our shelves, finding iconic voices like Ursula K. Le Guin, Robert Bringhurst, Nora Marks Keixwnéi Dauenhauer, and William Stafford. They are here. Then, we wanted to invite this-generation writers like Rick Barot, Rebecca Hoogs, and Xavier Cavazos. We reached out, asking writers if they had work right for this guide and if they could recommend others we might want to contact. And so on and so on. We wanted to cast a wide net, and we have.

Even after all that, we found that we had forty-four beings still in need of poems. This presented an opportunity for us to include voices important to the region, such as Garrett Hongo, Rob Taylor, Claudia Castro Luna, and Dorianne Laux. These poets, along with forty others, answered our call and created poems specifically for this anthology.

In seeking artists, we followed a similar route, thinking of people whose artistic practice ties them to the land and whose art embodies a range of aesthetic styles. *Cascadia*'s artists work in ink, cut paper, pencil, and pen; their styles range from realistic to fanciful. The work you find here was created especially for this guide. We are honored to have art from widely celebrated artists like Joe Feddersen and Justin Gibbens, and we are equally thrilled to honor work by artists who have to date received less recognition in the art world, such as Travis London and Sarah Van Sanden. We love, visually, how their work ties the beings of each community more closely to one another.

These amazing Humans represent the beautiful diversity of Cascadia.

THE WORDS THAT SHAPE HOW WE ARE HERE AND WITH WHOM

Throughout the creation of this anthology, in the search for poems and artists, and in our writing, we have worked to reflect Cascadia inclusively—culturally and historically. The stories, knowledge, and language of the Native people of this region are crucial to the work of science and understanding. Part of the work, then, of this anthology, is to offer some of the Native uses, names, and stories of beings herein. This text is by no means exhaustive, but merely an introduction, a reminder of the rich cultural and scientific history that lives in the languages (both awake and sleeping), the people, and the beings of Cascadia. There exist wonderful texts and storytellers that can expand your knowledge should you wish to learn more about any one of the beings, cultures, poets, and artworks in this volume. In the Resources section, we've listed the print and online references we've relied upon. We have also crafted a shorter, introductory set of resources for you. The artist and writer biographies in the back of the book will open doors for you to walk through as well. We invite you to further your understanding—as we look forward to increasing our own.

In regard to our use of Indigenous names and words, our intention is to honor the First People's knowledge of the beings of Cascadia. We also don't want to assume a knowledge that we, as editors, do not have. For that reason, we only use Indigenous names for beings in cases where we feel sure that we are honoring the people and beings correctly. Because different people prefer different language when referring to themselves, we use the words Native, Indigenous, First People, and First Nations interchangeably and with the understanding that these collective terms hold within them distinctive cultures.

We recognize the deep, diverse Native landscape and the hundreds of tribes that have called this place home for thousands of years. Throughout this book, you will encounter words and names from the first languages of Cascadia. It is our hope that these offerings add a richness to the text and a reminder of the many people who have relationships with these beings and the many names given them. In every instance that uses names or words of a first language, we have done our best to give the most widely accepted spelling and capitalization. We know these ideas may change over time, and we encourage all to seek out the history and names that beings have known for thousands of years, to nurture an understanding of First People's relationships—and to deepen your own, whoever you are. Perhaps also you might wonder, what do these beings call themselves?

Welcome to Cascadia. We are so excited for the connections you will build as you spend time with the beings and stories of this place. We hope that this book inspires you to start making stories, poems, and images of your own.

—*Elizabeth Bradfield, CMarie Fuhrman, and Derek Sheffield*

Tidewater Glacier

Art by Chloey Cavanaugh

At the end of an ice-carved and twisting fjord, miles inland, you meet a rugged, raw, crevassed, vertical wall of ice rising from the sea. Slivers of brilliant blue and dark lines texture the ice face, which might be miles wide and hundreds of feet tall. The water below the ice is milk jade, clouded with finely ground rock.

A crack, a momentous crash and splash, then ice rebounds upward from beneath the sea's surface. Terns and gulls hover above the roil, awaiting the stunned fish that a glacial calving—for that's what this is—might offer. Harbor Seal rests on previously broken-off floating ice chunks, safe from Bigg's Killer Whale. Ice pops, rolls, melts, and tinkles as it moves with tides, winds, and currents. At the fjord's edges, just above the glacier: newly exposed land, rock untouched by air or sun for thousands of years, unsoftened by mosses, grasses, shrubs, or trees.

In Cascadia, there are many glaciers high in the mountains, but only a few of these rivers of ice flow down and touch the sea, thus becoming Tidewater Glaciers. Patagonia, Greenland, Nunavut, Cascadia—there are not many places in the world that are home to this remarkable community. This is a special space. A place that asks for deep reverence and awe. The southernmost Tidewater Glacier in western North America is Le Conte Glacier, just outside Petersburg, Alaska. Glacier Bay National Park and Preserve, in the northern edge of Cascadia, is famous for the presence, influence, and rapid advance then retreat of glaciers. Each year, millions of people travel to see Margerie and Grand Pacific, the living, moving glacial boundaries of Glacier Bay's northern reach.

Thousands of years ago, most of Cascadia was covered by ice. The great Cordilleran ice sheet began near Denali in Southcentral Alaska, flowed down over British Columbia, then squeezed east of the Olympic Mountains to carve what is now the Salish Sea. The eastern edge of the sheet reached nearly as far as Missoula, Montana. As the ice advanced and melted, it shaped valleys and fjords, flatlands and rivers. This glacial retreat continues to this day—both part of a natural cycle and at a rate now accelerated by Human-caused climate change. Some glaciers from that transformational time remain. Some of them still kiss the sea.

In the realm of Tidewater Glacier, adventurous beings thrive: beings willing to travel into untested spaces. Chum Salmon takes an odd turn and finds a new stream to spawn in, Wolf ranges along the shore and discovers a new source of fish, Fireweed shoots up in the hardscrabble scree of moraines, and Red Alder starts fixing nitrogen, creating soil for plants who will follow. This is a place of action, transition, and flux. It's a thrilling place. A place of beginnings . . . and endings.

EVA SAULITIS

It Begins in Ice

I don't know what we expect to find: something blue
& pretty, not how the world begins in ice, not how it's still
being created. Here past & future exactly the same.

How we float in between slickensides, our fingers poking
out of fingerless gloves. We belong to the older world,
clad & lush. This creation of our country, chaotic, wild,

doesn't recognize us. We weren't born yet. The ice pulls back
unlike a tide, exposing nothing alive, just natal parts:
Rock flour, newborn scree, a template for the first lichen.

The glacier's intelligence is unfathomable to us.
Who, hiking up the moraine to where the ground's barren
could feel at home pitching a tent in a field of debris?

Even the alder thickets don't invite us to build a fire,
squat with a mug of smoky tea, listening to the one
sparrow claim his undisputed terrain over & over.

In the morning, we pack to go & we're relieved, hearing
sudden cracks as a face gives way, unloading another wall
of Jesus ice into the innocent milk of the fjord.

There are places on earth that aren't our home, scenery
about which, cameras cocked, we can't say, "When you look
at this, you can see forever," and not be afraid.

Here past and future always backing away, leave us
marooned. If we put our ear to the ground,
we won't be reassured. We don't belong here. We never did.

Common Raven

(Corvus corax)

You know Raven. Raven screams, swoops, sings watery clucks, makes guttural
trills, and can mimic Human speech. Trickster Raven gave us (and has sto-
len from us) the sun and is the second of two moieties (or sides) in Tlingit
and Haida cultures (for Tsimshian, Raven is one of four phaitries). Raven is
supremely powerful and iconic in Cascadia—and, indeed, anywhere they range.

You can distinguish Raven from Crow by tail shape: Raven's is slightly pointed
at the tip, like a diamond or spearpoint; Crow's is flat. Shaggy of neck, heavy
of bill. Raven. How big? Nearly two feet long with a wingspan twice that. How
long-lived? Up to thirty years. What does Raven eat? Seeds, rodents, nestlings,
eggs, carrion, and more. Hunters (Wolf or Human) will follow Raven to find
food, and Raven will hunt in groups to bring down larger prey such as Hare.

What remarkable details are left to discover of this well-known bird? The four
or five young fledged each year to life-mated Raven couples often stay together
through their first winter. Raven is the largest of the "perching birds," a group

that includes diminutive Kinglets and suburban Robin. Raven, as with their cousin corvids like Crows and Jays, are the most recently evolved avian order with the largest number of species—which some say is a reason for (or perhaps an indicator of) their high intelligence.

To come upon Raven roosting in the Cascadian winter can be a haunting experience: in the cold air, a tree rustles, jockeys, and mutters with birds (up to eight hundred have been counted in a roost, though there could be a mere dozen). Come day, Raven will depart and disperse to forage, but at night, they gather . . . Who knows what stories they tell.

ROBERT DAVIS HOFFMANN

from "Saginaw Bay: I Keep Going Back"

He dazzles you right out of water,
right out of the moon, the sun and fire.
Cocksure smooth talker, good looker,
Raven makes a name for himself
up and down the coast from Nass River,
stirs things up.

Hurling the first light, it lodges
in the ceiling of the sky,
everything takes form—
creatures flee to forest animals,
hide in fur. Some choose the sea,
turn to salmon, always escaping.
Those remaining in the light
stand as men, dumb and full of fear.

Raven turns his head
and laughs in amazement,
then dives off the landscape,
dividing the air
into moment before
and instant after.

He moves north, Kuiu Island, Saginaw Bay—
wind country, rain country,
its voices trying to rise through fog.
The long tongue of the sea
slides beneath the bay.
Raven is taken in by it all:
sticky mudflats horseclams squirting,
rockpool water bugs skitting,
bulge-eyed bullheads staring through shadow,
incessant drizzle hissing.
Oilslick Raven
fixed against the glossy surface of infinity.

Map Lichen

(Rhizocarpon geographicum)

When scrambling over rocks, pause to examine what's beneath your feet. It's quite possible that the patches of gray, black, white, or green that you notice underfoot are not the rock itself, but actually lichens pasting the stone.

What's a lichen? A rhyme will guide you: Freddie the Fungus met Alice the Algae, and they took a Lichen to each other (with some side help from Cyndi Cyanobacteria and sometimes Yanni Yeast). Lichens are incredibly complex; they're actually a few different beings living intertwined lives. Basically, a fungus provides structure and protection from the elements, and an algae offers sugars

via photosynthesis. With this pairing, a lichen is a self-sustaining organism able to thrive where most other beings cannot.

While many lichens are difficult to identify to the species level, Map Lichen is an exception. Map Lichen grows in continuous, loosely oval patches made of black circles filled with slightly raised neon-green centers spreading in a tile-like pattern. As with many crustose lichens (lichens firmly cemented to a surface without any liftable edges), Map Lichen grows slowly and steadily, annually increasing by about one millimeter. How slow is that? For comparison, the earth's tectonic plates move about fifty times that rate. In fact, Map Lichen's growth is so predictable that patches of them can be used to estimate how long a given rock may have been exposed to air by glacial retreat, rockslides, or other processes. The arrival and establishment of lichen is one of the ways newly exposed rubble moves toward soil, as the lichen traps dust and provides usable nitrogen.

As with all lichens, Map Lichen is both hearty (they can survive in dormancy for long periods, withstand extremes of heat and cold or wet and dry, and exist solely from what is wafted to them through air) and vulnerable (they pick up whatever pollutants are around them).

Lichens are an indicator species for air quality: areas with poor air have a dearth of lichen diversity, while clean air supports an abundance of different lichens. Look around, wherever you are, and consider what Lichen is telling you.

REBECCA HOOGS

What Eats Around Itself

My great-uncle Larry was, for a minute,
the oldest living man in America at 111.

I explain DNA to my son as a code.
We have the code, he brags

to people who do not have the code,
as if we could break into the safe

of ourselves, unlock a long life.
The oldest living organism is the map lichen,

a lichen that looks like
it knows something about somewhere,

a map licking Sharpie-black.
How is the air quality index back

home? A map lichen went to space
like dog or monkey or man

and was exposed to the map-less lack
of atmosphere, and shrugged:

I felt nothing. Extremophile.
The west burns for a third summer.

My backyard is solid with smoke, a gravestone
like the ones we played on as a kid, my mom

tracking the genealogy of other families
while we hopped from grave

to grave or scraped away lichen
growing into the grooves

where names once were.
Ash from the crematorium

of the sky snows onto the Subaru.
Linnaeus called lichens the "poor peasants

of the plant world" and was wrong.
They care nothing for our likes,

which they will long out-live,
out-eat, out-like.

Fireweed

(Chamaenerion angustifolium)

"When fireweed turns to cotton, summer's soon forgotten" is a common saying in Cascadia. The iconic visibility of Fireweed is a bright part of the Tidewater Glacier community and of any disturbed habitat like recent burns or roadsides. Indeed, Fireweed was one of the first plants to appear after the eruption of Loowit (Mount St. Helens). This beautiful being is nearly everywhere in North America, except the southeast. Fireweed is also found in Europe and into Russia and was one of the first flowers to bring color to London's bombed lands in the wake of World War II. There, one of the names for this being is Bombweed. Other plants eventually crowd out this bold trailblazer; five years after a fire, Fireweed's presence begins to wane as other beings edge in (it takes longer in more challenging ecologies, like Tidewater Glacier, where soil is just developing and new habitat is always available as the glacier churns on).

Fireweed is unmistakable: a tall, bright spear of magenta blossoms that go to fluff and drift from long, splayed pods in late summer. Look into Fireweed's blooms and you might surprise Bee bumbling in the turquoise pollen. Fireweed begins blossoming low on the stalk, then color and blooms steadily climb; each flower lasts about two days, and within the bright bowl of petals, the male organs (stamens) mature first, then the female organs (pistils) develop. This timing helps ensure that pollen is dispersed to other flowers in the area. By late summer, the blooms are gone, and the seeds, like those of Dande-lion or Milkweed, float out on breezes to find new, open soil. A single Fireweed plant can produce eighty thousand seeds!

Fireweed is used by many people in Cascadia: Haida make cord or twine for fishing nets from the stalk's fibers; Coast Salish find the seed fluff useful in weaving and padding. In British Columbia, excellent Fireweed patches can be owned by First Nations families. Fireweed's flowers provide ample nectar and thus excellent honey. Fireweed's tender spring shoots are a fantastic source of vitamin C; when steamed, they taste like asparagus and are an important early spring vegetable in Cascadia.

NANCY SLAVIN

Fireweed

—for Angela

> You are a new soul
> sprouted like a seedling
> that for eons wind has blown
> on white fluffy wings.
> Abandoned on earth
> bereft of your home,
> left only the hurt
> of blood-red rhizomes
> rooting in plots
> of industrial waste.
> You wonder if this lot
> is a perennial mistake.
> For the ache of your body
> stretched toward the sun
> with primroses budding
> positively burns.
> But all around, each hour,
> more are being captured.
> Bright pink flowers
> swell into capsules
> which, in spite of fear,

by the light on which they feed
open to the air
millions of angelic seeds.

Chum Salmon

(Oncorhynchus keta)

Chum, Calico, or Dog Salmon gets one of their names from the Chinook Jargon word *tzum*, meaning "spotted" or "blazed," and another from the fact that most people feed their dogs with this fish. Salmon for dogs? Such extravagance speaks to Cascadia's abundance of fishy riches. Five Salmon live in Cascadia, one for each finger, and there's a rhyme to help you remember them: Chum/Dog rhymes with thumb, and a dog is a chum; Sockeye/Red, sock 'em in the eye with your first finger; King/Chinook, biggest fish, biggest finger; Silver/Coho, silver on your ring finger; Pink/Humpies, for your pinkie finger. The whimsy of this belies the deep, spiritual presence of Salmon in Cascadian cultures. Without Salmon, Cascadia's rivers, art, forests, songs, seas, and feasts, past and present, would be shadows of themselves.

Is that Chum Salmon thrashing in the shallows of a river where fresh meets salt? Look for a greenish body barred vertically with reddish-purple, zebralike streaks. At sea, Chum is metallic green blue along their back and has black speckles, similar to both Sockeye and Coho; a large fish, only Chinook surpasses Chum in size, though the two Salmon have very different life histories. Chinook is the long-distance river runner, and Chum likes it near the mixing zone where rivers come into the sea.

Chum Salmon spends very little time in freshwater. Newly emerged Chum fry are ready to enter bays and estuaries as soon as they have absorbed their yolk sac; this takes about three months, during which they keep themselves safe by living within the gravel of the riverbed. At fry stage, four thousand Chum would weigh only two pounds, about as much as two loaves of sliced bread. When they return as adults three and four years later after swimming and foraging through the wild Pacific (usually only 1 percent survive), a spawning mass of four thousand adult Chum has a biomass equivalent to over two male Elephants!

Chum is able to spawn in the shallows and intertidal areas of streams, unlike their cousins, and is the most widely distributed of all the Pacific Salmon. Chum does not usually travel miles and miles upriver—they rarely go farther than one hundred miles inland, which may sound like a lot but is nothing compared to King Salmon, who may swim as much as two thousand miles upstream to spawn. Chum is an ideal firstcomer to newly revealed streams and rivers, such as those created by the retreat of Tidewater Glaciers.

LUCIA PERILLO

Chum

How come we all don't have the luxury of our ghosts?
The way some paintings of salmon
show their spectral versions of flying.
License, you might say,
for the artist to put dead fish in the sky.
Instead of leaving them as they are
when you see them wilting in the eddy:
two tons of major spent-sex stink.
Yet see how everyone skips so giddily around the trail—
eyeballing the spawning from this cedar bridge.
As if they're sure we will be cohorts
in the rapture about which the bumper stickers speak,
as if we really will ascend someday to swim among the fishes.
All of us: see how good we are,
so careful not to kick stones down into the creek.
I'm just trying to get a handle on how it would be
if we made love one time in our lives
(after days spent on the interstate)

before we lay down to die so publicly in shallow pools?
While the other forms pass by and point
to educate their frenzied children:
See the odd species. They chose love.

Red Alder

(Alnus rubra)

Are you approaching a shoreside wall of green? Work your way in beyond the trunks and branches that have grown since a Tidewater Glacier retreated, and you'll probably find a trail made by Brown Bear or Sitka Black-tailed Deer just inside the shadows. That living fence? That lush, thick barrier of green-leaved and many-branched shrubby bushes? This is most likely Red Alder (or Sitka Alder, a close cousin). Red Alder thrives along the margins, whether a slide, a shore edge, a trail, or the raw ground revealed by a glacier's retreat.

How will you know Red Alder? This tree's catkins dangle golden from bare branches before they have leafed out with their characteristic eye-shaped, serrated leaves, and their lima-bean-sized cones hang on through winter. You won't see a flashy show of color from this tree in fall—Red Alder clings to green. Don't be fooled by Red Alder's pale bark, which looks almost birch-like. The true bark is a lovely brown, but lichens cover Red Alder's older limbs and trunk, not hurting the tree—on the contrary, this lichen cloak most likely helps protect Alder from sun and wind. Still, look for a smooth, pale trunk if you're seeking Red Alder.

Given time, Alder can grow as tall as a six-story building, and Red Alder shines as a being that can, with the help of a bacterial partner, make a living in nitrogen-poor areas, such as the recently exposed rubble of a retreating glacier. In fact, Red Alder gives nitrogen back to the soil and so prepares the earth for other plants that need richer dirt to thrive. Alder is critically important to the succession from bare ground to forest.

The significance of Red Alder to Cascadian people can be counted in many ways. Red Alder is the best wood for smoking Salmon; for feast bowls, dishes, rattles, and masks; for reddish dye used on fishing nets to hide them from Salmon; and for medicine to treat respiratory ailments or as an antibiotic. For forest beings, Red Alder provides important shelter and sustenance. Small birds eat the seeds and nest in the branches. Deer love to browse the young branches and leaves. In so many ways, this tree marks the beginning of a sense of *home*.

DONALD J. MITCHELL

Red Alder

Even the buckled hearts of rockfish
deep under the Sound
pound the barrel drum of red alder.

Far out at sea, salmon gather
from alder
their pink slices of pie. In the rivers,
they bear their rosy pearls home
disguised
in alder's mendicant robes.

And the nitrogen-hunger
dirt feels for alder
is greater than the hunger of James or John;
it's hunger like Shiva's, like Eve's
as she bites down on the ruddy,
troubled flesh
of the universe.

Alexander Archipelago Wolf

(Canis lupus ligoni)

While you are unlikely to see subtle, quiet Wolf as you walk within the shrubby brush near a Tidewater Glacier, you might be rewarded if you scan the shore from a boat as you approach. That smallish form trotting along the tidal edge or lying in the shelter of a bleached beach log, perked ears standing up like two knobs? That's Wolf.

Wolves live elsewhere in Cascadia, but in the islands and along the coastal beaches—from Dixon Entrance in the south to Yakutat in the north—this unique Wolf, smaller and darker than Gray Wolf of elsewhere, thrives primarily

on Sitka Black-tailed Deer. They also eat Beaver, Salmon, and even marine invertebrates and fish. Wolves eating Salmon? Yes. Here, particularly in late summer, when Pink and Chum Salmon are running, you might catch Wolf's family fishing along shallows and pools. In fact, Salmon's plenty might be why the young of this Wolf are more likely to survive than their cousins living in the interior.

Alexander Archipelago Wolf is isolated from the interior Gray Wolf by the Coast Mountains. A strong swimmer, Wolf can move easily between islands in Cascadia. Like most Wolves, these beings live together in dynamic packs of seven to nine individuals and often den beneath old-growth trees near fresh water. They rear their three to seven pups from April to August and have a life span of six to eight years—so short for such a potent being! Legal and illegal hunting, as well as habitat fragmentation, are Wolf's biggest threats, and Wolf's presence and health are tied to that of Deer and Salmon.

Wolf is important to Cascadian people not only as sustenance and a shaper of ecology but also culturally. For Tlingit people, Wolf is a partner to Raven in social structure. Every person's clan is either descended from Yeil (Raven) or Gooch (Wolf), and the balance of these two moieties (or sides) is intrinsic to the culture in all ways, from marriages to funeral rites to potlatches. In other cultures of Cascadia's First People, such as Haida and Nisga'a, Wolf holds an important place as well. What pleasure to consider the life of Wolf as teacher and cultural symbol, what delight to consider how Raven guides us differently. The more we learn about these beings, the more we learn about both ourselves and the worlds—physical and social—that shape us.

VIVIAN FAITH PRESCOTT

šalka

—Sámi: firm path in snow, a marked place.

He reshaped the moon
bit it—chewed light—

played with what remained,
flicked it around

with his tail, tossed it into a pond.
Wolf,

why can't you just leave me alone?
You lure me from this windowsill

with your nightly chant, leaving teeth marks
on my spiny-edged dreams.

Salmonberry

(Rubus spectabilis)

While there are many berries in Cascadia,
only one transforms into a butterfly. Hold
Salmonberry's triad of leaflets in your
hand, and fold the central one back;
suddenly you're holding a butterfly in
flight. If you know this, even before the
bright magenta blossoms, even before the
roe-like cone of berries that range in color
from cantaloupe to crimson appears, you
will know Salmonberry.

Patches of Salmonberry can be owned by
Indigenous families even if they are on lands
designated by the government as public, so take
care to respect local gatherers if you seek to know
this fruit on your tongue. Salmonberry's flavor is delicate:
not the tart astringency of Raspberry, not the sugar punch of Blackberry, but
sweet, tart, and strange with a slight alkaline aftertaste. Collect Salmonberry,
which only grows wild and is not cultivated, gently: these berries do not want to
be squooshed in a bucket. They will turn to mush. For maximum deliciousness,
eat Salmonberry from the branch after a dry spell anytime between June and
August, when the flavor is concentrated and the fruits are firm.

These early-ripening berries are associated with the rising, whirled call of Swainson's Thrush, who is called Salmonberry Bird in many languages. Not only the berries are prized; peeled young sprouts can be eaten as a spring vegetable. As medicine, Salmonberry tea can be used to treat diarrhea, and a Salmonberry poultice of leaves and bark serves as an astringent for burns and sores.

Found throughout Cascadia and endemic to the region—thus both widespread and locally unique—look for Salmonberry in exposed areas such as road edges, recent slides, and glacial retreats as well as in marshy areas alongside Red Alder.

RENA PRIEST

Tour of a Salmonberry

A salmonberry is a
luminous spiral,
a golden basket,
woven of sunshine,
water, and birdsong.

I'm told that the birds
sing so sweet because
of all the berries they eat
and that is how you
can have a sweet voice too.

In my Native language,
the word for salmonberry
is *Alile'*. In Sanskrit, *Lila* means
'*God plays.*' Salmonberries
sometimes look that way.

Every year, they debut,
spectacular in the landscape,
worthy of their genus name:
Rubus spectabilis, meaning,
red sight worth seeing.

Each drupelet holds a seed
and the shimmering secret
kept by rain, of how to rise,
float above the earth, feel
the sun, and return.

Eulachon

(Thaleichthys pacificus)

A run of Eulachon in early spring is an awakening throughout Cascadia.
Before Salmon has returned, before Herring, Eulachon—also known as Can-
dlefish, Ooligan, Hooligan, and Saak—arrives. People wade out into rivers with
wide nets to dip for fish, or they set out traps and hooks to snare these hand-
sized, oily, silver beings who nourish people in more ways than one. Aside
from being a food source, Ooligan is also fatty enough to provide a source of
light. People would—and do—travel hundreds of miles to meet Eulachon when
they run in early spring. In British Columbia's Naas River, people brave the
still-iced waters to catch, share, and trade these fish—a spring bonanza after
the spare months of winter for Human and non-Human alike. Hooligan runs
up other big rivers in Cascadia, like the Columbia and Cowlitz, and wherever

they do, people harvest them. In fact, Eulachon may well be the origin of the word Oregon.

Ooligan is prepared every way you can imagine: baked, fried, steamed, dried, and more. The oil from Eulachon, which has the same consistency as vegetable oil, is traditionally just as important as their flesh and is prized as a dipping sauce and a preservative for berries. Historically, "grease trails" deep into Cascadia's interior allowed people to exchange Ooligan oil with inland, Athabaskan-speaking people.

Like Salmon, Eulachon spends years at sea but is born in and returns to die in freshwater rivers. Ooligan lives three to five years, and at sea is an important food for other fish, seabirds, Seal, Sea Lion, Orca, Eagle, and Bear. Near Tidewater Glaciers, they are recent arrivals, taking advantage of new streams and welcoming other beings to follow.

PAULANN PETERSEN

The Eulachon

Before vine maple leaves
have swollen enough to unfurl,
your sliver-blue glints
leave the salty Pacific.
In flashing masses,
you surge upstream,
muscling against
Cascadia's currents.

With welcome and praise,
with fine-gauge nets,
the people hasten to you,
        their rivers
alight with your life-giving fire.

Bull Kelp

(Nereocystis luetkeana)

Walk along nearly any seaside beach in Cascadia and you'll find cast-up tangles of seaborne ropes—some fresh and gleaming golden brown, some slimy with decay, some salty pale and dried hard by sun. This is Bull Kelp ashore, the flexible, strong strands of which can grow to the length of three school buses in one season and have been used by generations of kids as jump ropes.

For adults, the long, hollow stems of Bull Kelp (or stipes, in biological parlance) historically served as ideal, flexible tubes for storing and transporting Eulachon oil. Dried Bull Kelp, once soaked, can be made into flexible, strong fishing lines; the hollow tube of Bull Kelp also makes an ideal steamer for bending slender wood into fishing hooks. Fresh Bull Kelp can be sliced into rings and pickled for a salty, crisp vegetable—it is delicious.

In the water, Bull Kelp creates a forest to rival that of the one ashore in the Temperate Rainforest and provides life and shelter for many beings: Sea Otter, nudibranchs, young fish, snails, and more. But consider this: it's a forest remade every year. Bull Kelp grows at astounding rates, reaching maximum length in only one growing season—that's an average of over four inches (a hand width) per day! Like many brown algae species, Bull Kelp is cemented to the seafloor with a holdfast, buoyed afloat by a gas-filled bulb (a pneumatocyst), and uses long, photosynthetic blades that fan from the top of the bulb to harvest the sun's energy. Bull Kelp dampens the surf, too, providing safe harbor for nearshore beings.

The life cycle of Bull Kelp is worth delving into, as it involves two distinct stages in wildly complex succession—algae is complicated! You won't find Bull Kelp near the ice of a Tidewater Glacier, as this macro-algae is a later arrival in the wake of a glacier's retreat, but every fjord entrance and island edge in Cascadia glistens with a fringe of Bull Kelp.

HOLLY J. HUGHES

Holdfast

Last week of August: too soon for falling
leaves, fog that rises at dawn, ghosts up
the beach, geese lining up in their ragtag V.

Beyond the sandstone ledge carved
like a torso by the waves, beyond
purple sea stars inching toward tide pools,

ribbons of bull kelp drift with the tide,
ebb and flow, anchored to the sea floor
by a half-inch barnacle called a *holdfast*.

It knows the principle of hunkering down,
riding out the storm, staying put. All
winter, beneath the sea's relentless chop

it holds fast, gives over to each storm,
flows with each rising tide. All winter
it lets go what it can, holds fast to the rest.

That's what we'll do come November.
Hold fast to what sustains: our friends,
a steaming bowl of soup, this beach.

Muskeg

Art by Cori Dantini

The world of Muskeg is otherly and magical. Pools of open water are dotted by bright Buckbean and ringed by Bulrush and minuscule Sundew; mist clings to vibrant green Old Man's Beard hanging from the knobby arms of Shore Pine and Yellow-cedar, trees which, in this challenging environment, grow short and gnarled; Varied Thrush perches and sounds a long, haunting trill over the clearing.

Muskeg is an open, sun-spattered world within the taller, more shaded Temperate Rainforest. Here, Sphagnum Moss (and the peat that Sphagnum becomes) rules all and shapes the landscape. Sphagnum's acidity and ability to hold water creates a soggy, nutrient-poor, fairly anaerobic, and challenging environment.

But crouch down and look closely at the edge of one of Muskeg's pools and you'll find a wonderland: threads of Bog Cranberry with leaves like so many tiny bulbs on a dollhouse-sized twinkly light strand, vibrant pink blossoms of Bog Laurel and Bog Rosemary, stunted sconces of Yellow Skunk Cabbage inviting Beetle to feed, globes of Bog Blueberry, and perhaps even a Rough-skinned Newt slowly making her way back to a natal pool to lay eggs. Deer Cabbage, a favorite forage of Sitka Black-tailed Deer, rises up from the pools where those same Deer, stepping delicately, bend to nibble and drink.

Muskeg, it may surprise you to know, makes up 10 percent of the Tongass National Forest of Cascadia's Southeast Alaska. Even when the forest slopes to the sea on dramatic inclines, Muskeg can cling to steep hillsides, thanks to Sphagnum. Some biologists think that

Muskeg is not a stepping-stone on the progress toward towering Rainforest, but a climax habitat of itself, shaped by water and Sphagnum.

"Muskeg" originally comes from the Cree word for *swamp*, and you'll find these wonderlands all over the boreal and subboreal forests of North America. Elsewhere, like in Scotland, they'd be called bogs—a term that basically means a body of acidified water. Here, we call them wondrous, strange, enchanting . . . a space of light in the forest, a pause in our understanding of the woods, a place we love to linger and consider what might come.

ALERIA JENSEN

Muskeg Speaks

Call me a pause.
A pocket of still
left by the actions of ice.

Call me deer cabbage,
nagoonberry,
cottongrass.

Call me the slow churn
of decomposition,
tannin and peat.

Here, a measure of something—
a lean into slope, a tending
to lowlands, a humility.

Instead of stagnant, acidic,
infertile, say accumulation,
reservoir, container.

We're all summoned
to purpose,
mine is to hold space, water.

You ask what resilience looks like,
where buoyancy lives—
well, consider this an invitation.

Here the eyelash hairs
of sundews catch rain,
labrador tea gives over its resin.

In pools, groundwater
shows itself at the surface,
water lilies swim over bedrock.

Among jackpines,
room for dragonfly-skim,
silhouettes, weightlessness.

You have a choice—sink or float,
negotiate saturation,
come to rest on sphagnum,

remember your shape.

Sphagnum Moss

(Sphagnum spp.)

Look around: Is the sky above you open? Does Moss beneath your feet rise into
star-shaped minarets? Is it wet? Truly soggy? Are those Moss tufts pale green
or rusty red? Have you sunk to your ankles in the softness?

If so, you might be standing in a Sphagnum-dominated landscape, and
if so, lucky you. Sphagnum creates a world of its own: dwarfed, moist, and
unique. Many have heard of the peat bogs of Europe. Well, that's all due to
Sphagnum, the very one and the same being that makes a Muskeg. There are
about forty species of Sphagnum in Cascadia; this special moss creates habitat,

supersaturated and acidic. Indeed, we would not have Muskeg without Sphagnum.

Sphagnum mosses, unlike other mosses, are constructed so that they are able to store massive amounts of water in their bodies: living cells alternate with "holding cells," allowing Sphagnum to absorb and hold thirty times their own weight.

On dry, sunny days, stand still and listen. The opercula of Sphagnum blow open and spray their spores into the air (you can hear them popping). The practical uses of Sphagnum—now and historically—are numerous: diapers, menstrual pads, bedding, and wound dressings. Contemporary plant nurseries, too, rely on Sphagnum. However, this is less than sustainable. Sphagnum grows slowly, and what's taken away from a bog or Muskeg can't be replaced in a Human life span. Sphagnum bogs are also carbon sinks; pulling out the Sphagnum releases carbon back into the carbon cycle, thus retracting its benefit.

Want to garden differently and with respect for Muskeg? Don't buy potted soil with Sphagnum. Instead, seek products with recycled paper fibers or coconut coir; they won't work as well as Sphagnum, but outside a Muskeg, Sphagnum itself won't work as well either. Want to meet Sphagnum in full Muskeg glory? Oh, do, do, do.

THEODORE ROETHKE

Moss-Gathering

To loosen with all ten fingers held wide and limber
And lift up a patch, dark-green, the kind for lining cemetery baskets,
Thick and cushiony, like an old-fashioned doormat,
The crumbling small hollow sticks on the underside mixed with roots,
And wintergreen berries and leaves still stuck to the top, —
That was moss-gathering.
But something always went out of me when I dug loose those carpets
Of green, or plunged to my elbows in the spongy yellowish moss of
    the marshes:
And afterwards I always felt mean, jogging back over the logging road,
As if I had broken the natural order of things in that swampland;
Disturbed some rhythm, old and of vast importance,
By pulling off flesh from the living planet;
As if I had committed, against the whole scheme of life, a desecration.

Buckbean

(Menyanthes trifoliata)

Muskeg's round pools are, for the most part, dark and open. Their tannin-rich waters are not hospitable to many plants. Buckbean is an exception. Buckbean's rhizome-connected stalks poke up from the water with three finger-length, lance-shaped leaves in each cluster. And the flowers: So frilly! So bright white! So stinky!

Bunches of Buckbean blooms cluster on taller stalks in the Muskeg, blossoming from the bottom up, each pink bud opening to five white petals with a blush of magenta. Long white hairs bristle from each petal so that they look like Stevie Nicks–fringed arms, and a dark quintet of arced anthers splays from the center like little comma afterthoughts. In late summer, those blooms turn to smooth (buck naked?) green seed capsules. They are wild!

There is only one member of the genus *Menyanthes*, and this being can be found widely—from northern Europe to Asia to northern Africa—wherever the right boggy conditions occur. How can there be only one? Perhaps because this plant is able to reproduce asexually, through rhizomes. Perhaps because the Muskeg is a challenging home for so many others. Perhaps because they are perfectly suited.

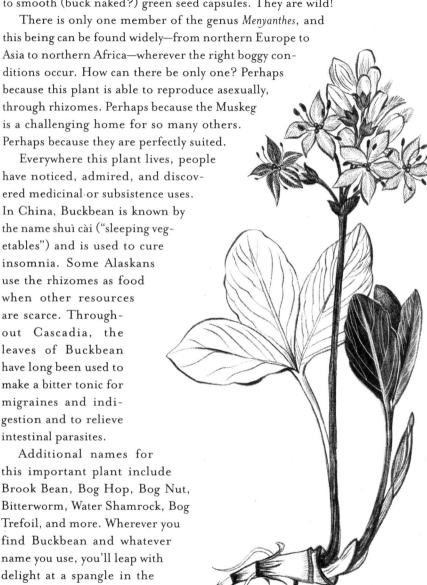

Everywhere this plant lives, people have noticed, admired, and discovered medicinal or subsistence uses. In China, Buckbean is known by the name shuì cài ("sleeping vegetables") and is used to cure insomnia. Some Alaskans use the rhizomes as food when other resources are scarce. Throughout Cascadia, the leaves of Buckbean have long been used to make a bitter tonic for migraines and indigestion and to relieve intestinal parasites.

Additional names for this important plant include Brook Bean, Bog Hop, Bog Nut, Bitterworm, Water Shamrock, Bog Trefoil, and more. Wherever you find Buckbean and whatever name you use, you'll leap with delight at a spangle in the bog.

ROBERT LASHLEY

The Homeboy Speaks to the Snake Lake Buckbeans

(while skipping school to avoid a gang beatdown)

Sway with me, water weeds. We are mimic
metaphors of exodus. Stuck among the woods
we waver, then hold and huddle
above the reflection of dirty water.
Stood still, our cores are meccas to thugs
snapped, our bones are medicine to people
who break us, then run away.

Do the swamps and marshes see our stars?
Do our bodies and fibers simulate light
or give timelines to our extinction?
Is the memory of dead in decaying kinfolk
in the fibers of our tenuous arms
drawn to and inescapable from the river?
Did our showing out our flamboyant selves
deem us vulnerable to the Darwinistic music
of yearly spring currents and rushes?

Oh buckbeans, my kinfolk buckbeans.
Blinding light from black and brown seeds,
Who knows the cost of our rooted pantomime?
Who knows the ubiquity of scrub or star
and the costs when we get spread out on earth?

Varied Thrush

(Ixoreus naevius)

Rain Robin, Gym Whistle Bird, T'án in Haida, you are so bright, beautiful, and iconic that you grace the cover of one of Sibley's early edition bird guides. Your throat and belly are saffron or burnt orange, and your wings and crown a streaked slate. You're like a banked fire.

"Gym whistle" best describes your long trill of a song, which is made of multiple tones ringing at once from the membranes of your syrinx. While we have heard you often and wondered if you were a distant referee at some deep-woods game, and while we know you to be gorgeously and brightly colored, you're rarely seen.

Insect eater in summer, berry eater in winter, ground-hopper, you inhabit the dim understories of Cascadia's forests and make your open-cup nests eye height (or higher) in conifers. You live fast and furious; the oldest Varied Thrush on record was four years, nine months old. (Robin, your close relative, usually lives two years; Bald Eagle, around twenty.)

In some areas you stay all year; in others, you move up and down in elevation as the seasons change. Either way, you're more homebodies than other thrushes.

Bird-watchers beyond Cascadia should keep an eye out—some odd wanderers show up in Robin flocks throughout North America during migration. Habitat loss in old-growth nesting forests has decreased your range over the past forty years. Without you, Varied Thrush, Cascadia's woods would be achingly, quietly unrecognizable.

JOHN WILLSON

Morning

There, again, piercing the chatter of other birds,
a long, single whistle, like a referee's whistle
stopping play, the bird itself hidden by salal
and the shadows of madrona and fir. An arrow
of sound shot back to an alpine dawn: sunlight

through tent fabric turned my hands
blue as the water where I swam until my eyes
opened to the same whistle. Creature that stays
from sight, how do you range from a mountain
down to this sea-level hawking
of crows, the finches gossip?
Again, your pure syllable

taut as a tent line from apex to ground.
Did you see the flap open, watch me crawl
out, scoop water to my face,
scratch my chin when glasses
turned a white blob into a goat
above the pass? First-Thing-in-the-Morning,
I have never seen the color of your soft
throat, but with a wingbeat's ease

you shuttle me across the distance, pump
thin air into my lungs, turn me

toward the dwarf lupine by my boot.
Though you remain anonymous as a painter
of ancient caves, I salute you with a cup of tea
and I would welcome your call as the signal,
the last sound before leaving the flesh, the whistle
bearing me into the wild blue.

Yellow-Cedar

(Chamaecyparis nootkatensis)

Redcedar and Yellow-cedar both have flattened needles and shaggy bark and are used to build canoes, totem poles, and more in Cascadia. How will you know if you're standing before Yellow-cedar? Stroke the branchlets away from the tip of the branch: Yellow-cedar will be prickly and shaggy. Also check the inner bark: if your fingernail exposes yellowish flesh that smells like raw potatoes, that's Yellow-cedar. And sniff again: Yellow-cedar has more of a mildewy smell than the marketed cedar of store candles. These are subtle differences, but they are everything.

Narrower in range than Redcedar, Yellow-cedar is almost entirely bounded within Cascadia, growing from sea level to near timberline from Yakutat to Northern California. Small, stunted trees are often found at the edges of Muskeg communities, even if none are found nearby in the taller Rainforest. Sometimes called Nootka Cedar or Canoe-cedar, in British Columbia this being is commonly called Yellow Cypress or sometimes simply Cypress.

It's hard to underestimate the importance of Yellow-cedar in Cascadia. As with Redcedar, Yellow-cedar is a significant being in Cascadia's Indigenous cultures. Although Yellow-cedar does not grow to the towering heights of Redcedar, their wood is rot-resistant and superb for paddles, masks, rattles, and other important cultural items. In fact, while the inner bark of Redcedar is widely prized, Yellow-cedar's is known to be more durable. Beyond the wood itself, people use Yellow-cedar's new, green needle tips as a tonic in tea. Both Brown Bear and Sitka Black-tailed Deer enjoy Yellow-cedar as forage.

Mature Yellow-cedar are typically 500 to 740 years old, and some can live to 1,500 years, one of the oldest trees in Cascadia. Dieback of Yellow-cedar has been documented since the late 1880s and is linked to climate change. Yellow-cedar has a fine, spreading network of rootlets that allows this tree to thrive in more nutrient-challenged spaces like Muskegs, but these shallow-spreading tendrils are also more susceptible to freezing, which has impacted trees since people have begun measuring them. Decreased snowpack has left the roots vulnerable.

SAMUEL GREEN

Yellow Cedar

i.m. George Sudworth, dendrologist, 1864–1927

We carry a hatchet when we walk the island
beaches, & test each suspect log by hacking
a blaze in its side. That yellow is like nothing
else, not sulphur, not the color of home-churned

butter. A blind man would know the smell
of it under a saw blade, cloying, like cutting
a sheet of hardened molasses. Sanded through
multiple grits, the knots, when oiled, become

exploding suns. What good is knowing
the inner bark of the live tree smells like the skin
of potatoes, that its leaves are tinted bluish-green, or
that its cones are shaped like clusters of tiny

umbrellas, when they come to us scoured
by beach stones, sun-bleached, limbless? Half
a dozen neighbors own lapstrake dories
of straight-grained yellow cedar planks. They float

on the chop like seabirds. Our house is filled
with shelves, desk tops, bench slats, window frames,
kitchen counters, a single bright stripe set in the center
of a table—all formed of island-milled boards

from logs broken free of their rafts. Each morning
that wood breathes out whatever light it took in
the day before, far from its high mountain
slopes, quiet, well-mannered as any good guest.

Roundleaf Sundew

(Drosera rotundifolia)

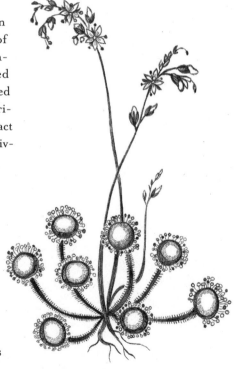

Look at Roundleaf Sundew. Bend down
or squat at the edge of an open pool of
water to see the tiny, beautiful, spoon-
shaped, yellow-green paddles fringed
with maroon eyelashes, each lash tipped
with a sticky teardrop that will trap a curi-
ous Midge or Gnat. Do you cry to attract
what you need? Observe Sundew's carniv-
orous lures.

Sundew lives on an edge, botani-
cally, in that they have less energy-
producing chlorophyll than
other plants, perhaps because
their environment is so challeng-
ing and nutrient-poor. To com-
pensate, Sundew relies on insects.
The presence of a trapped insect
triggers a Sundew leaf to curl inward
and digest the flesh. Ants in the Mus-
keg take advantage of this, in some cases

scavenging nearly two-thirds of Sundew's horde. In Sweden, these acidic leaves are used to curdle milks for cheese and treat warts.

What about Sundew's flowers? They don't get as much attention as the hungry, sticky-tipped leaves, but they are delicate, white, and ephemeral, blooming on a spindly stalk above the low-spread leaves, opening one at a time, day by day, starting from the bottom of the stalk. Wind and hovering insects can pollinate Sundew when the flowers are open, and in evening, when they close, Sundew self-pollinates. If conditions are too challenging for the production of seeds, Sundew can reproduce vegetatively from leaf buds. Sundew truly has found many ways to thrive! You won't find Sundew in the shade, though; they flourish only in sun.

ANNE HAVEN MCDONNELL

Edge Lover

> I call you edge of the floating logs
> lover, edge of the roadless north end,
> edge of loons under cliffs whose babies,
> I pray, survive the eagles this year.
> I call you edge where the wolves den,
> edge of the lake where rough-skinned newts
> float up in dream, limbs and fingers spread,
> then swivel back to depths.
> I call you edge we heard a deer scream,
> a scrape of wet humpback breath.
> I call you edge we had to work for,
> paddling miles against chop. Edge
> where we undress worry, shed our human
> regret. Edge of hunger, lover of edges,
> of rangy bog, of this big floater,
> a cedar log that doesn't spin
> but sinks a bit beneath our feet. I call
> you edge lover, flirting in your floating
> garden of moss, your open mouth
> of leaves, fringed in red hairs, tipped
> in sunlit drops of sticky sap. Off the edge

of your world, we dive deep, open
water bottles underneath, sit with you
on the sun-drenched log,
drinking lake.

Yellow Skunk Cabbage

(*Lysichiton americanus*)

The deep, lush, paddle-shaped leaves of Skunk Cabbage are one of the first greens to green in Cascadia's spring, pushing up even through snow with a metabolic heat of their own creation. In fact, the bright yellow "bog lanterns" of Skunk Cabbage emerge even before the leaves and glow in understory light. Their warmth, shelter, and smell draw in Beetle and Fly, Skunk Cabbage's prime pollinators. These early lights are a message to people, too, as traditional wisdom says that, in Alaska, when Skunk Cabbage appears, it's time to fish for King Salmon.

One of the first flowering plants to evolve, Skunk Cabbage was on Earth before Bee and birds and other sweet-lured, nectar-loving pollinators. Shelter and a slight carrion scent are Skunk Cabbage's enticements. Peer into Skunk Cabbage's yellow sconce and examine the spadix, that club studded with over one hundred greenish-yellow, petal-less flowers—surely you'll find many small beings inside. In Cascadia, our Yellow Skunk Cabbage does not have the stink of their Eastern, Radicchio-colored cousins, though they do offer a pleasant musk.

If you notice a uniform scallop taken from each tip in a splay of Skunk Cabbage greens, that's a sign of Deer nipping the young leaves when they were furled together (Deer also likes the tips of the flower stalks). Do you see upturned earth and shreds of white tubers in a patch of Skunk Cabbage? That was probably Brown Bear digging for a good meal. While people don't savor the lush vegetation because of intense oxalic acid, which causes a burning sensation similar to what some feel upon eating mounds of Spinach, there are a multitude of uses for these large, resilient leaves: food storage, steaming wraps, and basket liners. The roots of Skunk Cabbage, which is related to Taro, a staple in

Hawaiian and Polynesian cultures, have traditional medicinal uses for treating respiratory issues.

In the Muskeg proper, Skunk Cabbage is small in response to more acidic conditions, but in a rich, damp area by a stream, they can grow as tall as your waist. Nothing more fully evokes the forest primeval than a swath of Skunk Cabbage.

MAYA JEWELL ZELLER

Skunk Cabbage

Your spiked
flower
hardly knows

its own allure. Like
lemon cookie, like
hooded

clitoris. Shake you
and you let go
dew.

Your name
means dew
in Hebrew,

my mother tells me
at thirteen.
I've spent

the day staring
at skunk
cabbage, rubbing

the stamen
glow
between fingers,

learning
its curve,
and ah!—the pulpy

bumped berries
fleshing
its core. If I

were water
I'd catch
in the cup of you,

swamp lantern,
I'd reside in the light,
the rosette

of your hips.

Rough-Skinned Newt

(Taricha granulosa)

Oh, sweet, low-bellied, goose-pimpled crawler of the Rainforest's moist fields
and Muskeg's edges. Your back is the color of Cedar bark, your belly of Yam
flesh. We crouch to find you under Skunk Cabbage leaves, snugged in Sphag-
num, but we don't pick you up, tender amphibian the length of a palm, both
because of what the goop on our skin (bug spray, lotion, salve) would do to you
and because of what your skin might do to us.

Tender-bellied as you are, your skin secretes a neurotoxin like that in the
famed Puffer Fish. Even big-handed and thick-skinned Humans have felt your
protest when we've handled you, rashing up at your touch. Ingested, you can kill
us, as one young man in Oregon discovered upon swallowing you on a dare. Only
certain toxin-resistant Garter Snakes can eat you unharmed. Your protection
is, in many ways, a gift to us: because you crawl unafraid, we get to see you. For

this particular Newt, if the orange belly is not enough for identification, check the eyes: Rough-skinned Newt has yellow upper and orange lower eyelids.

Rough-skinned Newt ranges along the wet edge of Cascadia, from California to Southeast Alaska, though populations are disparate enough to be called subspecies. Like other salamanders, Rough-skinned Newt needs water to live, especially in breeding season, when they become partially aquatic. After a male Newt deposits a spermatophore, a female picks it up, then lays her fertilized eggs, attaching them one by one to moss or other aquatic vegetation.

Science doesn't know how long this Newt lives as they hunt insects in the damp Muskeg (maybe twenty years?) or how they navigate to mating sites. They may well use the stars.

MALEEA ACKER

Salamander

Tumbles from my fingers to my cuff
and burrows. Emerald lumined eye, jelly paws,
bark body and tiger belly bright. His tail a blade
of thick sedge. Each ponderous, stop motion limb,
the crook'd elbow, the fan of the toes, the gentle flick
at conclusion of each watery step. Coolness,
the Mogami River. His head nudges
my wrist, no momentum,
the fourth beat rest in tetrameter. How long?
      The back foot lifts,
hovers, a boneless, incandescent home.
I set him on my knee.
I am a bad person, too curious, too eager to touch.
He turns his head to see, then away,
the little mechanism of his thought-calm unpacks itself
      as he leaps to brush,
becomes akin to leaf litter, stick or sunlit shaft.

Pacific Wren

(Troglodytes pacificus)

Over there, out of sight, that liquid warbling and absurdly long, loud, complex
song? Who is that? Of course, it is Pacific Wren. For such a small bird, Pacific
Wren throws a mighty voice. And as he sings (males sing during breeding sea-
son to establish territory), his body trembles, his bill tilts skyward, and his tail
feathers are cocked up, as if alert to his own wild importance.

    A small brown bird with delicate pale spots, Wren is a dapple in the under-
story. To see Pacific Wren, you must be patient; you must seek by staying still.

Look for a flick of movement, or, when the song comes, check each nearby stump and stob, for Wren likes to sing from a stage.

Pacific Wren takes advantage of the abundance Salmon offers, building nests alongside streams that are bound to attract Salmon-carcass-eating insects, their most desired food. Pacific Wren males are hard workers, building multiple nests in hopes that one (or more!) might meet the criteria of a mate, who ultimately chooses which nest to settle upon. This nonmigratory bird maintains their territory all year, though in winter they relax a bit and shrink their boundaries. Although Pacific Wren doesn't live long—the oldest-known bird lived only six years—their songs proclaim an exuberant presence in the shaded woods and over the Muskeg's open pools.

DENISE LEVERTOV

A Wren

Quiet among the leaves, a wren,
fearless as if I were invisible
or moved with a silence like its own.

From bush to bush
it flies without hesitation,
no flutter or whirring of wings.
I feel myself lifted,
lightened, dispersed:

it has turned me to air,
it can fly right through me.

Sitka Black-Tailed Deer

(Odocoileus hemionus sitkensis)

If you know Deer—Mule Deer, White-tailed—you'll be struck by the redness, the smallness, the shore-ness of Sitka Black-tailed Deer. On a boat in Cascadia's inside passages, scan the shore edge if you seek Deer. Sitka Black-tail can often be spotted along the high-tide line, browsing on Sedge or Kelp. It's hard to imagine how the fine bones of their legs don't turn on the slick rocks. The Muskeg, where they browse on Deer Cabbage and Sedge, gives Sitka Black-tailed Deer, quiet and wary as most deer are, open areas to view approaching predators.

Found only in Southeast Alaska and adjacent British Columbia (plus a few transplant populations in Prince William Sound and on Kodiak Island), this Deer is a good swimmer. A Sitka Black-tailed doe only gets to be 80 pounds or so, a buck 120, and his antlers, too, are comparatively small. Wolf and Bear (both Black and Brown) are this Deer's predators, as are Humans. Today, Sitka Black-tailed Deer is the most hunted species of big game in Southeast Alaska. Traditionally (and still), the meat, hide, grease, bones, and antlers are all valuable to hunters and foragers.

Good winter snow is important to this Deer: too much and they can't dig down in winter for browse, too little and the good stuff that persists in winter freezes hard. You may be surprised by how much space Sitka Black-tailed Deer needs to forage and thrive. Studies on Prince of Wales Island show each needs open space roughly the size of twenty-two football fields.

RICHARD NELSON

from *Heart and Blood*

The doe lifts her head and gazes absentmindedly toward me, without blinking, as I stare back through the binoculars. She has enormous, elegantly curved lashes. Her globed eyes stand out from her face so she can look forward along her snout. And the morning sky reflects on their polished ebony surface the way clouds shimmer on still water.

I look from her eyes to the landscape they encompass: the green tangle at her feet; the surrounding meadows; the sodden muskegs that bed and nourish her; the forest that shelters her from rain and wind and snow; the dense thickets that shade and conceal her; the nearby shore, where kelp left by winter storms helps to carry her through the lean months; and the veering tundra heights of Kluksa Mountain, where she finds lush browse and seclusion in the long summer days.

During these moments, I sense—in a way that lies beyond words—how the deer is made from the world in which she lives, how this world is shaped by her existence within it, and how each is deeply infused with each other's wildness.

Salish Sea

Art by Carmen Selam

Protected and wild. Wet and dry. Miles and miles of inlets, bays, islands, river outlets, and even a few rough, ocean-influenced shores. Cascadia's Salish Sea holds all this as well as small shoreside towns and major urban cities such as Vancouver and Seattle, where Great Blue Heron and Bald Eagle fly. Halibut, Geoduck, Salmon, and other beings, including Humans, have flourished in the mild climate, rich forage, and easy waterways of the Salish Sea for thousands of years.

The Salish Sea embraces both the dry San Juan and Gulf Islands, where Garry Oak grows, and the wet edges of Puget Sound and Vancouver Island. What unifies this community is a connection to and shelter from the rough insistence of the Pacific Ocean, as well as the outflow of many mighty rivers, like the Fraser, bringing nutrients and sediments from inland Cascadia. In the Salish Sea, islands buffer, currents roil, and waves rarely break high and hard. Look into the clear, cool water and you might see Moon Jelly pulsing along. On a still day, dark fins of a pod of Southern Resident Killer Whales might slice up alongside a ferry transporting people from one evergreen shore to another. The urban density along much of the Salish Sea today holds an uneasy balance: city dwellers love to look out to the open waters, a respite from the built world, but our contemporary shipping, fishing, and other industries impact the non-Human beings we so appreciate.

The term Salish Sea, which acknowledges the Original People of this region, the Coast Salish, has gained momentum since it was proposed in the 1980s. It has been officially adopted by governments in both Washington State and British Columbia. The name is a wonderful corrective to the former patchwork of names (and international boundaries) that denied the wholeness of these interconnected waters: glacier-made routes that for millennia have given residents shelter, passage, and access to mile upon mile of rich intertidal and coastal edges.

JAN ZWICKY

Small song for the offshore breeze

Sunday, out on my bike,
I drop down from the hill's
brow and you come to meet me: wing
off the water, or two hands
at arms' length, grasping the shoulders—
you're here!—unlooked-for
plunge into the present:
                           quenching thirst
when I had not known I was thirsty.

Southern Resident Killer Whale

(Orcinus orca)

Calm day. Glossy sea. Evergreens reflected along the shore. The world breaks open as the tip of Killer Whale's dorsal fin rises through the surface. Evening light glows the exhaled plume of breath . . . then another, and another, and another, because Southern Resident Killer Whale travels in large family groups. These long-lived whales, the largest member of the dolphin family, have highly structured societies and spend all their lives in matriarchal groups. Older, post-menopausal females are incredibly valuable as teachers and leaders in Orca clans.

It is impossible to overstate the importance of Killer Whale to Native coastal people throughout Cascadia. Blackfish is a spiritually and physically powerful being and can appear threatening, but they are also an ally and teacher. This makes even more wrenching the deep harm done to Southern Residents of the Salish Sea by captures for aquaria in the 1970s. Blackfish families swimming among us now are still reckoning with that trauma. Today, noise pollution, depleted Salmon populations, and the accumulation of environmental pollutants threaten these beings, who are listed as endangered in all of Cascadia.

Worldwide, there are many ecotypes of *Orcinus orca*. Science classifies them all as the same species, though that may well change. Each ecotype is slightly different visually and *very* different from one another culturally: in life history, diet, social structure, and language. Three ecotypes swim the Salish Sea, though they rarely engage with one another and have not mingled genetically for thousands of years.

Called "Resident" because people observe them close to shore as they take advantage of Chinook Salmon runs and because they generally remain in or near coastal waters, this Orca actually roams widely and spends time offshore as well.

For the huge psychic space they occupy, it might surprise you to learn that there are fewer than one hundred Southern Resident Orca in existence (there are also Northern Residents beyond the Salish Sea). Local Humans know their local Orca clans: J pod, K pod, L pod. We track their presence and grieve with them when they experience loss, such as when Tahlequah's calf died after just thirty minutes of life and she, in mourning, carried the body with her for seventeen days.

JEREMY VOIGT

Lime Kiln

We watched the pod pass at Lime Kiln point,
standing together, a family of five, as an otter
emerged and remained fixed on the waterline;

his eyes not towards the milling people in the park,
but eying those larger black and white bodies
making their ponderous way north, mostly invisible,

but the machines tracking their movements told
the Ranger who told us to stay, so we stayed.
They came, with a few boats behind, everything else

out of the way, like the otter flapping his paws
quietly in the water, watching. The black fins
rising straight up, sinking, like a machine needle,

or exclamation points, and I thought of Merwin's
extinction poem, one must always pretend something
among the dying, and have always thought thus.

One must always pretend, though under summer skies
today, and high clouds there is nothing staged
in the otter's caution, in the breaths from the sea—

relief, shock, awe, or all three, percussive as they came.
Then gone, they were gone. And the otter. Though
we know where they are, like stars turning back to stone.

And of the mother carrying her still-born the captain
said, "it's almost human," but after seventeen days
every parent knows, that's the most animal in us all.

Pink Salmon

(Oncorhynchus gorbuscha)

How will you know if the fish before you is Pink Salmon? At sea, the distinction
takes a trained eye, but as the fish return to their homewater river to spawn, Pink
Salmon (like all other Salmon) transforms distinctively. Freckles dot their back
and tail, and males grow a tall hump behind their heads (hence their nickname
"Humpies")—a trait attractive to females that also makes them a bit vulnerable to
predators—and their flanks develop beautiful watercolor-like markings ranging
from pink to gold.

Pink Salmon is the smallest of Cascadia's Salmon and the shortest-lived,
going from egg to spawning in just two years. Even-year and odd-year fish
might use the same river, but because of their predictable life spans, they remain
genetically distinct. You will not likely find Pink Salmon more than forty miles
inland from the sea, and most spawn quite close to river mouths. Like many of
their cousins, Pink Salmon dies after spawning, and their body feeds both future
fish, animals, and the entire ecosystem along the river: trees, Raccoon, Heron,
Fly, and more. Pink Salmon populations have been rising since the 1970s in
Alaska while California and Washington have seen decreases; one theory is that
warming oceans have actually benefited them in northerly parts of their range.

The fishing culture centered on Salmon is sophisticated—nets, spears, weirs,
and other tools were long ago developed to take advantage of the seasonal abun-
dance of Salmon. For thousands of years, people have been catching and feasting
on this fish, which is eaten dried or smoked as well as fresh. Some people, such
as the Nuxalk, consider fermented Salmon roe a delicacy.

NORA MARKS K̲EIXWNÉI DAUENHAUER

from "How to Make Good Baked Salmon from the River"

—for Simon Ortiz, and for all our friends and relatives who love it

INGREDIENTS
Bar-b-q sticks of alder wood.
In this case the oven will do.
Salmon: River salmon,
current super market cost
$4.99 a pound.
In this case, salmon poached from river.
Seal oil or hooligan oil.
In this case, butter or Wesson oil,
if available.

DIRECTIONS
To butcher, split head up the jaw. Cut through.
Remove gills. Split from throat down the belly.
Gut, but make sure you toss all to the seagulls
and the ravens, because they're your kin,
and make sure you speak to them
while you're feeding them.
Then split down along the back bone
and through the skin.
Enjoy how nice it looks when it's split. [. . .]

Mash some fresh berries to go along for dessert.
Pour seal oil in with a little water. Set aside. [. . .]

Then go out by the cool stream
and get some skunk cabbage,
because it's biodegradable,
to serve the salmon from.
Before you take back the skunk cabbage,
you can make a cup out of one
to drink from the cool stream.

In this case, plastic forks,
paper plates and cups will do,
and drink cool water from the faucet.

TO SERVE
After smelling smoke and fish and watching
the cooking, smelling the skunk cabbage
and the berries mixed with seal oil,
when the salmon is done,
put salmon on stakes on the skunk cabbage
and pour some seal oil over it
and watch the oil run
into the nice cooked flakey flesh
which has now turned pink.

Shoo mosquitoes off the salmon,
and shoo the ravens away,
but don't insult them, because mosquitoes
are known to be the ashes of the cannibal giant,
and Raven is known to take off
with just about anything. [. . .]

TO EAT
Everyone knows that you can eat
just about every part of the salmon,
so I don't have to tell you
that you start from the head,
because it's everyone's favorite.
You take it apart,
bone by bone,
but be sure you don't miss
the eyes,
the cheeks,
the nose,
and the very best part—
the jawbone.

You start on the mandible
with a glottalized alveolar fricative action
as expressed in the Tlingit verb als'óos'.

Chew on the tasty, crispy skins
before you start on the bones.
Eiiiiiii!!!!!!
How delicious. [. . .]

Have some cool water from the stream
with the salmon.

In this case,
water from the faucet will do.
Enjoy how the water tastes sweeter with salmon.

When done, toss the bones to the ravens
and seagulls, and mosquitoes,
but don't throw them in the salmon stream
because the salmon have spirits
and don't like to see the remains
of their kin thrown in by us
among them in the stream.

In this case, put bones in plastic bag
to put in dumpster.

Now settle back to a story telling session
while someone feeds the fire.

In this case,
small talk and jokes with friends will do
while you drink beer.
If you shouldn't drink beer,
tea or coffee will do nicely.

Gunalchéesh for coming to my bar-b-q.

Bald Eagle

(Haliaeetus leucocephalus)

Did you know that, once, there was a Bald Eagle nest every mile along the Chesapeake Bay shoreline? That, in the central plains of the United States, Bald Eagle followed Buffalo's herds, taking advantage of what Indigenous hunters left behind? Bounties and the devastation of DDT reduced their number, but with protection, Bald Eagle is coming back across North America. Cascadia, where they have had a stronghold thanks to Salmon and lower pesticide use, is no exception.

Bald Eagle thrives along Cascadia's Salmon shores and is a significantly important being to many First People of Cascadia. In Tlingit, Haida, and Eyak cultures, for example, Eagle is, alongside Raven, one of two moieties between which all people are grouped.

Do you hear a high chittering, somewhat like a guitar pick skipping down a steel string? That, not the arched *skeeeer* that often sounds in commercials alongside a soaring, white-headed, white-tailed raptor, is Bald Eagle's true cry. (*Skeeeer* is the call of Red-Tailed Hawk, or as some like to joke, the Hollywood Hawk.)

Don't worry if you've been fooled; Bald Eagle is a bit of a shape-shifter. Bald Eagle (who takes about four years to reach adult plumage) has larger wings as a juvenile than they will as an adult because their wing feathers are longer to compensate for their lack of experience and skill. That, plus their brown, mottled plumage, causes them to be often confused with Golden Eagle.

Bald Eagle can travel tremendous distances, and in Cascadia, most migrate southward in fall, following food sources. This large raptor, with the wingspan of an NBA basketball player and weighing about as much as a gallon of paint, lives about twenty years, has long-term pair bonds, and returns to the same nest year after year, adding to the structure as part of their courtship ritual. This can really add up! One nature center compares Bald Eagle's nest to the size of a VW Bug. Look for "golf balls" high in the evergreens along Cascadian shores—you'll hopefully spot Bald Eagle perched and watching.

RAYMOND CARVER

Eagles

It was a sixteen-inch ling cod that the eagle
dropped near our feet
at the top of Bagley Creek canyon,
at the edge of the green woods.
Puncture marks in the sides of the fish
where the bird gripped with its talons!
That and a piece torn out of the fish's back.
Like an old painting recalled,
or an ancient memory coming back,
that eagle flew with the fish from the Strait
of Juan de Fuca up the canyon to where
the woods begin, and we stood watching.
It lost the fish above our heads,
dropped for it, missed it, and soared on
over the valley where wind beats all day.
We watched it keep going until it was
a speck, then gone. I picked up
the fish. That miraculous ling cod.
Came home from the walk and—
why the hell not?—cooked it
lightly in oil and ate it
with boiled potatoes and peas and biscuits.
Over dinner, talking about eagles
and an older, fiercer order of things.

Pacific Halibut

(Hippoglossus stenolepis)

Maybe you've seen the photos: a person lying alongside a just-caught fish that is taller than them. Or maybe you've felt the hard tug of Halibut at the end of your line. Was it a "barn door" or a "chicken"? Either way, you reeled and reeled up from the seafloor where Halibut had been. Then, at last, in the dark water, a flash of white: the belly of Halibut.

Halibut lives a long and fascinating life. When born, they look like most other fish finning along through the water, narrow and with their dorsal fins pointing toward sky. But by the time they are six months old, their left eye has moved to the right side of their head, and they spend the rest of their lives on their sides.

Halibut likes to stay on or near the seafloor, where their mottled brown upper skin camouflages them well. Halibut can travel long distances and form spawning groups in deeper waters off the edge of the continental shelf in winter. Females don't reach sexual maturity until they are eight to twelve years old, and the oldest documented Halibut was fifty-five.

As with other important foods, many Native people honor rituals centered on how to prepare and treat the first Halibut of the season. A Kwakwaka'wakw woman traditionally prepares the first Halibut using four different, special knives. When a Nootka fisher catches Halibut, the fish must be put in the canoe with the head pointing toward the fisher and the tail away.

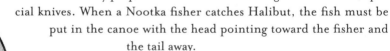

Čibu.d, as traditional Halibut hooks are called by Makah people, are an art form and a conservation tool, due to their specific size and construction. Halibut is a suction feeder, pulling in prey with quick huffs, and the čibu.d design ensures that only fish of the right size will be taken: too small, and they won't be able to fit the hook in their mouths; too big, and the barb won't set.

NANCY PAGH

Among the Vegetarians

(apologies to WW)

Sometimes I would like to turn and live
among the vegetarians—
they are so placid, and so self-contained.

They understand the eggplant's secret
firmness, the *tabula rasa* the bean curd is.

I contemplate them long and long.
Death does not linger on their breath.
The darker crevices
of their cutting boards are safe.

They exist without asking another
animal to kneel and spill itself.

The gentle eyes of the vegetarian
flash liquid revelations
to me and I accept them.

Theirs is an appetite to know and be filled
with the scallop the coho the razor
clam's dignity apart.

My hunger takes
the cream-white flesh of the halibut
the migrating eye of the halibut
the scythe-mouthed strike of the halibut
the graveled bed of the halibut
the cold gray sea of the halibut
in every bite.

It is incised, protean, unassuaged
by toast.

My hunger wants more than the halibut
and finds it in the halibut.

Believe me sometimes
I think if you were as much of this world
as the halibut
I would have to eat you too.

Great Blue Heron

(Ardea herodias)

Like Bald Eagle, Great Blue Heron is not unique
to Cascadia—they are widely distributed across
the Northern Hemisphere—but Heron is so
iconic! Who hasn't thrilled to the leggy sil-
houette of Heron standing in the shal-
lows, stock-still and waiting for prey
to fin by, or overhead, stretched out
and slow-flapping, perhaps sound-
ing an intensely prehistoric croak?

In British Columbia, Great
Blue Heron often builds their
nest near nesting Bald Eagle, one
of their predators. Why? Well, in
coastal British Columbia, Heron
is a local, nonmigratory bird, and
rich Salmon streams provide Eagle
and Heron alike plenty of forage.
Bald Eagle, even though they can be

a predator of Heron, provides protection for Heron from other, non-avian predators, a dynamic called the predator protection hypothesis.

Great Blue lives fifteen or so years, and even though they are large, they are sensitive to disturbance. In Cascadia, they are a year-round resident, and in Canada, coastal populations are listed as a species of special concern. Whether you see them solitarily as they forage in shallows or communally in their Heronry, a cacophonous and intense-smelling place where they build their nest and lay their three to six pale blue-gray eggs, even the most bird-averse viewer can't help but gawk at Blue Heron.

SAM HAMILL

Black Marsh Eclogue

Although it is midsummer, the great blue heron
holds darkest winter in his hunched shoulders,
those blue-turning-gray clouds
rising over him like a storm from the Pacific.

He stands in the black marsh
more monument than bird, a wizened prophet
returned from a vanished mythology.
He watches the hearts of things

and does not move or speak. But when
at last he flies, his great wings
cover the darkening sky, and slowly,
as though praying, he lifts, almost motionless,

as he pushes the world away.

Garry Oak

(Quercus garryana)

Are you a Pokémon fan? You might think you know Gary Oak (grandson of Professor Oak, friend of Ash, and, by all accounts, an arrogant Trainer humbled by his losses). But *Garry* Oak has no reason to be humbled; this being does and should stand proud! If you see a tall, deciduous tree with a broad canopy growing on a dry, rocky slope or in a lush meadow, you may have found Garry Oak, a tree unique in Cascadia—the only native oak north of Eugene, Oregon (another name for this being is Oregon White Oak). Not sure if what you see is this Oak? Look at the bark: it will be silver gray and deeply furrowed. Look at the branches: they will twist and corkscrew. And the leaves: in spring and summer, they'll be shiny green and smallish, with rounded lobes.

It takes about thirty years for Garry Oak to begin producing acorns. Once they do, Garry Oak offers delicious food to Turkey, Squirrel, Vole, other birds, and Deer. Salish people soak the acorns to take out tannins and then grind them for flour; some also roast and bury the acorns in mud to prepare them for feasts. The Cowlitz and W̱SÁNEĆ "four barks" medicine, used against tuberculosis, includes Garry Oak.

Indigenous people of the San Juan Islands, the Gulf Islands, and elsewhere historically kept Oak's savanna habitat healthy through careful burning, and contemporary land care is catching up to this Traditional Ecological Knowledge. Today, Garry Oak habitat is largely taken over by farming, and in the absence of burning, fir trees have encroached, shading the meadows that Garry Oak thrives in. The tree needs light.

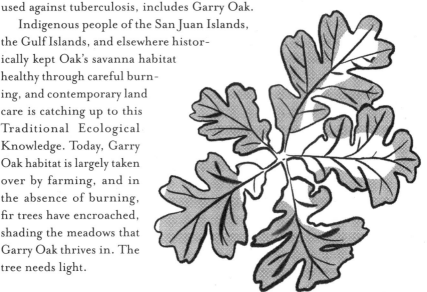

GREG DARMS

In the Last Oak Meadows

The *Large Marble* is extinct, unknown
why, probably fed on wild mustard.
Thirteen specimens held
around the world.

The *Zerene Fritillary* ate violets
as a larva. It can't be found.
It's a name no one can trace.

Propertius Dusky Wings hides in ground debris
over winter. They're raked
and bagged, they're burned
with trash from urban forests.

Moss's Elfin lives with rocks.
The *Ringlet* prefers grass.
Where we see such empty space
we build.

The *Common Banded Skipper*—but try
to find one.

The last meadows are fenced.
The ministry would like to spray, and will.
And will we know
when iridescent wings,
quiet as the oaks,
are gone?

Look close by lupines—
Icarioides Blue is possible.
They say one lives
in a recent clearcut near Shawnigan.

Mardon Skipper

(Polites mardon)

Fuzzy, rusty, small, this flutterer loves to move through fields of Prairie Lupine and Blue Violet (their favorites), sipping nectar. Once, the prairies of South Puget Sound offered Mardon Skipper an excellent home, but those grasslands are largely gone now.

Not sure the butterfly you're looking at is a Skipper? Watch closely: Skipper has a quick, bounding flight (hence the name). Mardon Skipper has antennae that look a bit like a cotton swab: there's a little bent bulge at the end. Their body is furred with subtle gold, and their wings are orange with light rectangular spots.

Mardon Skipper is closely associated with Bunchgrass—they love to lay their eggs on types of fescue, upon which the young larvae munch. Researchers don't know historic populations of Mardon Skipper, because systematic studies were not conducted until the 1980s. Today, there are only thirty-seven known places in southern Washington along the southern Salish Sea, the Oregon Cascades, and north coastal California where you might find Mardon Skipper, and in those places, you won't find many, perhaps fifty or so. If you happen to see Skipper resting in their characteristic pose—forewings at a forty-five-degree angle, back wings splayed wide—sit quietly for a moment and appreciate the subtle beauty of this small, rare being.

Mardon Skipper

We have come here for you,
Small orange blur among the wildflowers
So easily confused with those other butterflies
The Woodland Skipper, the Sandhill, the Sonoran
We come lumbering out of the trees
Too coarse to do anything that you do:

> Fly
> Alight upon a blade of grass
> Sip the nectar from a violet
> Know our place in the world

But with our long-handled nets
Our guides and keys, our close-focus binoculars
We are confident that we will find you
That our witness will make you real
And so then you will be, somehow, safe

Cascade Oregon-Grape

(Mahonia nervosa)

Close your eyes and reach down through the understory at shin level. You'll know Oregon-grape by feel alone: the leaf edges are prickly, unlike any other Cascadian plant. Even in winter you can enjoy this evergreen's shiny, Holly-like leaves, some of which turn a deep, rich red. Mahonia's clusters of yellow flowers, energetic as starbursts, are a welcome brightness in spring, as are the rich, dusky, tart, seedy, purple berries that follow in late summer. Rub your fingers after you pick a berry and you'll find a bit of wax has been given to you by the fruit—a technique to discourage pests and to keep the fruit from drying.

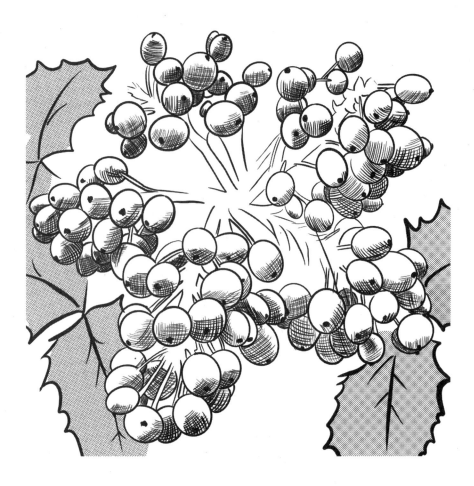

Scratch Oregon-grape's bark and you'll see chartreuse. A bright dye can be made by boiling the bark. If you see a yellow, traditionally woven basket, it is most likely colored by Mahonia. Wool and porcupine quills are also dyed in this way.

In the forest, Deer and Elk may browse on Oregon-grape in winter when other forage is scarce, and White-footed Vole in Oregon's Coast Range eats quite a bit of it. That sunny-blossom nectar? Delicious to Hummingbird. Those berries? Food for birds. That winter foliage? Perfect for tucking under for shelter.

While you won't find the fruit in most supermarkets, Native people have a special relationship with Oregon-grape. The berries, mixed with Salal and Huckleberry, make a delicious jam. The roots, stem, and berries of this plant have long been used medicinally. Medicines from Mahonia, both traditional and newly developed, include those for treating gonorrhea and syphilis, liver disease, canker sores, and more.

RUBY HANSEN MURRAY

A Couple Walks Up the Logging Road

Mid-morning in early summer fog haloes float off whaleback
ridges along the Columbia. A skein of moisture overhead
promises to cool the day a little longer.

We park at the juncture of roads that lead up Nelson Creek or
Alger Creek and walk to the locked metal gate where Camp-
bell Global has posted a list of rules. It's Sunday, no log
trucks will pass, no hunters this time of year.

He wants to see a snake and a bear. Honey bees and a bumble-
bee nectar along the road. She wants to lose weight, to float
up the hill, to walk all day.

We name the points, knobs with scraggly trees like a cowlick.
Crown Point, Wickiup, Skamokawa. Power lines and a
tower.

On the way back to the truck, down the rolling pebbles and
ankle-turning rocks, a black lump of licorice slug.

He says, "If we had taken the other road, we would have con-
nected with the road on the next creek." He draws the road
to the north in the air. "Around that curve is where I saw the
cougar."

Brambles. She says, "Salmonberry."
He points and says, "Oregon grape."
A pause. "Salal."
"Aren't they the same?" he asks.
Mahonia aquifolium, she thinks, smelling the yellow stickiness of it.
"No, Oregon grape has pointed leaves."

He looks for language they can speak, for a project, for joy.
   She studies the sides of the road for paths the elk might have
   taken. She wants to bring a chair, a picnic lunch, to walk
   into the woods left standing, to smell the ground where the
   elk rested.

Off Risk Road, white windows on a shingle wall, a porch the
   length of the house, two chairs ready for evening. The diesel
   engines of ghost trucks and men shouting.

Pigeon Guillemot

(Cepphus columba)

What's that sound, almost out of range, high and piercing, like a dog whistle?
It's Pigeon Guillemot, opening a black bill to reveal a bright red mouth and
sound a message to the world.

Look for Pigeon Guillemot paddling in an eddy by a ferry dock or perched
on the low rocks above tide line where she may have laid two mottled eggs in a
bare, rocky crevice. While eggs are vulnerable to Crow, Raccoon, and others,
once at sea Pigeon Guillemot is not hunted by many, though Orca and Octopus
have been said to sometimes take a few.

You'll know Pigeon Guillemot in breeding season by their black body punc-
tuated by white wing patches and, when they take off from the water with their
heavy flight, their bright red feet with goth-black toenails. Pigeon Guillemot
will be near you in the waters from Alaska down into California, loving the
turbulence of the Outer Coast but generally staying closer to shore and inland
waters than Murre, Auklet, and Puffin (other members of the alcid family).

Most of Pigeon Guillemot's relatives are long-lived (fifteen years) compared
to songbirds, monogamous, and show no visible differences in size or coloration
between males and females—and Pigeon Guillemot is no exception. Like other
alcids, Pigeon Guillemot uses their wings to swim underwater as they chase

small fish. Piggy Gilly (as one editor calls them) hunts closer to the seafloor than most other birds. In winter, Pigeon Guillemot shifts to a more mottled, white-black plumage that is almost a reverse of their summer smartness, but their feet remain gloriously red.

KEVIN CRAFT

Pigeon Guillemots

Dangle bright red legs
floating and diving
like simple sentences
by the ferry terminal—

so close, and closing in—
their glidepaths trimming
acrobatic pilings,
rounding off the long division

of the tide. Spring: Saturday
opens a beer and passes it
around. Dear sunlight,
we missed your clean throw rugs

beating on the bay.
There's no place to get to
but we're going anyway.
Compact. Glossy.

The world still has a thing
or two to show us,
much of which passes
for guillemots today.

Moon Jelly

(Aurelia aurita)

Below you, almost invisible through the surface sheen, a bit of more solid sea, pulsing and pancake-sized: Moon Jelly. Go ahead, reach. Moon Jelly won't sting you, even though there are stinging cells on the delicate short tentacles—your Human skin is too tough to feel them. If you lift Moon Jelly out of the water, they will have a hard time with gravity. Although able to survive the wildest storm, air, skin warmth, and weight will do Moon Jelly harm. You say there's a tinge of lavender in the four horseshoes clustered at this being's center? Yes—though they could also be white or blue, depending on what Moon Jelly is eating—these are the gonads. From here, males and females will send forth their eggs or sperm to find one another in the wide sea.

We have only to look to the sea for the widest array of possibilities of how to live a life. Moon Jelly, like other jellies, has two different forms in their life cycle: a sexual one, adrift at the mercy of the currents, and an asexual one, moored to the seafloor. Clones of upside-down Moon Jelly bud off a seafloor polyp, becoming the floating moons we know. July or August is when you're more likely to see a large number of this delicate being pulsing in the water.

Despite their delicacy, Moon Jelly thrives in conditions that challenge other marine life—namely, seas with lower than normal dissolved oxygen (often correlated with pollution or warm water). Moon Jelly is a carnivore, eating zooplankton, which they trap in a mucus snare and move along toward their mouths by cilia. People eat Moon Jelly, though they're not traditionally a favored food in Cascadia, and creatures such as Ocean Sunfish and Leatherback Sea Turtle rely on Moon Jelly as a cornerstone of their diet.

EMILY WALL

Grace Harbour, Desolation Sound

When we wake the next morning
and look over the side to check the anchor:

jellies, jellies, jellies!
The water around us is a thick carpet

of moon jellies, each little orb pulsing,
rising and falling in the tide swell.

Even though we know better, we can't help
stretching out our hands, reaching down.

Who could resist touching the moon,
if it came down, in its thousand little bodies,

and surrounded us? Sometimes we need
to be chosen. Sometimes we need for belief

to be out of our hands.

Pacific Geoduck

(Panopea generosa)

Low tide. Sandy shore. A sudden squirt arcs into the air above bright green
Sea Lettuce or splayed Eelgrass. Then another a few feet away. And another.
That's Geoduck (pronounced "Gooey-duck"), the largest bivalve in the world,
ejecting wastewater from a siphon. There are many impressive clams in Cas-
cadia: Horse Clam, Piddock, Cockle, Razor Clam. All delicious. But there is

only one Geoduck, a being that can live over 160 years and, after a brief larval drift, never leaves their one chosen, deep-dug home.

If you're wondering whether the brown-tan hose you're looking at in the intertidal is Geoduck or some other sand dweller, examine the inner lining of the siphon. Geoduck's will be smooth, white, and without tentacles around the opening or a harder cap at the top.

You'd like to taste one? Dig deep. Geoduck can extend their long neck to baseball bat length, so to reach the clam's body, you'll have to kneel and stretch down to armpit depth. Typically Geoduck weighs two to three pounds, and while the white shell might fit in your hand like a pocketbook, the body and neck spill over, unable to fit—no need to tuck the soft flesh in the shell when protected by so much sand. Cut the neck into rings and quick fry them with butter and white wine or stir the meat into a rich chowder.

In recent decades, Geoduck harvest has been commercialized, which is controversial. The "farming" involves studding the intertidal with PVC pipes around Geoduck's holes and then, when the time is right, jetting high-pressure water to extract them. Wild Geoduck has few natural predators, though Sea Otter, Dogfish, and Sea Star attack the siphon. For all their iconic presence, our full understanding of Geoduck's role in the ecosystem is poorly understood. What a delicious invitation to study and learn!

ISAAC YUEN

Geoduck

Shell and mantle, foot and siphon, the geoduck buffers itself against the current of time. Entombs its body beneath the ocean floor. Filters the world's tidings over a lifespan normally reserved for land tortoises and bowhead whales. The clam does what it can with this given gift, laying down with dull diligence a growth ring on its shell every year, like its land neighbour the cedar does with its trunk every season, growing out sapwood, building up heartwood. Both are markers of bygone eras and bygone climes. Keepers of records stretching beyond the range of our sapient lives so roiled with love and regret, joys and sorrows. Geoduck safety comes at a cost. Juveniles are free to choose. Free to float in planktonic abandon. Free to link up with and detach from prospective polychaete partners. Yet most will settle upon choice sandy estate to remain for their life's remainder, growing too fat for their foot to ever move them again. If unearthed, a geoduck is unable to rebury itself. Some choices in life can only be made once.

The Nisqually name for geoduck is gʷídəq. Translated from Lushootseed it means "dig deep." In 2009, the British Columbia Supreme Court ruled that the Nuu-chah-nulth people of Western Vancouver Island had no constitutional right to fish their ancestral lands for geoducks, citing that the species was not known until European arrival. In 2019, archeologists uncovered on Keith Island a clambake site containing shells dating back at least half a millennia. Gʷídəq at low tide where the water jets up. Gʷídəq into the past to where the truth lies.

The Chinese name for geoduck is 象拔蚌. Translated literally it means "elephant trunk clam." In Hong Kong where I was born it is prized for its flesh. In Canada I tasted it as a new settler to the Coast Salish lands. My mom brought some home one winter night, weary from waitressing at a sushi restaurant. That first year. That hard house. Where the bathwater in the tub slanted left. Clam sliced thin, blanched quick, no more. Served with a soy and wasabi dipping sauce. A taste and time I can still recall: So sweet, crisp, then gone. Like a childhood, an ebbed memory.

Coastal Urban Woods

Art by Sarah Van Sanden

To stand in the Coastal Urban Woods of Cascadia is to stand in two worlds: in one, the roads, strip malls, and skyscrapers of the built world threaded by medians, parks, and yards and, in the other, a wild tangle of Sword Fern and Salal still towered by Redcedar and buzzed by Mason Bee in secret nooks and crannies. For many Cascadians, this is where our connection to the non-Human world begins.

Steller's Jay, bright and alert as any city kid, hops among the peeling branches of shoreside Madrona, maybe sussing out the developing berries, maybe just curious in a particular corvid way. At night, mostly unnoticed, small Mountain Beaver emerges from an intricate system of burrows to forage, perhaps seeking young Vine Maple (a favorite food), though they must be careful of Barred Owl swooping down from above or Coyote padding the now-quiet greenways.

Wild beings still thrive here in the Coastal Urban Woods, linking cities and suburbs to the places that existed long before the first windowsill or paved driveway. Take a moment. Stand on a curb near the edge of a vacant lot or ravine. There are so many lives going on above and below you in the shadows of branches—yearning, as branches, toward light.

COLLEEN J. MCELROY

The Lost Breath of Trees

an oratorio for vanishing voices, collapsing
universes, and a falling tree . . .
—Lena Herzog, *Last Whispers*

1.

in the days before urban sprawl this town
remained no more than cow pastures
logs skidding down to the harbor
gulls riding them like surfboards
a green belt embraced the one road north
a hundred years they say until the lease expired
in those days trees lining each side threw shade over
hippies and geese bound to the same direction
this was the rain forest and we took
for granted the trees that sheltered the sun
in shimmering light the music of wind
and leaves that left air breathable
we thought the developers would never come
that Eden would last forever

2.

if I remember well the first to go
was the old growth Ponderosa near the school
what a racket all that sawing and sawing
no sapling that one stubborn tough
from thick outer ring to the core
on overhead wires larks crows and common wrens
lined up like jurors surveying a crime scene
chortling and cackling a chorus of *what's*
this what's this come see come see
every so often one broke rank
and swooped toward the cantilevered trunk
as if they could bring back to life those limbs

where each night they had fought to gain purchase
circling as if remembering the canopy
before the thieving ravens evicted them
swirling in all directions birds
leaves one and the same into a vortex until
the tree shivered one last time and fell
still I listen for the rustle of leaves
sweeping clean the air

3.

one morning on the sun-drenched asphalt
a blue feather lay as if fallen by magic
from some child's dream of angels
was there ever a bird so blue so
cobalt perfect from downy barbs to vanes
to fall undamaged by progress
among the squalor of high-rises and noise
of backhoes awakening each morning
was this an omen an augury a straw in the wind
to land here where few trees thrive
you look up at the birdless sky think:
this is a city this a mountain
this a remnant of the rain forest

Steller's Jay

(Cyanocitta stelleri)

With tail and outer wings of indigo and a shawl, head, and spunky crest of
smoky black, Steller's Jay is utterly unique in Cascadia—boldly visible and yet
also able to blend into the shadowed forests of home. Like most members of
the corvid family, the bright-eyed Steller's Jay is inquisitive, noisy, social, and
a good mimic, as well as a member of complex societies, including pair bonds

that appear to be monogamous and maintained all year (rather than only in the breeding season).

Listen for rapid, repeated *wek wek wek* calls or a more melodious, high *chew chew chew chew*, but know that Steller's Jay might also mimic Osprey, Cooper's Hawk, or a water sprinkler. Look for Steller's Jay in the woods or in residential or agricultural areas, gleaning insects, seeds, nuts, eggs, and even small vertebrates (their diet is about one-third carnivorous). Usually, Steller's Jay nests on horizontal branches close to the trunk of an evergreen, building a bulky cup of stems, leaves, Moss, and sticks held together with mud and lined with Pine needles or fur. Inside, two to six blue-white, specked eggs lead to hatchlings who can fledge in only sixteen days and may live for sixteen years.

This beautiful bird, named after German biologist Georg Steller, is the only crested jay west of the Rocky Mountains. There are sixteen subspecies of Steller's Jay in North and Central America. Haida Gwaii, in British Columbia, is home to the largest and darkest group. The Makah of Washington State's Olympic Peninsula have a wonderful story about how Kwish-kwishee got a crest. Seek an Elder who may share it with you and whom you can then thank for keeping such stories—and the connections they honor—alive.

OLIVER DE LA PAZ

from "Autumn Songs in Four Variations"

STELLER'S JAYS
There's one of them, beak upright,
and crown black as a demon's eye.

There's another on the branch above, a lookout.

He's singing to her as the forked alders
sway like sea grass. Meanwhile

the birds barely settle, their blue wings

rising this way and that for balance.
It is November, love, and the jays are hungry.

Winds have knocked over the feeders

and I've stopped setting out suet but still they come—
like little nudges, little threads tied to my thumb.

Soon the mountain passes will fill with snow

and my diligence with the seed will matter
just as these hours with you matter.

How can I keep you safe, knowing

each wayward tree could fall?
Where each evening's breeze rattles the panes?

Where a Steller's Jay calling to the horizon means everything?

Pacific Madrona

(Arbutus menziesii)

Madrona's skin—smooth and bright chartreuse when young, then aging to a brittle cinnamon red that curls from their trunk in delicate papers perfect for writing secret notes—is unmistakable. This tree's white, urn-shaped flowers hang in large, drooping sprays that, in fall, become bumpy orange-red berries prized by Robin, Cedar Waxwing, Varied Thrush, and Quail. People find Madrona's berries bitter, though they can be used as bait for Steelhead, perhaps because of their resemblance to fish roe.

Also called Madrone, Madroño, and Arbutus, Madrona grows tall as a three-story building and bears evergreen leaves that are oval, shiny, and dark (no wonder Madrona was mistaken by interloper George Vancouver as Magnolia). In fact, Madrona is the only broadleaf evergreen native to Cascadia and is North America's most northerly broadleaf evergreen. Madrona does shed their leaves, but not all at once . . . bit by bit, like Sitka Spruce or Douglas-fir. Madrona grows along the coast from southern British Columbia to San Diego, tolerating a wide range of temperatures and rainfall.

You think Madrona is hearty? Think again. Although tough in their ideal conditions, this tree is fragile outside them. It turns out Madrona's health is incompatible with modern, Human land development such as pavement and lawns. Madrona likes sunny, well-drained areas and is fire-adapted, resprouting quickly after a burn. Notoriously difficult to transplant (most likely because of their critical relationship with mycorrhizal fungi), Madrona resists Human interference, so we must learn about their historic ecology in order to nurture them.

Some people call Madrona the "refrigerator tree" because the trunk is always, even in the height of summer, cool. Straits Salish tribes say that survivors of the Great Flood anchored their canoe to Madrona at the mountaintop, and in gratitude for Madrona's help, they do not use the wood as fuel. The tree is sacred.

ELIZABETH BRADFIELD

Succession

In the neighborhood called Magnolia
they've planted magnolia trees
to right an old mistake
made when George Vancouver's crew
saw thick-leaved madronas
on bluffs over Elliott Bay
and misnamed them. Magnolia trees
outside the coffee shop,
magnolia trees—
                    native to this continent
but not its northwest coast, land of cedar
and salal. They are leafed-out,
staked-up witness to our desire
for truthmaking—
                    outside
the post office on Magnolia,
magnolias. Magnolias glossy
and tended by the antique store, fenced
in the sidewalk by the bus stop.

Meanwhile, the madronas,
whose peeling trunks, burnt-orange and sleek,
colors layering from granny smith to pomegranate,
papery with curls I've peeled and scrawled,
here since the last glaciation,
slow-growing and picky,
                    waste away

in neighborhood parks while
beautification committees worry,
worry and try, unable to hear what for madronas
is truth: what the tree wants is burning. To burn

among huckleberry and Oregon grape
then bud from the leftover roots. Moldered
by lawn and dogs and all we've brought
with us to make things nice,
                    the madronas wait
for lightning, for some untended spark
to argue their need against our clipped
and tended ideas of care.

Salal

(Gaultheria shallon)

What is more beautiful, important, iconic,
surprising, and delicious than Salal? Salal's
white-pink, urn-shaped flowers grow in an
arched row along their branch ends, opening
toward earth and beckoning pollinators such
as Bee and Fly into their warmed globes, a
trait shared by many other heath family
plants. Salal's evergreen, leathery, egg-
shaped leaves carpet the gappy under-
story of most western Cascadian forest
communities at shin height, though Salal
can grow to tower at twice the height of
a tall person, given the right conditions.
Because of partnerships with mycorrhizal fungi, Salal can obtain nitrogen and
phosphorus from their surroundings, allowing them to make even clayey soils
a welcome home.

In recent years, Salal's beautiful foliage has become wildly important to the commercial florist trade—so much so that in 1998 a murder was attributed to a fight over Salal fronds. As with any wild being made into a commodity, we must protect Salal as we have protected Sea Otter, Redcedar, Sockeye Salmon, and other beings vulnerable to overharvest.

In late summer, Salal's blueberry-sized fruit ripens to a dusky, deep purple. Somewhat spicy, seedy, and utterly delicious, Salal's berries are traditionally dried into cakes, stored wrapped in skunk cabbage leaves, and then eaten dipped in Eulachon oil. Haida uses of Salal's berries include thickening Salmon eggs, and Salal berry jam is a perfect topping for any pancake, biscuit, or scone. Beware, though: gather only enough for your family. This wild plant, like many others, can't bear the demands of those who live far afield of their rooting—local birds and other beings rely on them!

TESS GALLAGHER

He Would Have

To speak for him is to leave a breath
pulled suddenly from an overlapping realm
suspended in the room. So this morning
snow lightly cupped in salal is raised against
the hillside by fresh ardor alone
because he would have called to me
while putting on the morning coffee
to look out and see it into its island moment,
spiraled double and darkly inward
by our pushing pleasure up another notch
until the world stays as beneficent as it is.
I stand at the window the better to amplify
cool underneath of petals a snow-lit green.
Any unexpected bounty adds him like seasoning
to the day, as when the eagle uses the frayed
sky-green of the neighboring hemlock to
beguile our paired attentions, his white head
at its topped crown washed clean of the past and
the future.

Alert raw knot of infinity.

Blue Orchard Mason Bee

(Osmia lignaria)

Do you like fruit? Send gratitude to Blue Orchard Mason Bee, rarely seen or acknowledged yet a critical fruit tree pollinator. Mason Bee is about the size of Honeybee but shaded a dark, metallic, Fly-like blue. Is that bumbler in a flower Fly or Bee? Watch them hovering over and within blooms, gathering pollen—flies don't do this—it's Mason Bee! Unlike Honeybee, known for their saddlebags of pollen, Mason Bee carries her flowery loot on her belly.

Blue Orchard Bee emerges in early spring to mate. One by one, as soon as temperatures steady out at 55 degrees Fahrenheit, they chew through the chamber where they've overwintered—a tube about the size of a pencil—and emerge. Males, last to be laid as eggs in fall, are first to appear, and they linger by the nest. As soon as females emerge, Blue Orchard Mason Bee mates, and with that accomplished, the males die and the females go on to enjoy their summers.

Mason Bee builds her nest alone rather than in colonies, though she tends to nest near others. She spends the summer collecting pollen, bringing it to her nest (most likely the same tube she emerged from), and kneading it into a ball mixed with nectar and her own saliva. Then she lays an egg on top of the

accumulated pollen. She fertilizes the first few eggs with sperm she's stored, ensuring that these eggs will produce female Bees. The last few, which she lays unfertilized, will become males—these outer-tube males are more vulnerable to predation, but if some are sacrificed to birds or other predators, there will still be females safe in the back to carry the population forward. Mason Bee compartmentalizes each egg chamber in the tube with mud, much as a stone-mason uses mortar.

Mason Bee rarely stings, and urban gardeners welcome them, just as orchardists do. You can make your neighborhood more hospitable to Mason Bee by providing houses—a little research will get you on your way to being a good Bee host.

SIERRA NELSON

Blue Orchard Mason Bee

The mason bee of my 20s
takes herself out to a disco and brings herself home again.
Goes wild in the orchard, 2,000 blooms, but dances
just to please herself, belly yellow with pollen.

She's got no time for honey,
metallic blue-green black sheen,
fly-like to an uncareful eye.

Solitary bee,
home just a little bigger than her body,
a piece of paper rolled around a pencil,
an old reed, a paper straw, really any tube will do.

Industrious,
she teaches herself to bake,
round little pollen cake, mixed with nectar,
a little spit, one egg right on top.

Works with clay,
everything she wants to say
ends in mud, just the way she likes it.

Works alone
but doesn't mind the nearby *zuzz*
of others, maybe even prefers it.

She lives a year, but 9 months you don't see.
She's reading, changing, studying up in her cell
till it's time to crunch out, get dirty.

With the fruit trees she debuts in early spring.
A fling or two, then learns to wall off
each compartment tenderly,
love notes to future selves.

Vine Maple

(Acer circinatum)

Vine Maple's spring cluster-bursts of four to twenty green-white flowers dangle
from maroon stems and cups beneath the season's fresh green leaves. In fall,
this tree's brilliant red foliage glows in open, moist habitats from Northern
California to southern British Columbia (in shady areas, the leaves are a warm
yellow). When planted in clearings or yards, a common practice for this beloved
tree, Vine Maple grows tall and straight to about twenty-five feet (or about the
height of four stacked refrigerators), but in shade the branches twist and turn
and the tree grows low. Vine Maple's flexible, strong shoots inspire Quinault
basket makers to weave carriers for firewood or shellfish, and Vine Maple's
larger limbs can be bent to swing baby cradles or build snowshoe frames and
drum hoops.

Vine Maple's hardiness and beauty have led people to cultivate and welcome
this tree into their lives. Vine Maple is supremely flexible and often bends so that
their crown touches the earth, where they then take root. These natural arches
(to some a tripping hazard), as well as Vine Maple's twisted, spreading limbs
in Cascadia's shaded understory, are a distinctive architecture in our forests.

DAVID WAGONER

For the Young Vine Maples

If they sprout deep in thickets,
Their branches grope
Upward crookedly left or down
And right among tanglefooted elders,
Their leaves stretched out
Through salal, through hazel
For the least light-hold.

If they find no sky halfway
Their own, they stay
Alive where they are, the green boughs
Dipping to root again and again, almost
Unbreakably supple
Under the treads and blades
Of loggers and earth-movers.

But even cut half through, bent
Backward, left for dead, fire-checked
With slash or buried
Crushed in snag-filled ditches,
They will break out by spring
In shadows, searching once more
For light they may never find.

If moved into a garden then, they rise
Slowly and slowly straighten
To a grove of slender trees,
The first to go blood-red and amber
By the end of summer, lingering
Long into every winter
For one death after another.

Mountain Beaver

(Aplodontia rufa)

Look and listen for Mountain Beaver at dawn or dusk in the damp, western lands of Cascadia. Tune your ear for gentle, purring queries. Peer into dim light and watch for the tremble of a tender green shoot. If the bough falls and disappears—tug, tug, tug!—into a burrow, you've seen Mountain Beaver at work storing bits of Fern, Alder, or other delicacies in one chamber of the intricate underground home they have built, and that's most likely all you'll see. Mountain Beaver is secretive and fairly nocturnal in urban areas, although in wilder spaces they forage and nap throughout the day and night.

Mountain Beaver's preference for tree seedlings may be unpopular with domestic gardeners and the logging industry, but there is much to appreciate about Mountain Beaver. Unchanged for forty thousand years, this large member of the rodent family is about the size, shape, and weight of a standard toaster (three pounds), with brown fur, a short tail, delicate hands of tender pink skin, and curved claws. Mountain Beaver's underground lair can range over half an acre and contains chambers for food storage, sleep, and latrines. Another amazing fact? Mountain Beaver hosts the world's largest Flea (*Hystrichopsylla schefferi*), which, unlike other Fleas, is picky and wants only Mountain Beaver as their host.

Traditionally, people hunted Mountain Beaver in the spring and traded their furs. One of Mountain Beaver's many names, Suwellel (or Sewellel) comes from Lewis and Clark, who both mistranslated and misunderstood the Chinook word for the robe made from Mountain Beaver's skins, which is called She-wal-lal in Chinook Jargon (Mountain Beaver is called Ogwoolal by the Chinook, Showt'l by the Nisqually, Squallal by the Yakimas, and Netate by the Tolowas of Northern California). The robe is not the being! Other names for this being are Boomer, Chehalis, and Kick Willy. Why Mountain Beaver for a creature who does not live wholly in the mountains nor is beaver-like? That is your story to invent.

LENA KHALAF TUFFAHA

Inside the Terrarium

At the edge is how I think of it,
our house overlooking a forest
hemmed by a low fence and signs
reminding us to protect the wetland, heart
of its own community. Coyote
and bird songs echo through the alders, frogs chorus
the stream. Bobcats strut along the fence
when they are so inclined, sometimes wandering
into the spaces we've claimed.

I wonder about you, mountain beaver—misnamed ancient,
elusive survivor. Is it you whose chatter and squealing rises up
from the underbrush on evenings when the windows
are open to the dampening air?
Do you burrow beneath the stubborn clay
I've amended for my peonies? Do you scoff
at my young habitation, you who have wandered
among oreodonts and sabre-tooth cats, witnessing
civilizations rise, gnawing on ferns as they crumbled. Which of us

is animal, compromising root systems as we forage,
mapping networks of roads, laying waste stretches
of seedling? You see the suburb best, our webs of pipe and wire,
the somber concrete and layers of lawn and lilacs, our garish
structures, their jaundiced lights blinking on just as you begin
your night rounds. I wonder about you, eyeing us,
how we spiral beyond the glass.

Sword Fern

(Polystichum munitum)

Any shady, moist, coniferous forest not too high above sea level in Cascadia might hold Sword Fern's thigh-high bundles of dark, leathery, evergreen leaves that stand like a strange bird buried in the ground but for an upthrust, brushy, quivering tail. In dry weather, the fronds—due to their rusty spores, which are a favorite food of Mouse—have a distinctive smell, not unlike the dust of sanded wood; in spring, the early growth pops up and unspools more than unfurls.

Sword Fern has never been favored for food by Humans, except for their rhizomes in spring, but Sword Fern's fronds work well as flooring or bedding and can be used as a layer in traditional pit ovens or for storage. Sword Fern is known in many Coast Salish cultures as pala-pala plant because of a children's game in which the contest is to see who can pull the most leaflets off a stem in a single breath while saying "pala" with each one. This game helped train young Nuu-chah-nulth and others to hold their breath, a skill essential in diving to harvest Bull Kelp.

There are at least six *Polystichum* species in Cascadia, but Western Sword Fern is the most abundant. Rusty-orange bumps of reproductive sporangia (spore cases) line the undersides of Sword Fern's leaves, looking like some wild version of candy dots on strips of paper. Sword Fern takes time maturing, and spores are not produced until Sword Fern is one to five years of age; then the hearty, wind-borne bits disperse in the millions.

KEVIN MILLER

Near Vashon Viewpoint

—Point Defiance Park

On the afternoon walk past the culvert
and its signature of small stones, the hill

is a shady mound of sword ferns
lapping at the boles of moss-shagged maple,

second-growth fir, and nurse stumps
big as VW bugs. At the road's edge,

another old man stands, watches
his white-eyed chocolate lab

romp through waist-high fronds
as my springer, as she did yesterday

and will tomorrow, tugs me into
that rustly jungle, her nose to the ground.

What is it about dogs and sword ferns?
I ask my almost twin. He laughs,

says his dog is blind, says
it's all about the mice.

Western Redcedar

(Thuja plicata)

Easily recognized, Western Redcedar is the ultimate icon of Cascadia and considered by many Nations and people as the "tree of life." Cedar's leaves are tiny and strongly flattened, their cones about one-half-inch long, and their bark (usually clear of Lichen or Moss) stretches up the trunk in long strips. The largest Redcedar tree recorded was over nineteen feet in diameter at breast height.

Although people have lived in what is now Cedar territory for over ten thousand years, Cedar was uncommon (and not much used) until 3,500 years ago, when the climate found an ideal balance in which Redcedar could thrive. Look for Redcedar in moist or wet areas below 4,200 feet. There is a population in the Coast Mountains and Cascade Range from Southeast Alaska to northwestern California and a Rocky Mountain population from the British Columbia Interior and Alberta to Montana. Wherever they grow, stand at the base and gawk up—Cedar. The straight trunk of Cedar will be clear of understory, and the wide, drooping limbs will shelter you.

Redcedar is foundational to everything about coastal living in Cascadia. Slow-growing and long-lived (commonly over one thousand years), Redcedar's wood is durable, if not strong, and resists both rot and pests. A single tree can make a canoe sixty feet long (about the length of a bowling lane) by eight feet wide. Totem pole carvers seek Cedar trunks for their impressive size, durability, and workability. The inner bark of Redcedar has been used more than any part of the tree: for clothing, absorbent padding, blankets, hats, and more. This remarkable fiber has clothed and protected generations upon generations of people in Cascadia.

Material for houses can be taken from the tree without felling them if the strips of wood are carefully harvested from standing trees. These culturally modified trees (CMTs) can be found throughout coastal Cascadia if you look closely. The work takes skill. Seek out a video of Jessica Silvey and Robert Joe sharing their Cedar harvest techniques and traditions on the Sechelt reserve to learn more about the details and the deep connection that such work embodies.

BREN SIMMERS

may there be giants

we lean on swaybacked cedar
lone remnant that soars over
second growth notched stumps
the size of hot tubs trunk
worn smooth by hands
exhales a brief flicker
of living memory
750 years old all the time
spent against a cedar tree
will be given back to us
we're told so
lean look up
what of the men
who logged this valley
woodsmen who knew
the scent of spring—
warmed sap
starting to run
the rhythm of their swing
not unlike the sway
of branches above
what gave them pause
to put down axes
and leave this one
giant untouched

this one giant untouched
by crosscut saws axes
what gave them pause
sway of branches
not unlike the rhythm
of their swing sap
starting to run spring—
warm scent of woodsmen
who knew this valley
in the '40s logged it
with horses
who leaned looked up
called her grandmother
exhales a brief flicker
in living memory
hands rough on
the smooth trunk
all around them
stumps
who leaned and left
this one remnant
to soar
above

ERIN FOX

Temperate Rainforest

Art by Erin Fox

Place of rains and water-glint, of deep shadow under tall, tall evergreens, of cool mists where Lungwort Lichen hardly ever dries enough to get crisp. This stronghold of Brown Bear is, beyond the rush of rivers, often a quiet place, though the calls of birds like Townsend's Warbler echo piercingly through the trees. A moss-soft floor eases the paths of Slug; the high, Moss-padded branches of Sitka Spruce host the single egg of Marbled Murrelet pairs. This is a place linked to ocean and interlinked in all ways by Salmon, who brings food to those living here as eggs, fry, and spawning adults.

Ease yourself. Listen to rain patter on the broad-spanning leaves of Devil's Club. Taste a berry, tart and bright, from Huckleberry, Blueberry, Salmonberry, and Twistedstalk. Leave hurry behind. The Temperate Rainforest is a slow-growing community, taking hundreds of years to reach the mixed, dappled maturity so important to Spotted Owl. A slow-rotting place too. Fallen trees here last long enough to serve as habitat for the next generation, which will eventually stand with wide-legged roots straddling the now-absent log they sprouted from, creating a perfect space for kids and Mink to crawl into.

For thousands of years, the lush fecundity of the Temperate Rainforest has nurtured people, and many diverse cultures acknowledge the weave of this relationship in art, ceremony, and song. Even when the earth inland of the coast was covered by glaciers, this sea edge was open.

Cascadia's Temperate Rainforest is the largest on the planet, stretching from Kodiak Island in Alaska down to Northern California's Redwoods. Within that span, there are forests within the forest—different nuances of community. In these pages, we honor northern Rainforest beings. Scientists mark a temperate rainforest as a place that sees at least fifty-five inches of rain a year (about the height of a midsized car) and averages between 39 and 54 degrees Fahrenheit in annual temperature. That's helpful to know. But, really, it's the cool shade, the dampened quiet, the bright green understory, and the sense of water, water, water in the air, in the nearby sea, and deep in the mosses that tell us we are here.

SHERRY SIMPSON

from "The Book of Being Lost"

There's a word that describes the texture of light in the rain forest: gloaming. Few people use this word anymore, except possibly the Scots, but it is the right word to describe the dreamy density of air, the sheen of rain, the way trees rise from the earth, their corrugated trunks weeping pitch, their crowns meshing so tightly that sky splinters into vagueness. A kind of vegetative hush cushions the air, broken only by the raven's thick dialect, the chime of a thrush, the rain percolating through the fine green needles. In the gloaming, it is not day, it is not night.

Biologists call the boundary where landscape changes an "edge"—that place where, for example, a deer might forage in a meadow and take shelter among adjoining trees. In Southeast Alaska the forest includes many internal edges, where one kind of habitat or vegetation eases into another. Animals and birds shift back and forth through these places, seeking what they need from different kinds of habitat.

In human history, too, edges mark the places where event and myth and legend rub together, where people move from one kind of story into another. It is humanity's pride and haunting that we stepped out of the dark woods, out of savagery, sexuality, instinct. We tamed ourselves by striking down frightening forests, flushing out wild animals, baring the horizons. But in the oldest part of our minds, a thick forest stands, inhabited by talking beasts, changelings, wild people and lost children; by nightmares, reveries, and profound silences; by trick of shadow and light; by everything we once were and never will be again.

Banana Slug

(Ariolimax columbianus)

It's all about the slime. Slime for sliding over sharp grit or clinging to smooth glass, strong slime for dangling like a spider, mouth-numbing slime for predator deterrence, body slime for keeping moist, scented slime for attracting mates, and more. Slug slime is an underappreciated and wondrous substance. Look down. Stretched on the path or to one side in Cascadia's wetter habitats, you're likely to see Banana Slug. Olive-skinned, black-dotted, sometimes ivory pale or overall green, Banana Slug is unmistakable and unmistakably large: up to the length of, well, a banana!

No other unshelled gastropod of this forest bests you, Banana Slug. Indeed, you are the second-largest slug in the world. If someone picks you up, your slime gunks to their hands like rubber cement. If we hunker and bend to you, you may relax, showing first your lower, sensory antennae, which search for the chemical signals of organic matter you seek as food, then your upper eyestalks, each topped with the bead of an eye that senses light and motion. You might

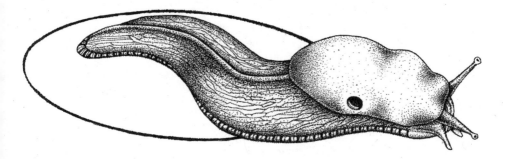

even, if you are feeling relaxed and unthreatened, open your pneumostome, a hole on the right side of your mantle through which you breathe.

Banana Slug is a key part of the Temperate Rainforest community, gliding along, spreading spores, scraping decaying matter on the forest floor with a rasp-like radula (a structure that is both teeth and tongue). While it might seem that such an unarmored, slow-moving being would be vulnerable, the slime (the slime!) protects Banana Slug. There's much more to say about this being, especially about their hermaphroditic nature and fascinating mating habits. For now, we'll stop, suggesting you look deeper at what perhaps once was thought of as a pest in your garden. These underfoot and often-maligned beings can live up to seven years and are very important recyclers of what falls to Cascadia's mossy earth.

THEODORE ROETHKE

Slug

How I loved one like you when I was little!—
With his stripes of silver and his small house on his back,
Making a slow journey around the well-curb.
I longed to be like him, and was,
In my way, close cousin
To the dirt, my knees scrubbing
The gravel, my nose wetter than his.

When I slip, just slightly, in the dark,
I know it isn't a wet leaf,
But you, loose toe from the old life,
The cold slime come into being,
A fat, five-inch appendage
Creeping slowly over the wet grass,
Eating the heart out of the garden.

And you refuse to die decently!—
Flying upward through the knives of my lawnmower
Like pieces of smoked eel or raw oyster,
And I go faster in my rage to get done with it,
Until I'm scraping and scratching at you, on the doormat,

The small dead pieces sticking under an instep;
Or, poisoned, dragging a white skein of spittle over a path—
Beautiful, in its way, like quicksilver—
You shrink to something less,
A rain-drenched fly or spider.

I'm sure I've been a toad, one time or another.
With bats, weasels, worms—I rejoice in the kinship.
Even the caterpillar I can love, and the various vermin.
But as for you, most odious—
Would Blake call you holy?

Northern Spotted Owl

(*Strix occidentalis*)

It's night. You're in the woods. Shush of wind through needles. Patting rain.
Then, improbably, what sounds like someone blowing on a stem of grass trapped
between their thumbs, an echo of a farmer's rising *Soooo-ee!* That's Spotted Owl
calling to a mate in the darkness as they hunt, keeping in touch through trees
and over distance. There are other sounds to attend, hoots similar in pitch to
Barred Owl's *Who cooks for you?* but with a different, slower rhythm. If you eye
Owl silently floating down near you, look for a bark-brown, Raven-sized body
with light spots and no tufted "horns": Spotted Owl.

Return to the area you first heard them any time of year to seek Spotted Owl;
they do not migrate. Sometime between February and April, nesting begins.
Don't look in old Pileated Woodpecker holes for Spotted Owl; rather, peer down
into broken-off tree trunks, old Goshawk nests, or Mistletoe snarls. There, she
will lay her one to four eggs, which she incubates for about a month. During this
time, she is fiercely protective of her nest. Wildlife biologist Janet Millard once
saw Spotted Owl dive-bombing Black Bear who had happened to wander too
close and was running away as fast as they could! After the eggs hatch, Spotted
Owl and her mate then spend another month raising their brood before the
young are ready to fly and forage, following and learning from their parents

for another two to three months. Spotted Owl doesn't necessarily breed every year, and in the wild they can live up to ten years. Lately, Barred Owl, who is more adaptable and more aggressive, has been displacing Spotted Owl. This, along with climate change and fire, is another threat to their voices in Cascadia's forests.

If you hear Spotted Owl, you're lucky. This beautiful being has been in steady decline since systematic counts began in the 1970s. People who lived in logging country during the 1980s may remember the vitriolic owl wars. Spotted Owl was a visible target for those in the logging industry impacted by new technologies and a changing economy, as Spotted Owl's "endangered" status put areas of old-growth forest off limits for logging. Though Spotted Owl can live in second-growth forests, their ideal habitat includes old trees for nesting and large tracts of forest to support enough of their favorite foods: Flying Squirrel, Red Tree Vole, and Bushy-tailed Woodrat. Forests with closed canopies, snags, and generally complex vegetation of differing ages are key—a habitat most often found in older forests. Protection of this forest, and of Owl, benefits all the lesser-noticed lives around them.

YVONNE BLOMER

Spotted Owl as Desire

—after Robert Bateman's painting, "Mossy Branches—Spotted Owl"

True owl. Old-growth owl. Nocturnal
owl. The clock turns by you.
Barking owl. Whistling.
Hooted notes fall from mossed trees.
Old-man moss. Knight's Plume moss. Creeping-
feather moss. Nothing human here except me.
Your eyes a lure. Shoulder-
hunched owl. Padded in your brown
mottled cloak, what are you
tracking? Fogged-in owl, muffle-
feathered owl, patience is
your domain. Bone-lichen
feathered. Lour-browed.
Old strix. What are you
making me into?

Sitka Spruce

(Picea sitchensis)

Is the evergreen branch before you Hemlock or Spruce? Reach out and grasp it.
If the needles hurt, if you flinch a bit, you're in the presence of Sitka Spruce. Is
it spring? Nip the Spruce tips, those bright green bundles of new needles, and
brew a vitamin C—rich tea. Look down, scrape a bit of humus away, and you're
looking at tradition: the thin rootlets of Sitka Spruce are an essential part of the
beautiful hats and baskets created by Haida, Tlingit, and Coast Salish weavers.

This tree's wood has been and is used to make many other specialty items such as concert pianos, guitars, ship planks and masts, and more.

In the Temperate Rainforest, wanderers will often come upon tall reddish mounds of cone flakes and cobs: these are the middens of Douglas Squirrel, who eats the Spruce seeds, then tunnels a home into the insulating hills of cone detritus. Sitka Spruce's shallow-rooting base permits trees to be knocked down by strong gusts, creating gaps of light for Devil's Club and Huckleberry, offering themselves as nurse logs for future generations. In the Temperate Rainforest, wind, not fire, is the forest's primary shaper.

Known also as Tideland Spruce, Coast Spruce, and Yellow Spruce, this being is the largest of the world's Spruces and, like many northern beings, is slow to mature, holding off twenty to forty years until first producing cones. That's okay, though; they've got seven hundred or more years to grow. The largest Sitka Spruce known is in coastal Oregon and stretches 216 feet tall (about the height of a fifteen-story building).

MATT RADER

Sitka Spruce

A Steinway soundboard at core. A knack
for pitch and cords. High strength-to-weight
ratio and knot-free rings mean I sing like
sunlight in honey when played by the right
wind, when let stand in the alluvial pitch,
in the tracks of avalanche, marine terraces,
or wherever else I'm found curing an itch
for sky. The age of true timber races
by on steel stretchers, borne to the ever after
in a pageantry of dust and gravel, machine
oil, the tuneless cackle of chainsaws leaping
to life in the woods. A pair of perfect wings
for that garage-built, jerry-rigged aeroplane,
you can almost hear me humming in the rafters.

Marbled Murrelet

(Brachyramphus marmoratus)

Sitting on the water in summer, squat and dun, looking like a mini-football,
you call, *Keeer*, and we know you, Fog Lark, with your sweet voice sounding over
the water. But how do we even begin to really know you? In summer, when most
other birds are bold, you are subtle: male or female, you're a sweet, mottled
brown, and always, as soon as someone focuses binoculars on you, you dive.
In winter, you're a more striking black and white, a coloration more typical of
your diving cousins, Murre and Puffin.

    Like all alcids (Puffin, Guillemot, Auklet), the water is as much your territory
as is sky, and your wings propel you deep toward fish or quick through forest air
at an improbable fifty miles an hour toward your nest: a high branch mossed
and wide enough for one single egg laid in dappled light. This is where your

summer plumage works to hide you. For years, until the 1970s, you foiled the notetakers who sought your secret nesting site. All of your cousin alcids nest on cliffs and islands near the ocean's waves, but you hunker in pairs up to fifty miles inland. Now, seekers track you by standing in the woods at dawn or dusk, listening for you as you make your crepuscular flights to and from the sea to trade out incubation and chick-tending duties with your long-term mate. When your chick fledges, their very first flight must cover all those miles; landing on forest floor rather than water means they won't be able to launch again. Once safely afloat that first time, they wander and forage for a few years before returning to the forest to mate and nest.

The intact forests of Southeast Alaska are a stronghold for you, though you range in lesser numbers from California to the Aleutian Islands. You are so much a part of the Temperate Rainforest that every part of your life embodies its huge, old-growth trees, shaded canyons, mossy limbs, and rich forage fish.

DAO STROM

nest/sea

nest   sea

a telemetry of our enigma

{ } } {

{
}
{
}

]   are you at home [in]
        or torn [between]
your two worlds, murrelet ?

]   or are you lesson of home
                            as
                        wavewinged-
                            marbleheart

            calledback

to birth
high
in
branch

Lungwort Lichen

(Lobaria pulmonaria)

Clinging loosely to boulders or tree trunks in large clusters of palm-sized "leaves," scattered on the ground as windfall, seafoam green on top and ivory underneath with distinctive melon-colored bumps and a netted texture of ridges, Lungwort Lichen is hard to mistake. Reach out to feel the surface: leathery, almost spongy. When the forest is moist, Lungwort will be supple and soft, providing shelter for invertebrates that, in turn, nourish birds and other beings. When Lungwort falls, their nitrogen enriches plants growing in the understory. These are slow-growing lichens, taking five to thirty years to reach full size, and they require mature, healthy, cool forests to thrive.

Lungwort, while iconic in Cascadia's Temperate Rainforest, is found in forests around the globe. The common name for Lungwort Lichen (and the Latin name, too) comes from the resemblance of this lichen to lungs. Lungwort's lung-related healing properties were recognized early on by Sechelt, European, and other people. However, because lichens in general, and Lungwort in particular, are sensitive to air pollution, the presence of Lungwort is much reduced outside Cascadia. In the United Kingdom, Lungwort now exists only on the wilder edges of Scotland and a few other isolated, pollution-free areas. If you find yourself standing near Lungwort, breathe deep. This is good, clean air.

LAURA DA'

Doctrine of Signatures

Like a figure
from an illuminated manuscript,

fingers elongated,
richly robed,
wide unfocused eyes,

toes pointed down as if bedbound,

lion at my feet,
ox over my shoulder,
bear in my belly.

> In this place
> I aestheticize meadow
> and anesthetize current.

Grisaille of Lungwort lichen
jockeys branches and boulders
across the ghost town.

On the cusp of
the flood meadow—

> a hop shed sweating
> hundred-year creosote.

To the west,
under the schoolhouse—
> the foundation
> of the longhouse.

In stock storytelling convention,
the revenant hero

upon fulfillment
of a divine purpose
draws a promise—

Next time, let me go to my rest.

If the three-kingdom city
of algae, fungus, and yeast
is never divided
into a severalty of parts,
lichen may live forever,
in misty seasonality.

Cover my eyes with
flat river stones
that remember
the press of canoes.
Open my lips.
Fold the molting world
under my tongue.

Next time, let me lichen.

Townsend's Warbler

(Setophaga townsendi)

Little bird, we know we are more likely to hear you first than see you as you forage up high overhead in the Rainforest's dim heights. Your song, *dee-do-dee-do tzee-tzee-TZEE*, strains hard toward an end, buzzy and bright, echoing the vivid yellow patches on your head and chest, the black-olive-gray barring on your wings. When you do stop still, we can see that you are masked like Catwoman, and the little yellow moon under your eye is a wink of color and a delight.

Do you get lonely in winter, those of you who come down from elevation into coastal forests and linger? Do you miss your friends who have flown farther south to Mexico and Central America? We know you, like most warblers, don't often sit still. You forage, glean, sing, hop, and  flit. Females of your kind nest seven times a Human's height above the ground, and you're particular about that nest. Sometimes you'll build one halved-grapefruit-sized nest only to move the entire thing, twig by twig and web by web and needle by needle, to another nearby (better?) tree. Maybe you're monogamous, maybe not. Only you know that secret still. We do know that you live at least ten years, which seems short for such a vivid brilliance in our lush shade. We also know that if we put out suet, mealworms, or peanut butter in our winter yards, you might grace us with a visit.

TIM MCNULTY

Tropical Sunlight

Smoke from wildfires fills the valleys,
and a high veil of cirrus
        dampens the morning sun.
Then a gift from Costa Rican forests—
Townsend's warbler drops by.

Sunlit yellow face and breast,
dark Zorro-like mask,
quickly, neatly, shakes down
        a subalpine fir crown
for bugs,

cleans his beak madly on a limb,
and takes leave south
        across the Skagit,
                heading back.

From the lookout steps,
three thousand miles north,
I'm warmed through.

Red Huckleberry

(*Vaccinium parvifolium*)

For people who live on the wet side of Cascadia, this tall, delicate plant is cherished. Others may scratch their heads at the name Huckleberry, thinking of the times they've stooped to pick blue-purple berries similar to Blueberry. But Red Huckleberry is different.

Reach out chest-high or higher to pick the glowing, pea-sized fruit of Red Huckleberry: tart, bright, and most often growing in shoreside edges near coniferous forests or from the stumps of conifers themselves (a clever spot, as this elevates the leaves into sun and also, being spongy, provides a source of moisture even in dry years). You'll pucker at them in your mouth, delicious and tart. Huckleberry's Latin species name, *parvifolium*, means small-leaved, and that's true. This being's leaves are dainty, soft, green, oval, and sweetly smooth. Huckleberry's twigs and leaves are delicious to Deer, Mountain Goat, Elk, and Mountain Beaver.

Some use the name Red Whortleberry or Red Bilberry for this being—either way, Red Huckleberry's berries look a little like Salmon roe and are used as bait for that reason. Gather them. Huckleberry makes great pies, can be dried into cakes for winter snacks rich with vitamins, are perfect for pancakes, or can be juiced for a cleansing tonic. If you're a Bear or small mammal, you're seeking them already. Traditional gathering methods include shaking the bush or removing berries with a comb. You could, if you wish, also reach up with open mouth and pluck one, then one, then one.

ALYSSA OGI

Pantoum for an Uncertain Future

At the edge of our new home,
I found huckleberries recovering from drought.
Red lights, open leaves, they stretched
in the shade of summer trees.

I found huckleberries recovering from drought
when I too needed strength
in the shade of summer trees.
Ancient fruit, I had heard the myth

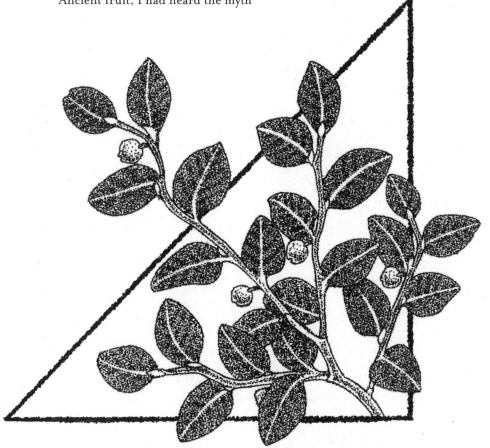

when I too needed strength:
that you cannot be domesticated.
Ancient fruit, I had heard the myth
that only you can choose where to root.

One cannot be domesticated
if each morning becomes a discovery
and I've chosen a northern soil
far from what I once knew:

each morning becomes a discovery—
dogwood, bleeding-hearts, irises
far from what I once knew—
is this not a kind of survival? As I look back

at redwoods, live-forevers, poppies,
I grieve what was promised to us.
Is this a kind of survival? As we look back
at a nation that was meant to be green

we grieve what was promised to us—
and I fear I'm holding on to the past.
A nation that was meant to be green
becomes autumn, hoping for winter again.

But fear, I'm holding on; past
red lights, open leaves, stretching
beyond autumn, hoping for winter rain
at the edge of our new home.

Coastal Tailed Frog

(Ascaphus truei)

If you find yourself resting alongside a step pool in a stream by a mountain trail through old-growth forest west of the Cascades and British Columbia's Coast Mountains (or in the Blue Mountains of Oregon and Washington, or in the Rockies of Idaho and Montana), take your shoes off and cool your feet. Dip your handkerchief and lay it across your neck. Linger. Listen to the rushing water. And look for Frog. Whether you are down low, close to the ocean, or up high near tree line, you'll only find Coastal Tailed Frog if the water's cool enough—anything over 71 degrees Fahrenheit is too hot.

Is the delicate, sensitive amphibian you've found Coastal Tailed Frog? Feel the toes: the tips will be slightly hardened to manage the rocky stream-beds they prefer. And look close: Coastal Tailed Frog is small, only (at most) the size of an Oreo cookie, nose to tail. Don't trust color— Coastal Tailed Frog does their best to blend in with whatever place they find themselves and can be tan to choc-olate to green. The tail? Only males have them, and they're short, used for internal fertilization in rushing streams (most other frogs fertilize eggs externally).

The absence of trilling or croaking might be one clue as to which Frog is near you. Coastal Tailed Frog is quiet. If you are still and other Frog voices have resumed after your arrival startled them into silence and still there is no frog sound from the being before you, perhaps this is Coastal Tailed Frog. Why silent? The loud rushing streams they live alongside make vocalizing an exercise in frustration. If you're looking for egg masses, dive in. They'll be attached to the undersides of large boulders. Tailed Frog tadpoles have suction-like mouths that allow them to grip rocks in the fast water they're born to.

Frog is a significant being in many Cascadian cultures, and all wonder at Frog's ability to hop between water and land, to survive the hard winter with such thin skin, to transform so easily through so many shapes: egg to tadpole to Frog.

BRITTNEY CORRIGAN

In Praise of the Coastal Tailed Frog

How to begin when the male has not tail but cloaca:
seed-deliverer, fertile bud. When what is on display
is not rudder but root, not appendage but unabashed
adaptation. Oh, glorious amplexus. Oh, pelvic clasp. In
turbulent waters, future-frogs are not swept downstream.

Hail the tadpoles with their flattened heads, mouths
agape in aureoles of folds. All suction and patience
as they cling to the undersides of rocks. Cold currents,
fast and clear, fail to dislodge their slow-morphing
bodies. Outside the water, we measure time by its loss.

Trees lean in quiet devotion toward ghost-frogs,
ancestor-frogs, who navigate wet rocks with primal claws.
Living-frogs, now-frogs, breathe through slickened skin.
Grainy-frogs, earth-bellied frogs, blend into mossy banks.
New-frogs emerge transparent in forest streams.

On land, we stand out. Muddy what we try to stand in.
We divide and multiply, measure time by its leggy strokes.
How to un-muck ourselves and exalt the golden-eyed beings
smaller than the palms of our hands? The no-voice-frogs
lift their faces from the rushing water and un-sing.

Devil's Club

(Oplopanax horridus)

Oh, sun shielder, with wide, flat, verdant, Maple-shaped leaves ready to patter loud in rain. Oh, bright, late-season cones of red berries, treat-on-a-stalk for Brown Bear. You grow shin-high to arm-stretch above. In fall, your yellowing leaves bring sun into the understory. And your spring blossoms? A cone of delicate, tiny white-green flowers. Guider of paths with your thorns, which break off and nudge into Human skin, how many plants have visible prickers not just on their stems but all along the undersides of their leaves? You're amazing! In Rainforest light, your delicate pale barbs glow. And you're found in the wild, and only in the wild; you resist cultivation.

This member of the ginseng family is known by many Native people throughout Cascadia as a potent healer and, as such, is a sacred being. It's the inner bark (not the roots) of Devil's Club that holds most healing properties: for tuberculosis, arthritis, diabetes, rheumatism, and more. Watch Tlingit Elder Helen Watkins in a video as she cuts the large stalks in spring, then scrapes off the outer bark to expose the bright green beneath. She shares that the berries are useful in combating lice and making hair shiny. The cleaned sticks can be used for walking, sounding drums, and fashioning various fishhooks and as beads. Ash from the stalks can be used to make a ceremonial and protective face paint. Devil's Club is a signal of your arrival to Cascadia's Temperate Rainforest.

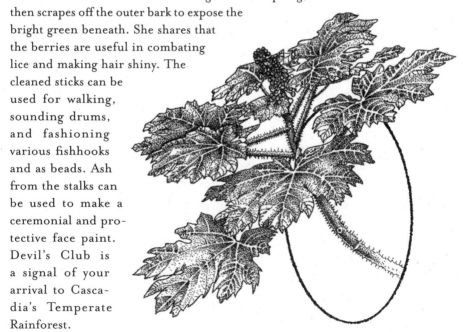

CLAUDIA CASTRO LUNA

Oplopanax Splendorous

Once upon a time
an intelligence disguised as seed
on an ancient forest floor descended
and rose up as a mighty bristled creature
with mighty healing prowess

To think of the human who
long ago communing with bird,
with fog, and verdant woods
first saw past thorn and spike
—from root to red fruit
by way of leaf and bark—
and thus the plant's
wisdom apprehended

Or, to think of the outsider
who saw on the large leaves
nothing more than his fears reflected
and named it "Devil's Club"

To think, now of she—
the mystery flowing through her,
generous and splendid,
and humbly ask,
what name she calls herself

Brown Bear

(Ursus arctos)

If, in the woods, you come upon a strange trail unlike any you've ever seen—
not a thin strip of worn-to-dirt, but plates of bare earth in alternating left-
right alignment—you've come upon the work of Brown Bear. The path won't go
far. Fifty feet or so. Where it stops and starts, look up. Most likely you'll find
kinked hair stuck in Spruce bark and sap, maybe even claw marks overhead. In
Southeast Alaska's biggest islands, where Brown Bear thrives in densities unlike
anywhere else on earth, these paths are calling cards, places where Bear leaves

scent for those who follow and smells the passages of others, discerning male from female, young from old. That nose leads Bear, as well, to Salmon, Deer, Sedge, Blueberry, and Currant.

Is the bear you see among the Sitka Spruce Black Bear or Brown Bear? Brown Bear can be black, glorious cinnamon, or blond. Brown Bear's ears are fairly small, their nose more doglike, and they have a rounded hump on their shoulders, all the better for digging. Grizzly Bear, Brown Bear, Bruin: all *Ursus arctos*, though there are differences between Coastal Brownies, who gather and grow to impressive size along Salmon runs, and Grizzlies of the interior mountains, who are smaller, blonder, and have larger ranges to compensate for their more dispersed food resources. Subspecies of Brown Bear live also on Kodiak Island, on the Kamchatka Peninsula, and in Europe. The "lumpers and splitters" have played with Brown Bear species and subspecies for centuries. What science knows is that Brown Bear walked into Cascadia from Asia, first arriving around sixty thousand years ago.

There is so much to learn and appreciate about the life of Brown Bear— from females' delayed implantation to the smallness of the cubs born in the winter den (about the size and weight of a bear-shaped squeeze bottle of honey). From the specialized fishing techniques of individuals to the ways they nurture forests alongside Salmon streams by carrying fish carcasses away to eat undisturbed. Bear is sheltered by and adds to the wealth of the forest they stroll through. People who live aware of Brown Bear alongside them have come to their own understandings of how to walk together in the woods, how to understand the relationships and the long histories we share with this being. Seek their wisdom.

LOIS RED ELK

from "We Call Them Hu Nunpa"

MATO PEJUTA
In early Spring Grandma would begin making offerings for the bear and the plants. She said it was during the days after hibernation that the plant nation would release their scent into the defrosting soil, an aroma so full that waves of awakening air vibrated above the stillness of melting snow. Grandma knew this as she studied the hungry bears, looking for healing nour-

ishment after long months with Mother Earth. She said the two nations worked together to sustain life, the animals and the plants. Bears can smell their medicine miles off, she said and knew where to dig for them thus sharing knowledge of the best roots or bear medicine (*Mato Pejuta*). Grandma would send her nephews to the mountains with handmade deerskin pouches filled with pemmican and wrapped in sage and sweet grass. These gifts were for those who harvested the bear medicine. She said this was proper, to appease the bear and the plants, as only they could begin the harvest of all sacred medicines.

Sockeye Salmon

(*Oncorhynchus nerka*)

Even though Salmon lives in water, this being is the forest as much as Spruce, Bear, Frog, or Lichen. In the Rainforest's rivers, cool and clear, shaded by trees and Devil's Club, Sockeye feed Bear and other beings who often take the fish up away from the water to enjoy them alongside a cozy Spruce, leaving fish bits behind to feed the trees. Scientists have measured this path of nutrients by looking at marine-based nitrogen in tree trunks, proving that much of the Rainforest's richness, even far from the rivers where Salmon thrive, is due to Salmon.

From traditional subsistence gathering to sport fishers to commercial fisheries, Sockeye is greatly valued by people. Are the fish in the river you're looking at Sockeye? If they're an adult headed upriver, their body will be scarlet and their head a mossy green. The name Sockeye comes from the Snuneymuxw First Nation of the Fraser River, who call them *sthuqi'*, meaning "red fish." In June and July, when Sockeye is heading home to spawn, river shallows can be a tumult of bodies, crimson and thrashing.

For people? Where shall we begin? Sockeye is one of the most prized Salmon, and subsistence and commercial fishers alike seek to capture some of this regular bounty without impeding the health of the system as a whole. Salmon numbers and calculations are astounding: a female Sockeye will lay 2,000 to 5,000 eggs in shallow scrapes (redds) she digs in river gravel near a lake before she dies. A male, hovering nearby, fighting off other males for the privilege, then releases his milt (sperm) above the eggs. Sockeye young grow under gravel. Some will feed predators, and some will emerge as fry and fin up to nearby lakes where they'll live and grow for a year or two before heading out to sea, transforming as they move from fresh to salt, swimming and feeding, then returning a few years later to spawn. For every thousand eggs laid by a Sockeye hen, one Salmon returns. But this is not waste! Every step of the way, someone benefits from Sockeye Salmon, both as sustenance and as inspiration as the bright, fierce fish return.

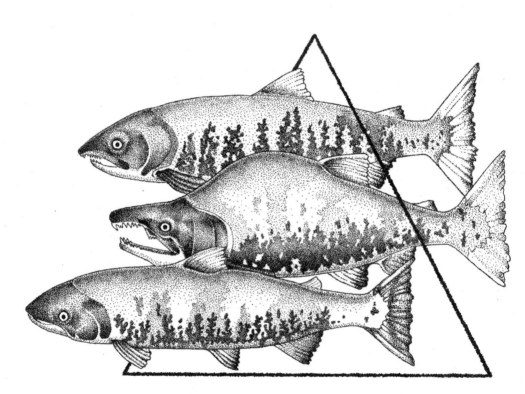

LINDA BIERDS

After-Image

Three weeks past my father's death
his surgeons, in pond-green smocks, linger,
trail after me from dream to porch, down
the bark and needle pathway toward the river.
One nudges me, explains, as he did weeks ago,
the eye's propensity for opposites, why green
displaced their bleached-white coats. Looking up
from the tablet of a patient's blood, he says,
the red-filled retina will cast a green
on every white it crosses. A phantom wash
on a neighboring sleeve. It startles us,
he tells me. And: Green absorbs the ghosting.
                              Then he is gone, the path
returning to boot brush and the squirrel ratchets
my father loved. It is noon, the sky
through the tree limbs a sunless white.
I have come to watch the spawning salmon
stalled in the shallow pools. Age
has burned them a smoky red, though
their heads are silver, like helmets. Just over
the mossy floor, they float unsupported,
or supported by the air their gills have winnowed.
I think I will gather them soon, deep
in the eye, red and red and red,
then turn to the canopy of sky and cedars.
It will support them soon, the green.

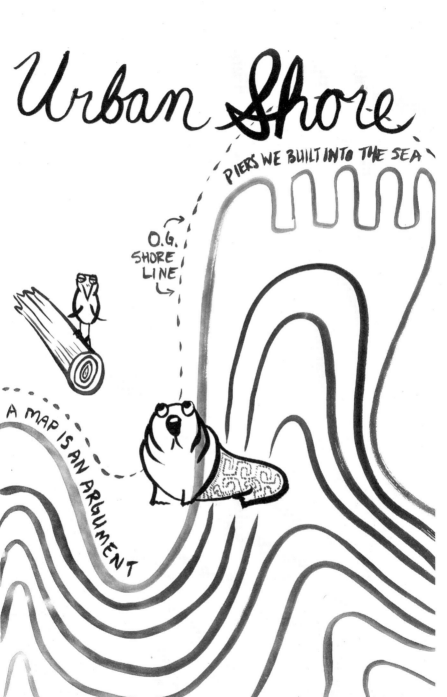

Urban Shore

Art by Rachel Kessler

Perhaps you could say that any salty shore in Cascadia is an Urban Shore, given how water and air mix and mingle around the globe, moving dust from the Sahara across the Atlantic, mercury over the Arctic, and plastic everywhere. Yet for cities by the sea—Seattle, Vancouver, Astoria, Juneau—the sea edge is a reminder that the paved world has boundaries, that forces and rhythms and movements of tides and currents pulse beyond rush hour traffic, school schedules, and holidays.

Even city creeks—overhung by Snowberry and overflown by Crow—can carry Salmon. Even city beaches find themselves pearled with Herring roe in spring or reveal, when the tide goes out, Ochre Star bright on dock pilings (which are often topped with little gardens of their own, afire with the red blooms of Scarlet Paintbrush). The raw growl of Steller Sea Lion, a denizen of wild water, can be heard from crowded marinas, their snorted breaths echoing off the sides of tankers, sailboats, and ferries.

Cities can crawl over forests and bury Snowberry in pavement, but they can't sprawl into the sea. Not much. Not yet. And that wildness shimmering at the edge of things, lidded and liquid, how lucky those who live near it are to have such a gorgeous reminder of our connection to the unbuilt world.

Ballard Locks

Air-struck, wound-gilled, ladder
    upon ladder of them thrashing
through froth, herds of us climb
    the cement stair to watch
this annual plunge back to dying, spawn;
    so much twisted light
the whole tank seethes in a welter of bubbles:
    more like sequined
purses than fish, champagned explosions
    beneath which the ever-moving
smolt fume smacks against glass, churns them up
    to lake from sea level, the way,
outside, fishing boats are dropped or raised
    in pressured chambers, hoses spraying
the salt-slicked undersides a cleaner clean.
    Now the vessels
can return to dock. Now the fish,
    in their similar chambers, rise and fall
along the weirs, smelling the place
    instinct makes for them,
city's pollutants sieved
    through grates: keeping fish
where fish will spawn; changing the physics of it,
    changing ours as well:
one giant world encased
    with plastic rock, seaweed transplanted
in thick ribbons for schools to rest in
    before they work their way up
the industrious journey: past shipyard, bus lot,
    train yard, past
bear-cave, past ice-valley; past the place
    my father's father once,
as a child, had stood with crowds
    and shot at them with guns

then scooped them from the river with a net, such
    silvers, pinks cross-hatched with black:
now there's protective glass
    behind which gray shapes shift: change
then change again. Can you see the jaws
    thickening with teeth, scales
beginning to plush themselves with blood; can you see
    there is so little distinction here
between beauty, violence, utility?
    The water looks like boiling sun.
A child has turned his finger into a gun.
    Bang, the ladders say
as they bring up fish into too-bright air, then down again,
    while the child watches the glass
revolve its shapes into a hiss of light.
    Bang, the boy repeats.
His finger points and points.

Scarlet Paintbrush

(Castilleja miniata)

In a mountain meadow, along an urban stream or roadside, at a tidal edge, if you spot a bright tuft of red (or orange, or even pale yellow), whether it's early spring or nudging into autumn, you've most likely found Scarlet Paintbrush. This colorful plant has long caught the eye of those living alongside them, and people such as the Gitxsan have found medicine for lungs, eyes, and more in Paintbrush's leaves.

    Hummingbird and Human alike find the nectar of Scarlet Paintbrush delicious, though you have to delve and poke to find it. The actual flowers of Paintbrush are buried deep within the fuzzy, colorful bracts (modified leaves that look like petals). To see them, bend close. Look for a greenish pod poking out from what you first registered as red petals, then look for a tendril of even paler

yellow green with a dark dot at its tip poking out from that. There. That's it. The flower.

Like other members of the broomrape family, Scarlet Paintbrush is semi-parasitic and relies on neighbors to thrive, most often Aster, Pea, and Grass. Scarlet Paintbrush is still able to get a little juice from their own chlorophyll, though, and isn't excessively picky about whom they partner with. *Miniata* in the Latin name comes from "minium," or "red lead," a rare form of lead tetroxide. Although red lead can be found here and there around the world, in Cascadia, you must search for it in Idaho's Salmon River Mountains. Or in Paintbrush.

GARRETT HONGO

Scarlet Paintbrush

My cousin, just married, came upon a field of them while
    hiking around Mt. Rainier.
She posted a selfie on Facebook, she and her husband both
    ruddy-cheeked,
Facing a brisk wind, their hair tousled, making whips like
    florets of paintbrush
Dancing around coronas of pure happiness visited upon them
    by the Everlasting.

And, one summer, I saw a field of paintbrush bent by a flat
    heel of wind
Sent from a black thunderhead scudding over Fish Lake near
    McKenzie Bridge.
They are alive in memory from when I drove to my brother's
    summer camp
On the southeastern edge of Mono Lake where he trained his
    string of birddogs.
There were patches of paintbrush popping up along a stream-
    bed, dandles of red
Rising from dry ground, surrounded by salt beds, tufa, and
    black lava sands.

In 1944, internees at Tule Lake gathered the blossoms to
   pound into paste,
A dye they mixed in *chawan* for painting flowers on burlap
   they'd scrounged
To make humble sleeves for chopsticks they'd fashioned from
   scrap pine,
A decorous touch at mealtimes while incarcerated during
   World War II.
Did Uncle Mas tell me this? At 95, the last time he'd visited?
   Away at college
In Stockton when war broke, he got rounded up by Executive
   Order 9066.

Over a century ago, in 1873, a shaman made a like paste from
   paintbrush blooms
To dye the red tule rope he wove for a sacred circle around the
   Ghost Dance
Of 52 warriors who would make their stand against 400 U.S.
   soldiers
And cavalry sent to remove the Modoc from the lava beds of
   their native land.
The rope was said to make them invisible, that their dancing
   would overturn
The Universe, exiling the whites, restoring a people to where
   they belonged.

The next morning, a thick tule fog rose from the land, engulf-
   ing the crags and trenches
Of the stronghold where the warriors hid, making their move-
   ments invisible.
After many days, the Modoc were victorious, the soldiers and
   cavalry rebuffed,
But more came and the medicine of the paintbrush faded,
   four Modoc were hanged,
And the rest removed to reservations in Oregon and Oklaho-
   ma, a scattered people.

My friend, their descendant, retold this story on my deck in
   back of my house,

Invoking the fragile promise of protection by the paintbrush,
the sleevelike florets
Of them inviolate in memory like monks gently genuflecting
toward the West
Through the firedamp of grey air and the final smudge of
scarlet that was the sun.

Ochre Star

(Pisaster ochraceus)

Look down into tide pools or onto rocks in the nearshore waters from Alaska to California. Do you see a thick, five-armed, royal-purple Starfish studded with white freckles? Is there a brick-orange Sea Star nearby, or another who is burnt umber? Any of these might be Ochre Star, a keystone species of the intertidal zone who keeps rocks clear of Mussel and thereby allows Kelp to grow into forests that nurture millions of beings.

Now bend closer and reach down. Notice how the white freckles all over the body stand out from the flesh, rough and sandpaper-like, arranged in a netted, star-map pattern. In actuality, these calcified spines are tiny pincers (pedicellariae), which Ochre Star uses to keep algae (as well as other would-be hitchhikers) from growing over their slow-moving back.

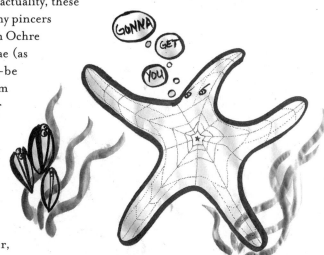

Sea star wasting syndrome, caused by what is thought to be a bacterial infection and lethal to Sea Star and exacerbated by warm water, has impacted twenty species of sea stars, including Ochre Star, from Alaska to Mexico. Scientists are working now to find more answers—and perhaps solutions. What would our oceans be without their stars?

If the Ochre Star you're watching is hunched up, the center mounded, then you've probably caught Ochre Star mid-meal, holding open Blue Mussel's shell with powerful suckers, pushing their own stomach into Mussel's shell and dissolving the meat there. This is how most Sea Stars eat their meals: out.

Ochre Star is long-lived—up to twenty years unless a gull or Sea Otter, their only real predators, intervenes. Gulls will choke down Ochre Star whole (it can take a while to fit all the arms into a gull's mouth), but Sea Otter usually only eats the tips of Ochre Star's arms, which Ochre Star can then regenerate. But did you know Sea Star has their eyes (really, light sensors) at the tips of their arms. So, when Sea Otter is munching on Ochre Star, they're going for the eyes.

FIONA TINWEI LAM

Sea Star

Similar die-offs had occurred before, but never at this scale. . . . [T]he stars were blinking out.

—"A Starfish-Killing Disease Is Remaking the Oceans," *The Atlantic*, January 2019

A fleck of constellation
studded in a blank swathe of shore.

No fragments of mollusk,
no green tendrils. No trace

of your undersea universe
beyond the ocean's shifting

border. I hover above you, ponder
your arrival. Do I imagine

your flinch as I wake you from stasis?
You freeze, rigid.

I gingerly lift and balance
your body between twigs,

reach water's edge, flip you
right side up. A blurred wriggle—

descent in a blink.
Shallow waves wash over

impassive sand. Galaxies
of your sunflower kin dissolving

on reefs from Alaska to Mexico.
Go where the tide takes you, sea star.

What will be left?

Pacific Herring

(Clupea pallasii)

Spring. Humpback Whale is coming inshore, and Sea Lion is patrolling closer too. It must be time for Herring to return and spawn. Get a Hemlock branch and sink it just beyond the tide line . . . and wait. Female Herring is seeking a place to lay her tens of thousands of pearly, seed-bead-sized eggs, and the soft needles and branchlets are a perfect invitation. Soon, the water will turn milky with milt from males.

Lift the laden branch out of the water. Put an egg into your mouth and bite: *Pop*, clean and salty. Now divvy up the harvest: some to eat fresh, some to dry, some to pack in salt. Your neighbors were busy with other tasks, so bring them some. Send some to friends up north in Whitehorse or down south in Seattle. This is tradition. Victoria is the "place of smoked herring" to the Lekwungen, and in 2014, a Sitka Sound study showed that 90 percent of people's Herring roe harvest was shared with immediate and extended community. Traditionally, you might trade your bounty for Eulachon oil, Mountain Goat meat, or beadwork. Such seasonal bounty and exchange is one of the cornerstones of traditional Cascadian coastal communities, and indeed, cities like Sitka were sited in part because of the rich Herring spawn along their shores.

Herring flashes blue-silver in large schools throughout the North Pacific, from California to Japan, and measures between a handspan and a foot. During the daylight hours, it would be unusual to see a school of Herring because the fish make a vertical migration every day—rising to the surface at night and subsiding at dawn. There are commercial fisheries for Herring too. The biggest is for sac roe—eggs held within a female—a harvest controversial around Vancouver Island, in particular, given the declining numbers of Herring in British Columbia's waters. Advocacy by Heiltsuk and several other First Nations have led to bans on that particular fishery. What Herring wants is clean waters offshore to feed and inshore to spawn, creating the next generation of this marvelous fish.

KIM HEACOX
Pacific Herring

For a while it seemed
it was the only thing anybody
talked about. The ocean had turned white
with herring spawn. In a world worn down
by the feet of too many people, nature could still erupt
with bounty. A fish could still astound us.
And give us hope. It happened
off Cape St. Elias, Alaska,
the place where Vitus Bering first
sighted North America in 1741, back when
the ocean was colder and thirty percent
less acidic than today.
And still, the small Pacific herring,
a fat-rich, forage fish, essential food
for whales, salmon, seabirds, sea lions and seals
astounded us. And we, watchers and harvesters, tourists
and Tlingit, gape as the heavy boughs
of hemlock are pulled from the bays and inlets,
studded with roe. Grateful. Grateful
for a small fish that gives us hope.

Copepod

(Calanus spp.*)*

Small but mighty, that's Copepod. If you have a cup of unfiltered water, you most likely have at least a few individuals of this type of zooplankton swimming around. Have you ever watched *SpongeBob SquarePants*? Then you've seen Copepod. Evil Mr. Plankton in the cartoon is a pretty accurate rendition: long body, red eye in the middle of the forehead, and two big antennae. In reality, Copepod is tiny, about the size of a grain of rice or smaller, and Copepod isn't evil! Copepod is essential. Cassin's Auklet, squid, Herring, Anchovy, Sand Lance, and Sei Whale, to name a few, rely on Copepod as a mainstay of their diets.

We hear a lot about Krill as a foundational member of the marine food web, particularly in the Southern Ocean around Antarctica. But in the north, Copepod rules. In fact, they rule overall. Scientists think Copepod may be one of the most abundant multicellular beings on planet Ocean. They are found worldwide and have thirteen thousand named species to their genus.

As a being, Copepod is quite fascinating. Officially a crustacean (like crabs), Copepod has thirteen life stages, some with radically different forms. Copepod has no heart or circulatory system, instead absorbing oxygen directly into their tiny body. Though small, Copepod can swim against a current and even make a quick dash to escape predators by using a second pair of long antennae on their head that serve as oars.

Although it takes some serious effort and a bit of equipment to actually see tiny Copepod, you might smell them. A thick Copepod patch at sea gives off a honeydew melon scent. They smell sweet.

KATHRYN SMITH

Dear Copepod

I'm sorry I don't think of you more often.
You have a name I love: three syllables,
a dactyl, its rhythm like skipping

or a problematic heart. You have no heart.
That's something else I love: you can't
love me back. My tears make the shape

of your body. Your body could fit
inside one. Could you live there, in my salt?
Already, you feed on what I shed—microplastics,

exhaled carbon. You know the carelessness of
my kind. I'm sorry. I thought maybe you
could teach me how to cope, how to climb

inside the pod of *I can do this*, and drift. But if
I would look closer, I'd see how swiftly
you pedal your single foot as the current

draws you to the mouths of predators,
and they consume you. Humans call this
the bottom of the food chain, and again,

I'm sorry, though by now my apologies
must seem feeble. Here I am trying
to set myself apart from the worst of

my species while I make assumptions
about the whole of yours. You don't care
about my excuses. You don't care at all.

You calculate. Your feathered antennae
fanning out, feeling.

Silver Salmon

(Oncorhynchus kisutch)

Some say you leap more than other Salmon, and we believe it. Like all the Pacific Salmon, Silver Salmon (or Coho) stitches together upstream and downstream, fresh and salt. Coho doesn't venture as far offshore as King or Sockeye. Once emerged from their redds, Silver Salmon fry spend their first year in the streams and lakes they came from, then move out into saltwater, returning to their natal streams after three or four years at sea. Look for Coho heading upstream to spawn in later summer or fall in Cascadia. At that time, males gain a deep red color, similar to though less dramatic than Sockeye.

As with other Salmon, it's not just the flesh of Coho that people seek. Traditionally and in today's high fashion, goods made from Salmon skin are prized for their beauty and durability. Coho are found in unexpected places in North America: stocked in the Great Lakes as early as the 1920s to control Alewife populations, stocked in the coastal Atlantic states of New Hampshire and Massachusetts in the 1960s, and introduced into Connecticut since the 1800s. Really, the only true Coho (*true* meaning living in their homewaters and not moved by Humans) are those in Cascadia, finning toward reproduction and harvest. Fish farming with Coho began in Cascadia around 1900 in Oregon and since has expanded to Chile and Japan. Is this good? It's . . . complicated. An Alaska bumper sticker reads "Friends Don't Let Friends Eat Farmed Fish," and any mindful market-goer can learn more from Seafood Watch, a site run by the Monterey Bay Aquarium.

JESSICA E. JOHNSON

Hatchery

Whatever you are
you are blue at
the fringes. You
wear the
cartoonish color
of cold.

Whatever you *are*,

sum of roe
and milk,

your blunted
noses align toward
me.

Whatever I am
here you come,

a one-brained riot,
an onslaught
of famished raindrops.

*

On the barn's wide roof,
one single-clone.

One bred rose
in a long, long hedge . . .

I track one Coho
in the tank

as if there could exist a further fact

behind her ball-peen nose
her cold electric skin

her complexion a sky
in mixed weather.

I want there to be something
single in her swim

a self in the planned
body.

I hold her in my eye.
There, and there, and then—

but she is gone
in the sibling-hover.

Steller Sea Lion

(Eumetopias jubatus)

The thrash and splash of Steller Sea Lion tearing bite-sized chunks from Coho, Halibut, or Pollock is a sight to behold. And this blond, huge, shaggy-necked (at least for the males) being is superlative in other ways: the growliest (Steller Sea Lion doesn't bark like their southern cousin, California Sea Lion; no, they gutter, roar, and growl) and the biggest (males can grow to eleven feet in length and weigh the equivalent of two grand pianos, while females are about a third of that).

If you've traveled the Salish Sea or the Inside Passage of Cascadia, you've met Steller Sea Lion. If you've visited the Sea Lion Caves of Oregon's coast, you've heard their amplified, rough music. Maybe you've met Steller Sea Lion outside the Ballard Locks in Seattle, where they wait for Salmon to congregate near the fish ladder, or if you've ventured out on a boat, you may have seen navigational buoys outside Victoria or Vancouver listing over and draped with big bodies: sea lions. In northern Cascadia, this is the most likely Sea Lion you'll see.

As anyone might imagine, such a large, fur-bearing, meaty, fat-rich being is incredibly valuable to Native coastal people. In addition to practical uses, ceremonial and spiritual significance abound in Steller Sea Lion, or Taan in Lingít. One example is the shakee.át, a ceremonial headdress, which uses Steller Sea Lion's whiskers to hold downy feathers of Eagle in its crown.

There are two populations of Steller Sea Lion in the North Pacific. In Cascadia, it's the healthier, eastern stock we mostly get to see (the western stock, which stretches from Prince William Sound across to Russia and Japan, is endangered). Steller Sea Lion travels wide distances when at sea, often solitarily, but they also need isolated spots to gather and rest onshore. In summer, females, pups, and dominant males can be found on offshore rookeries where

they breed. Juveniles and past-their-prime bulls gather on haul-outs in more protected waters.

Steller Sea Lion is surprisingly agile: on land they can sometimes be spotted napping on a ledge several stories above the tide line, and in water they swim by powerful strokes of their large foreflippers. To look down from your kayak or small boat and see Steller Sea Lion gliding below you, rolling one large brown eye up to meet yours, is a thrilling and terrifying experience.

URSULA K. LE GUIN

Found Poem

However, Bruce Baird, Laguna Beach's chief lifeguard, doubts that
sea lions could ever replace, or even really aid, his staff. "If you were
someone from Ohio, and you were in the water having trouble and a
sea lion approached you, well, it would require a whole lot more public
education," he told the Orange County Register.
                                        —Paul Simon, for AP, 17 December 1984

If I am ever someone from Ohio
in the water having trouble
off a continent's west edge
and am translated to my element
by a sudden warm great animal
with sea-dark fur sleek shining
and the eyes of Shiva,
I hope to sink my troubles like a stone
and all uneducated ride
her inshore shouting with the foam
praises of the freedom to be saved.

                                        (1986)

American Crow

(Corvus brachyrhynchos)

Crow? We know Crow. Black, noisy, complaining, excellent harasser of Bald Eagle and Great Horned Owl. Sly and glint-eyed, Crow is able to recognize and remember individual Humans for years, particularly if someone does Crow some injury. Airborne trickster, Crow tosses sticks and nabs them as they fall.

For decades, birders distinguished between (and puzzled over the difference between) Northwestern Crow and nearly identical American Crow. Their ranges overlapped, but Northwesterners were described as slightly smaller and found only along the coast between Alaska and northern Washington. Any Crow hopping on Kelp or digging in the sand for Clam on Vancouver Island was likely to be Northwestern Crow. The distinction is still in debate. In 2020, the American Ornithological Society decided that, in fact, the two are one and the same. The glaciers that had separated them had long ago receded, and DNA revealed that, through interbreeding, the distinctions between them had been erased. Then, in 2022, they proposed to reinstate the Northwestern Crow as a separate species. Honestly, where it will all end is anyone's guess. But don't roll your eyes.

This kind of reconsideration happens all the time. Sooty and Dusky Grouse, for example, were first described and listed as separate in the 1800s; then, in the 1900s, they were joined as a single species (Blue Grouse) until 2006, when they were split again. Such determinations are more than theoretical. Underlying the process is a quest for understanding that has broad implications for conservation, protection, and management.

Crow pairs up for the breeding season, sometimes getting help with nest-building and chick-raising from one of the previous year's young. After chicks are fledged, the whole process of which takes nearly three months from egg-laying to independence, Crow usually gathers into large roosting communities. Omnivorous opportunist, Crow eats whatever's at hand, though they favor clams, crabs, and Sand Dollar, and in berry season, they really love Blackberry and disperse seeds wherever they roam. You can thank Crow, too, for rich and diverse tide pools, as they keep Crab populations in check, allowing beings that would otherwise be Crab food to thrive.

SANDY SHREVE

Crows

"Cras" *(Latin) means "tomorrow."*

Out of all four corners of the world,
these ancients with tomorrow on their tongues
gather one by one,

cackle from whatever throne
they find to occupy—
at the edges of our eyes, the crows'

feet etch our every smile,
as if the only thing in life that matters
is our laughter.

Creatures of both earth and sky, they do not
care if we believe them evil,
dread them as death's messengers

or simply scorn them for the mess they make
scavenging through garbage in the park.
Always dressed for funerals,

crows know they are the pallbearers for our souls,
their gift, to find the glitter in what we leave behind.

Mosquito

(Culicidae spp.*)*

Let's face it, Mosquito has a bad rap. The whine, the itch, the blood meals sought by females (and only females!). Malaria, Zika, West Nile, the list goes on. More than one person has asked aloud what on earth is Mosquito's purpose . . . Wouldn't the world be better without them? No! We need Mosquito.

Mosquito feeds birds, fish, Bat, Dragonfly, Newt, and other beautiful beings. If you love wild orchids, you have to thank Mosquito for their presence, particularly in the north. The beautiful chartreuse Blunt-leaved Orchid is pollinated almost exclusively by Mosquito.

This powerful being is a Haida and Gitxsan clan crest—look for the upraised wings and down-pointing needle on totem poles—and stories of Mosquito are told by many Indigenous people of Cascadia. It would be surprising if such an attention-demanding being *didn't* have spiritual potency.

If such arguments are not persuasive, perhaps the fact that Mosquito's phenomenally sophisticated needle has inspired important innovations in medical instruments and techniques might do the trick. When that ouchless needle is finally perfected by Humans, you'll have Mosquito to thank.

JAMES GRABILL

Mosquito

Mosquito, you're drilling at high speeds into the living drum of my ear.
We've reached the place where we stand, whatever we do, as standing
    flies in back of the seen and holding still comes over us
    from before, as stillness revolves around quickening of light.

We've faced the mirror by diving through space to the future unknown,
    with our hungers grown in the open cracking into red-violet
    heights come down to where day thickens in spite of itself,
    burning out in flares along the rims of flying global water.

For this is the time before razor-blade dusk is severing ties to the day,
    when night exudes from the underground.
I'm not a scout familiar with stagnant waters in which transformations
    occur, your wigglers turning into tumblers that burst
    into oil-drill helicopters out for blood to keep you
    making ova, rafts, and underwater snowfalls
    of tiny eggs in the possibility a future here exists.

Of course, it's being alive that knows what it sees, that uses these eyes.
And knowing holds onto the side of the world for which it was created,
    however crossed our purposes have been, as small as we are.

Mosquito, where our cells have gone, we merge with time that's easy
    to forget when caught in the middle of it.

Mosquito, with your fifty varieties in this region alone, your kind spreads
all the more fever the hotter it is—while people spill their unnatural
80,000+ chemicals.

Mosquito, you're the product of flowing under-flowers hidden in swamps,
tiny blooms so green and quick they blend with the mosses
that power into the unknowable nutshell around gravity,
where you've been the protector of still waters and wild time.

For we participate, don't we, mosquito, from our cells out through light.

Rufous Hummingbird

(Selasphorus rufus)

Zip! Chit chit chit chit! And a terrifyingly loud wing buzz. Whether
you're on an apartment balcony with hanging baskets of flow-
ers, along a shoreside, or in a yard, hang out long enough and
the wild flit of Rufous Hummingbird will find you. Smaller
than other hummingbirds, this feisty and territorial being
breeds as far north as Southeast Alaska, farther than any
other hummingbird in the world, and winters as far
south as Mexico. This means that (ounce
for ounce) Rufous Hummingbird
has the longest migration of any
bird—over seventy-eight million
body lengths. Another astound-
ing number: their wings can
beat more than fifty-two times
per *second*.

Is the quick flitter, zip fighter, sugar sipper you see Rufous Hummingbird? Males are a glowing rust, females and young birds a much more subtle gray green, and both (unlike Anna's Hummingbird) have bright white chests. In coastal cultures, Hummingbird has inspired many stories that honor their quick flight and ability to hover, and Hummingbird is seen by many as a sign of good luck. And not just a sign: don't you feel lucky every time you see one?

Bright flowers like Scarlet Paintbrush and Red Currant lure Rufous Hummingbird in for nectar, and Hummingbird also enjoys a bit of protein with their sugar, primarily from small insects caught on the wing. You'll have to search carefully to find Rufous Hummingbird's nest. Most likely well above your head—maybe even three stories in the air—the cup is formed with Grasses, Lichen, spiderwebs, and bark and is only as wide as a soda can on the outside. The egg site? Merely a thumb pad. The eggs themselves are about the size and color of a white Tic Tac.

ELIZABETH AUSTEN

Neighbors

> her nest   a forest flotsam eggcup
> lichen   moss   bark-bits knit
> with spider thread   floats on a branch-end
> like a rowboat on the open ocean
> riding the swells
>
> what would she see if she looked
> back at me   glassed-in
> gaping

Snowberry

(Symphoricarpos albus)

In spring, you might see the Blueberry-like pink blooms that lead to Snowberry's pale fruits. In summer, the berries disappear behind dusty-green, oval leaves, but once the leaves are down in late fall, Snowberry shines. The clusters of bright white berries, tightly grouped in bundles of seven or more, each with a sweet button of a navel, pop from winter's brown canes like little glowing lights, whether in woodlands, along riverbanks, or in city parks. Snowberry is not endemic to Cascadia—they grow throughout temperate North America—but they are iconic in our Coastal Urban Woods where they thrive in city parks and ungroomed lots. A resourceful being, Snowberry propagates both by seeds and by underground rhizomes, which are particularly helpful after fire. The rhizomes are buried two to five inches in the soil, just enough to protect them. After the aboveground vegetation has burned away, Snowberry's new shoots

are among the first to rise, providing much-needed forage and shade in a burned landscape.

"Can you eat them?" is a question we often ask of berries. In Cascadia, there are very few berries that are not delicious. Some consider Snowberry one, though traditionally berries are eaten fresh or dried and stored for winter. Indigenous names for the plant include those translated as "Corpse Berry" or "Snake's Berry." Intimidating as that may be, the bark of Snowberry is used traditionally by Coast Salish tribes to treat skin problems, the berries as a shampoo, and the light, hollow canes as arrow shafts or pipe stems.

Deer, Bear, Bighorn Sheep, and many, many birds rely on Snowberry for forage, and even more beings find shelter in Snowberry's thickets. As you wander the winter shore, sea to one side and a chaos of brown brambles and shrubs to the other, you'll delight in Snowberry's bright glow along your path.

KATHARINE WHITCOMB

Snowberry in Drought Season

Chinook winds dry out the eastern
    slopes of the Cascades. Snowberry

        thickets' pale pink flowers give over
    in August to bone-white berries.

Good full brush stays green for
    deer, elk & bighorns. Black bears

        browse the berries. Drought season
    is a hard season after a hard season

& a hard one again. Snowberry
    lives, rain-less, wind-battered, no matter.

        Grouse, quail & thrushes in their arms.
    Gophers chew root stems in the dark;

rabbits sleep curled underneath
       burrowed all winter. Snowberry

           holds up hillsides in their root nets,
      thick catch-all webs covering

abandoned land. Devastation & ruins from
       old mines taken back. Even burned, snowberry

          revives with a little sleet-melt.
     Seeds cracked, seeds spread

by birds up & down the dry eastern slopes.

Pine Forest

Art by Xena Lunsford

Welcome to the Pine Forest. Here is a landscape vibrant with towering Ponderosa Pine, chattering Yellow-pine Chipmunk, the taps of various members of the Woodpecker clan, and the oh-so-sweet smell of Pine in sun. This is a community whose tallest trees, save for Western Larch, don't change color with the season but whose foliage, thanks to beings such as Arrowleaf Balsamroot and Mountain Ash, runs from bright yellow in summer to bright red in autumn. In spring, when the breeze is just right, you might spy a saffron-yellow cloud rising from the crown of every Pine tree. Even the *thought* of so much pollen released into the air might make some sneeze.

The Pine Forest offers so much to so many, from cone seeds for sustenance to shelter from sun, wind, and snow, to nesting habitat. As snags (also called wildlife trees), Pine offers the ideal home for beings who nest in cavities, such as Northern Flying Squirrel, Western Bluebird, Raccoon, Pygmy Nuthatch, Pine Marten, and Flammulated Owl. Up and down their trunks and draping their branches, you will typically find several kinds of lichen happily growing, from the tiny, chartreuse, shrub-like forms of Wolf Lichen to the long, dark strands of Horsehair.

Cascadian Pine Forests have provided homes and nourished people for millennia. And as we still harvest trees from this community, we can also look to it for connection. As in all forests, that connection is sustained by the communication and sharing of resources provided by fungal networks within the soil itself.

In Japan, many people receive this spiritual gift as they practice shinrin-yoku, or "forest bathing." Not only do we feel the spiritual enrichment of time within the forest, but researchers have also studied and documented the many health benefits of taking one's body among the trees to simply be: to breathe the living air, listen to the voices of other beings, smell sun-warmed duff, see light glinting along a strand of silk, and feel at home. Those of us who know the Pine Forest have felt this in our bones.

BILL YAKE

The Tree as Verb

> The true formula for thought is: The cherry tree is all that it does.
> —Ernest Fenollosa

Seed, swell, press and push, sprout, bud, curl, bloom, unfurl, quicken, ripen, and dispense.

Remain.

Blotch, ferment, rot and mushroom.

Germinate.

Probe, grope, root, draw in, draw up, dole out, absorb, allot, assimilate, respire, reconstitute, release.

Senesce.

Reach, brace, resist, avoid, deflect, split, notch, rustle, shake, bend and shimmy.

Occupy.

Cover, mask, obscure, protect, enclose and hide; tolerate, support, feed, shade, harbor and disguise.

Stand, sketch out, stretch out, fork, reach, branch, divide,
    incline and sway.

Reclaim, endure and burn.

Return, leaf out, green up, synthesize, digest, night-quiver,
    yellow, wilt and wither, abscise,

and collapse to root and rise.

Ponderosa Pine

(Pinus ponderosa)

When you come across Ponderosa Pine, make sure to find a sun-warmed fissure in the orange-brown bark and take a good long sniff. Many people smell vanilla; others whiff butterscotch or even cream soda.

This thick, jigsaw-puzzle bark, along with a high crown, helps make Ponderosa Pine one of the most fire-resistant trees in Cascadia. Some trunks still hold sign of fires that burned over five hundred years ago. When standing next to the long-needled Pondo, check for claw marks. The great size of the older trees (the biggest being seven feet in diameter and two hundred feet tall) makes them ideal pillars for Black Bear to use in climbing exercises or as an escape route. They also make fantastic back scratchers. Their awe-inspiring size is what earned them the *ponderous* part of their name.

These forests tend to be open and welcoming and full of light. Ponderosa flourishes on the dry side of Cascadia, and during drought, they can (amazingly) close their leaf pores to prevent water loss. Because they are adapted to the dry side, they grow best when frequent, low-intensity fires sweep through their understory, burning the small brush and dead branches.

Ponderosa Pine, also known as Western Yellow Pine, is an essential source of high-grade lumber because of the uniform grain of mature trees. You will

find Ponderosa Pine in the trim around doors and windows and the structural frames of houses. Indigenous people have over two hundred uses for Ponderosa Pine, including using the sap for chewing gum and the inner bark, or cambium, as a sugar-rich food in early spring. Yellow-pine Chipmunk and other beings make caches of the seeds to eat through winter. However, they don't use all their stores, and those seeds can become little groves that tend to thrive better than wind-planted seedlings.

ROBERT WRIGLEY

In Time

The great pine fallen by the wind
lay across the game trail down
from the ridge to the creek
and has in all the years since been

leaped, scratched, and scrambled over—
tenderized, hoof-chiseled—
until today, when down all its half-limbed
unbroken length there is only this

one gap to pass through,
and I do, for the hundredth time
I've walked here, going always back
through deeper seasons of drought and fire

seasons of plenty and seasons of want,
to the pummeled heart of its long death
and longer life, to when it first rose up into the sun
which had just the day before shown Keats his pale shadow.

Yellow-Pine Chipmunk

(Tamias amoenus)

The bird you think you hear as you stroll through the inviting understory of a
Pine Forest might turn out to be the cinnamon-furred, bushy-tailed, and black-
and-white-striped Yellow-pine Chipmunk! Chipmunk utters a fantastic array
of repeated chirps, chips, and tisks. Chipmunk is rarely still and seems always
to be dashing through the brush, tail-twitching from a tree limb or boulder,
or standing and using their handlike forefeet to chew their way through a cone

just as a Human toddler would a corncob. Their bright colors and voices (and perhaps their diminutive industry) earned them the second part of their Latin name, which means "delightful."

During warmer months, Chipmunk gathers seeds and stores them in various caches (hence the first part of the Latin name, which means "storer"). Then, as winter approaches, these jelly jar–sized, semiarboreal beings use their ample cheek pouches to carry seeds to their nests, which are typically located under logs and rocks or in stumps and snags. Instead of hibernating through winter like Golden-mantled Ground Squirrel (who has a similar appearance but no facial stripes), they wake from their torpor every four or five days to eat and defecate and, on milder days, emerge to forage.

CHARLES FINN

Yellow-Pine Chipmunk

When the warm heart of day
and thin wrist of luck
offer you a Yellow-Pine Chipmunk
squatting on its haunches
cinnamon sides panting
in the phosphorus sun—take it.
Take it and its question mark tail
into your heart
its five black and white racing stripes
and forepaws clutched to its chest.
Take it and count your blessings
humble yourself before this tiny king
resting on its midden of cones
its polite wedge of face
like a worn arrowhead narrowing
to a twitching nose and nonexistent chin.
There is a world out there
larger than any imagined
take it and fill the cheeks of your mouth
with the seeds of thanks
for the tiny paws, the stop and go mentality
for the frozen moment of time
when those almond-shaped, oil-drop eyes
look back into yours.

Horsehair Lichen

(Bryoria fuscescens)

This being has a name in at least twenty different Indigenous languages in North America. In Secwépemc language, they are wila, a word also used for the dish made from this being. This being is so well known, perhaps, because it is such an important part of many diets. Packed in those long ten-drils hanging from tree branches is a dense serving of carbohydrates that Indigenous families and others harvest and store by the pound. Horse-hair Lichen is usually soaked for several hours to overnight in water, often in running water. While soaking, Lichen is sometimes worked with hands or pounded with a paddle-shaped tool.

Horsehair Lichen looks exactly as you might think. Up there, in the branches of Lodgepole Pine, those long, thick, dark brown tendrils swaying in the breeze like the mane of Horse, are living things. Unlike other single-organism beings, Horsehair Lichen, like all lichens, combines two organisms, fungal and algal.

Bunch them to your chin like a beard, make them the hair on a forest snow-man, let your fingers twist and play with them as you pass by or under, and maybe you will give them yet another name.

EMMA NOYES

Sqʷlip

Once you've found a stick long enough
Modified to twirl and hook hair like a finger
Raise it and rake through wispy remnants
Of another one of coyote's great escapes

Your other hand should shield your baby's crown and eyes
From bark and bits of lichen and gossip
Loosened by your efforts and the lonesome winds
Young untrained tongues cannot be trusted
Your samples should be delivered promptly
To the laboratory housed within the perfect palate
Of an elder's practiced mouth
Between a lifetime clinging to pine
And the next life hung over rafters
Lies the knowledge of transformation
Sustenance of bears and birds and deer
Baked into great blankets barring hunger
This is where you might find yourself lost
A pit oven and pocket knife away from nourishment
I was taught to microwave moss pudding
Hints of honey and rose mixed with fungus and algae
Forming a sea of steam and dark jelly
This is what happens when one elder sheds spores
of ancient teachings to take hold on new branches

Cassia Crossbill

(Loxia sinesciuris)

The only place in the world you can hear the burry, finchy warble of Cassia Crossbill and see their bright bodies—reddish-orange-yellow in males and greenish-gray in females—dangling upside down from Pine cones is in Idaho's South Hills and Albion Mountains.

Cassia Crossbill looks like the other nine varieties of Red Crossbill in size and coloration and the characteristic shape of their bills, which appear twisted. In crossbills, the top bill curves one way and the bottom bill the other, like bent pliers. One important difference, however, appears in the thicker bill that Cassia Crossbill uses to pry open the scales of Lodgepole Pine cones as they slip a dexterous tongue in to retrieve their primary food source: Lodgepole Pine

seeds. When hundreds of Cassia Crossbills are feeding this way, you can hear the lightest rain of the diaphanous husks falling to the forest floor and an occasional softly called *kip*. The second part of their Latin name, *sinesciuris*, means "without squirrels" and refers to the absence of Red Squirrel in their habitat, a key condition that has led to the amazing coevolution happening between their bill and Lodgepole Pine's cones.

Although others in Cascadia have surely known Cassia Crossbill for a very long time, contemporary scientists became aware of them only recently. And in 2020, the Badger Fire in the Sawtooth National Forest burned through about a third of their habitat. What other beings, we might wonder, have so far escaped our awareness, and will they survive long enough for us to meet them?

NICK NEELY

The Looking Glass

I tucked myself into a threadbare willow beside a cabin and tried not to flinch. The leaves cut my shape, just enough, and the birds came. The putters of their wingbeats announced three species: Cassin's finches, somehow saccharine in their scarlet crowns; pine siskins, yellow-barred; and Cassia crossbills, elephantine by comparison, a heavier burst and slowing as they landed, *brr-rump*. They'd come for salt extruded from the concrete foundation. Slowly, I raised my binoculars. Beside a few old planks and crushed beer cans, they hopped, scratched, jostled—mouthed and digested this earth.

European folklore holds that, while Jesus hung on the cross, a roaming finch came to his aid, pulling at the nails in vain, bathing its plumage in blood, wounding itself, mangling its bill forever. The evolutionary explanation for the crossbill is simpler and no less miraculous: They are adapted for opening conifer cones.

Curl your index finger over the knuckle of your thumb, and you shape this bird's namesake anomaly, which it jams between two scaly bracts. As it bites, its bill's curved tips press in opposite directions, forcing the scales apart. Next it flexes its lower mandible (your thumb) sideways, using a hyper-developed muscle on one side of its face to pry the scales wider. The bird's pink tongue—so long that it wraps behind its skull when retracted, as in hummingbirds and woodpeckers—slips in for the seed in its papery skin. The bird husks the nut using a special groove on its upper palate. The crossbill performs this ritual, this chore, about 1,500 times a day.

As the birds lifted their heads from the dust, I studied those beaks. Cassia crossbills are found only in these mountains and the neighboring range. They have co-evolved with the lodgepole pines here, so that their bills have grown larger, on average, along with the cones. There are perhaps only four or five thousand Cassia crossbills in the world. They're not likely to survive this century. Warmer temperatures are causing the South Hills' cones to open prematurely and shed their seeds, the bird's one and only staple. From under my willow I looked into those charismatic black reflective eyes. You could say they looked like coal.

Ten-Lined June Beetle

(Polyphylla decemlineata)

Ten-lined June Beetle is common throughout Cascadia, the adults feeding on conifers and the larvae specializing on plant roots. They are drawn to light, which is usually where you will find them, day or night. They are a striking being, relatively large—about as long as two standard paper clips—and the white lines striping their elytra (wing covers) are hard to miss. If you get a close look, you will find that each elytra has one long and four short lines.

If you come across a male June Beetle, you will also see how his antennae, made of what are called lamellate plates, appear quite large, like a grandiose mustache on a Human male. These antennae aren't a fashion statement but rather how males detect the pheromones released by females.

When disturbed, they emit a distinct sound that some have compared to the hissing of Bat. Don't worry. They aren't throwing a hissy fit, and they aren't spraying you like Skunk might. The hiss comes when they push their wings rapidly against their back, expelling only air. If you are lucky enough to have June Beetle land on you, you might feel the soft tickle of the golden-brown hairs covering their belly as they explore the place that is you.

MARTHA SILANO

To the Ten-Lined June Beetle

Feed them to your chickens or simply squish . . .
—*The Daily Garden*

Nights you're drawn to our electric lights, to the scent
of a mate. Into the ground you go to lay your eggs,
into the ground your babies, feeding

on the roots of trees—almond, apple, cherry, plum.
You do your damage quietly, until it's too late.
But aren't we both pretty? Determined?

Industrious? But aren't you saving us
from ourselves as you destroy a crop
requiring a trillion gallons of water, three gallons per nut?

Oh, little scarab, Egyptian god of the rising sun, creator and protector,
symbol of resurrection, your lines resemble the parched ground
where pumped-dry rivers flowed.

Lodgepole Pine

(*Pinus contorta*)

You know Lodgepole Pine in this way: the needles cluster in pairs. On the coast, Lodgepoles are shorter and grow in a twisted fashion (hence the second part of their Latin name, *contorta*). But inland, even on an eighty-foot being, their trunks are slender and straight, and the bark is thin and will peel with your thumbnail like orange-brown, gray, and black scales.

When you think of Lodgepole, think of home. This being's name comes from the way Coastal Tribes first used Lodgepole: in the building of their lodges. To Nimiipuu, Lodgepole is known as Qalámgalam, and makes perfect tepee poles. Lodgepole is also used to manufacture contemporary homes—there is a good chance that if your home is constructed with wood, you can knock on your wall and hear Lodgepole within.

Lodgepole is less fire-resistant than other Pines because of their thin bark, smaller-diameter trunk, and delicate branches. But fire works wonders for the tree. After a blaze, serotinous cones release seeds by the millions, and stands can come back thicker and denser than before. Lodgepole is also an excellent shelter for the weary traveler. Take a rest under this being's branches, and there find another being that makes a home with the tree: Grouse Whortleberry. Pick a

handful of these cousins to Huckleberry and taste a summer forest. If the year is right and the breeze is blowing, watch for the seeds that drop from Lodgepole's cone—they will flutter through the air on a single spinning wing and rest on the humus until they awaken again.

JACKSON HOLBERT

A Short Note on the Names of Trees

I knew none of them, save for one—lodgepole pine. I'd heard many, certainly. Dozens. But when my sister said maple, I thought lodgepole pine, and when my sister said sycamore, I thought lodgepole pine. Even when she said *blackberry lilac tarragon bitterbrush*. Lodgepole pine lodgepole pine, etc. It didn't matter. One day it was suddenly the seventh grade and I was in Spanish and I had to say jacarandá, but couldn't. Our small, wheezing teacher steered me to the front of the class and made me say it fifty times. Jacarandá jacarandá jacarandá and I got it! All I had to do was imagine the beautiful pictures of jacarandás that inhabited our ancient textbooks. But by the twelfth jacarandá I lost it, heard only the soft music of my boy voice. I kept saying it, I made it to fifty, but in my head I was singing lodgepole pine lodgepole pine.

White-Headed Woodpecker

(Dryobates albolarvatus)

When you encounter White-headed Woodpecker, it will often be because you catch sight of this characteristically silent being flying an undulant path with rapid wing beats and brief glides from one Pine trunk to another. Aside from being visually stunning, their glossy black body and bright white head make them easy to distinguish from others of the Woodpecker clan and provide cryptic

coloring, mimicking the way shade plays through a sun-dappled forest.

If you do hear White-headed Woodpecker, instead of their sharp, high-pitched calls, it might be the crackling sounds they make when prying insects from tree bark or Pine cones. Not only does Pine provide them their primary food of seeds, but crevices in the bark also make a kind of vise to hold larger seeds for them to break into edible bits.

Using their powerful beak to drum on particularly resonant trunks, White-headed Woodpecker signals his territory and attracts potential mates. It is almost as if their sharply demarcated coloration symbolizes their roles in parenting: the male incubates the eggs all night, while the female takes the day shift. During incubation (about two weeks), the parents are attentive to each other, frequently communicating by softly drumming inside and out of the nest cavity, not unlike Human siblings tapping to each other through a shared wall.

Birders fly from all over the world to catch a glimpse of this being endemic to Cascadia and Southern California.

SEAN HILL

The White-Headed Woodpecker

Quiet. Given to prying more than pecking, an odd member of the family, lives only in the high pine forests of western

mountains like the Cascades, where I spent an afternoon almost a decade ago in Roslyn, Washington looking for what

I could find of Black people who'd migrated from the South
almost a century and a quarter prior. The white-headed

woodpecker doesn't migrate and so is found in its
home range year-round when it can be found. Roslyn,

founded as a coal mining town, drew miners from all over
Europe—as far away as Croatia—across the ocean, with

opportunities. With their hammering and drilling to extract
a living, woodpeckers could be considered arboreal miners.

A habitat, a home range, is where one can feed and house
oneself—meet the requirements of life—and propagate.

In 1888, those miners from many lands all in Roslyn came
together to go on strike against the mine management.

And so, from Southern states, a few hundred Black miners
were recruited with the promise of opportunities in Roslyn,

many with their families in tow, to break the strike. They
faced resentment and armed resistance, left in the dark

until their arrival, unwitting scabs—that healing that happens
after lacerations or abrasions. Things settled down as they do

sometimes, and eventually Blacks and whites entered a union
as equals. Black save for a white face and crown and a sliver

of white on its wings that flares to a crescent when they
spread for flight, the white-headed woodpecker is a study

in stark contrasts. Males have a patch of red feathers
on the back of their crowns, and I can't help but see blood.

Pinedrops

(Pterospora andromedea)

It is a rare and wonderful opportunity to spot Pine-
drops! When you do, step carefully toward the toe-
high cluster. Maybe it is merely the stalk you've
spotted, which is the predominant state of Pine-
drops, or perhaps
you have lucked into
a blossoming flock. If
so, bend down to look at
the reddish stems produc-
ing similarly reddish flowers
that resemble tiny urns. Note
the sticky petals, and stop to thank
Pine for harboring this being, as the
two have a particularly important rela-
tionship.

The Latin genus name, *Pterospora*, comes
from Greek for "winged seeds," referring
to the netlike wing at one end of each tear-
drop-sized seed that carries it to a new site as it
is sprinkled from the cup that held it. Unlike most
other Pine Forest plants, Pterospora doesn't photosyn-
thesize and so lacks the familiar green of many plants.
Instead, Woodland Pinedrops utilizes unique mycorrhizal fungi to obtain carbon
from the roots of coniferous trees. Most of Woodland Pinedrops's life happens
underground in a series of brittle but fleshy roots.

Original stewards of Pine Forest have used Pinedrops medicinally in a fusion
of ground berries and stems as an astringent or as snuff to prevent nosebleeds.
Today, because of their rarity, we enjoy them where they are and celebrate the
unique characteristics of a plant whose appearance makes a forest walk magical.

ELIZABETH AOKI

When they looked at you breathing, they saw scarlet wings

Luck-borne,
how else can the clustered thought
of you fly so far? So many pine cones drop dead
but not you. So sticky.

The pale open mouth
of my jacket cuff
mimics the curve of your blossoms,
seed bells trilling, a forest's tintinnabulum.

So secretly you feed, down through your roots
to the fungi that also dine on this ancient pine:
oldster of the forest, towering sun eater.

Below its canopy,
all your tiny winged seeds
flare translucent triangles of hope,
struggling where they fall askew.

It's so damn hard to sprout alone.

Pinedrops, teach us to love
what we already know:
we're all slipping, sliding, arms intertwined,
reaching for whatever we can
in the dark.

Black Bear

(Ursus americanus)

You know them by what they leave behind—scat, prints, claw marks. In summer, feces mounds sport seeds of berries, which Black Bear eats by the pound. In fall, tracks left in first snow wander into the woods or drainages where Bear will sleep for up to seven and a half months in caves or dens dug into earth. Come spring, they crawl out, stretch, and scratch the trunk of Aspen and Pine, leaving scent messages for others of their kin.

Born blind in a den during the darkest days of winter and weighing less than a pound, Black Bear will grow to be anywhere from three feet tall on all fours to an average of six feet standing upright. Sows can have up to ten litters of cubs and live as many as thirty years, though most die in their early twenties.

If you look up a tree trunk and see claw marks high above you, that's most likely the sign left by a cub, whose scramble to safety might have taken her hundreds of yards up a tall Ponderosa Pine. Lean into the trunk, smell the musk, then turn and rub your back against it as Bear does.

People harvest Bear for food, as well as bedding, blankets, robes, and moccasins. Today Black Bear is a ubiquitous marketing symbol in mountain towns all over Cascadia, but nothing beats the thrill of seeing her, ambling on turned-in forepaws, mouth full of moths she might eat by the pawful, and close behind, trundling cubs, which will stay with her this winter too.

BARBARA DRAKE

The Bear

Seeing a black bear by the road
I shout, "It's a bear, it's a bear,"
and cover my eyes, I think
because I like seeing it so much.

Arrowleaf Balsamroot

(Balsamorhiza sagittata)

Don't be surprised if you find yourself suddenly singing, "The hills are alive" when you catch sight of Arrowleaf Balsamroot blooming by the thousands in early spring. Their Sunflower-like petals splash great patches of gold across the still-green slopes of Cascadia's dry interior.

Others, however, may see the same sight and think, "Dinnertime!" Deer and Elk graze on the wide, arrow-shaped leaves throughout the year. All parts of Arrowleaf Balsamroot, in fact, are edible. Motorists, hikers, and bikers admiring their annual spring show may have little idea of how essential this being has been as a food source for Native people.

Arrowleaf Balsamroot's young leaves can be eaten raw or steamed, and Okanagan people smoke them like tobacco. The slightly woody aromatic taproots (roots that grow straight down) can be nearly nine feet long and help this being survive both fire and drought. Arrowleaf Balsamroot's seeds look and feel and taste like smaller, darker, pointier sunflower seeds. They can be dried and pounded to make flour. Mid-June is usually the best time to harvest the seeds.

In addition to eating and smoking Arrowleaf Balsamroot, many Native people use them medicinally. Blackfeet use the root smoke to treat body aches and make a poultice of the roots to treat blisters, sores, insect bites, bruises, and wounds.

When you get a chance, give Arrowleaf Balsamroot's flowers a good sniff. See if you, like many others, think they smell like chocolate.

DAVID OATES

Arrowleaf Balsamroot

If in a dry land there be a balm
yellow by eye and bright as sun
in stony ground or gulch,
in oak-choked kolk or basalt standing,
arrayed across arroyos
as a green rustle balsamwise
at noonday and by starshine . . .

if in a dry mind a balsam root
then is the desert secret known for a time—
no drought but this one, no blazing heat
except what the day bring
and is always bringing.

If in a dry time, and getting dryer,
we need these gay green suns
clustered by ditch or dike
or out among the clinkered scablands
or down in bee-hummed hummocks
by weather-rinded rocks and slim sly lichen
beside the neverstoppingness of lupine
and the coming and going folks who wonder

at so healing a yellow, so seeing a green
arrowing us into our own time to come
out on dusty ridges
and between the long-spaced rains.

Western Rattlesnake

(Crotalus oreganus)

In Nez Perce tradition, a charm against evil is invoked by placing a Wéexpus head on hot coals in the earth and covering it with fresh liver and gall from other wild beings. During the steaming, the liver is thought to absorb venom from the head, which is then carried as a talisman. But it is not the head we usually think of when we think of Western Rattlesnake.

Many traditions, myths, and beliefs center around this being, whose tail is often a charm and bite is sometimes deadly. Though the hinged fangs carry a deadly venom, the tail is surprisingly empty. Instead of functioning like a maraca to make its namesake sound, the outer shell of the rattle, made of keratin, clicks together. Special shaker muscles in the tail allow the tip to vibrate up to ninety times per second. Though this rattle often evokes fear, as it should, Rattlesnake wants to avoid conflict. They are generally quite docile and run (slither!) from you as quickly as you do from them.

Though most of what we think about when Rattlesnake comes to mind is sound and bite, it is actually smell that is their strongest sensory organ. Those nostrils are great for breathing, but that split tongue does the smelling—almost. It reaches out and grabs molecules from the air and brings them to Snake's Jacobson's organ, a chemoreceptor located in the nasal cavity. This organ helps decode the molecules into smells.

Rattlesnake, who can live up to twenty years, has few natural predators, but they have long been persecuted by Humans. In some areas, Snake populations have adapted by cutting down on their warning rattles, which makes them harder to find and kill—a good reminder that when in Rattlesnake's community, you should watch where you step!

JACK JOHNSON

Leaving the Garden

When a Great Northern swallows the tracks,
we work in the garden without talking.

We leave our weed pulling
to walk the fire trail to the river.

A car's wheels hiss up Derby Canyon.
The Wenatchee crawls below the rail bed,

snakes toward the Columbia.
We glimpse an osprey overhead

and try to spot a catbird
meowing high in pine branches.

We hear quail rattle the wild roses,
the snowberries. So—

he sees us before we see him—
a brown and yellow spotted snake—

his flat head balanced above his tail,
the sudden rattle

a Rainbird sprinkler striking tin.
All things move in coils.

In smooth roots and yellow grass,
the sky disappears.

Bitterbrush

(Purshia tridentata)

Bitterbrush. To say the word seems to limit this magnificent plant, a hardy thriver of arid regions who blooms from April through July and is typically a dominant shrub in the Pine Forest. Bitterbrush is often sporting hundreds of five-petaled, sweet-smelling suns on long, scruff-leafed branches and seems anything but bitter. In fact, this being flourishes, sending taproots deep into the soil and blooming for decades—some are well over a century old!

The full common name of Bitterbrush is Antelope Bitterbrush, which signifies the importance of this being as food for Deer, Elk, Bighorn Sheep, and of course, Pronghorn Antelope, who find the leaves very palatable (though to Humans the taste is, indeed, quite bitter). In winter, Bitterbrush's long branches reach above the snowpack and provide one of the few food sources for these browsers. And though the teeth of these mammals often browse Bitterbrush's small, hairy, green leaves, those leaves have teeth too—look for three at the tip (hence the second part of their Latin name)—but don't expect any bite. Bitterbrush is quite friendly, lending small birds and other beings a home and cover and helping to reclaim areas where mining or fire has disturbed the soil.

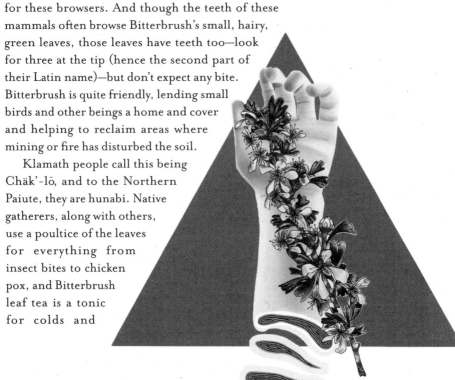

Klamath people call this being Chäk'-lō, and to the Northern Paiute, they are hunabi. Native gatherers, along with others, use a poultice of the leaves for everything from insect bites to chicken pox, and Bitterbrush leaf tea is a tonic for colds and constipation. A purplish dye can be made from the seeds. For many Pine Forest walkers, the greatest gift of Bitterbrush is the joy this being exudes on summer slopes at 3,100 to 10,000 feet in elevation.

ALLEN BRADEN

Fable of Greasewood

Ringleader of the Old West's status quo,
it has more aliases than a wanted poster.
Bitterbrush. Buckbrush. Call it creosote's

cousin, grouse hotel or antelope salad.
Whenever the guide says *greasewood*,
I imagine shrubs lubing the zerks

of deer and longhorn that chaparral
from drought to arroyo wash
for bitterness enough to live.

Paiute, Pima, and Colville
pestle its good medicine for the pox,
brew away fever, boil worm tonic.

Ticks, deerflies, pioneers, soldiers,
hunters, everyone who passes through
itching for blood in scablands and scrub.

In the New West, we plunder dirt.
That's right. We plow under the thorns,
along with the succulence.

Eastern Rivers

Art by Justin Gibbens

Say you are the golden leaf of Black Cottonwood. A fall breeze pulls you from the limb, and you sashay through the cool air and land in a river. Maybe it is the Snake River. Maybe the Salmon. Or perhaps the mighty Columbia. Whichever the river, it carries you on its slower-moving water through a land that has sustained people for thousands of years. As you rock gently on the water, you look below to see a flash of crimson, Chinook Salmon, moving in the opposite direction, heading home to make her redd. And then, looking up, another crimson, this of Red-osier Dogwood leaning toward the water as if looking for you.

On this journey of hundreds of miles, you glide over juvenile Idaho Giant Salamander, but only as you pass through Idaho. Caddisfly larvae will be scraping their way along the river's bottom. At the same time, Western Ridged Mussel will be doing the kind work of cleaning the river's water. You'll hear the song of Chukar and the whispers of Humans walking the banks in awe of the beautiful canyons and drainages through which the Eastern Rivers of Cascadia flow.

Dipper will tickle the stream, Pack Rat will take a nighttime sip, and with a breeze, seeds of the ever-important Biscuit Root will join you on the journey. Like the sun runs over the backs of the Salmon River Mountains, so shall your imagination run the ridges of the White Sturgeon before drifting into the open sea.

"Eventually," as Norman Maclean writes, "all things merge into one, and a river runs through it." And so it is for Cascadia. The

Eastern Rivers community is the network of veins carrying life to and from and around Cascadia. To know these river communities is to know much about how to be, who to be, and how to thrive within them.

DAVID JAMES DUNCAN
from "Hearts Like Mountains"

When I was four years old I stood at Celilo Falls in its last month above slackwater, feeling the dip net inside me spring to life, scoop down. The faces of those tribal fishermen; the oceanic roar so far from the sea: they wreck me still. When I was five I had my first close encounter with a big male coho in a ruined urban stream: his totem red, white and black face assails me still. When I was eight I hooked my first winter steelhead in a little tributary of the Clackamas. She exploded the creek and my heart both at once. It hurts, it hurts, it hurts to remember how much wild wealth and beauty and joy has been lost, diminished, unloved, destroyed. But when it's the loving heart that hurts, I say, *Let it.* Mountains, broken and broken and broken again, become the pebbles of our beloved salmon's birth houses. May our hearts be like the mountains.

King Salmon
(*Oncorhynchus tshawytscha*)

One of the First People's legends goes something like this: When Coyote came to this area known as Cascadia, he saw the People required some help. So Coyote created the Columbia River, and with it connected the Pacific Ocean and an inland pond where women had been keeping two fish. Knowing the river would bring more Humans, Coyote declared the fish as "the people's food." Salmon began to make their journey from the pond to the ocean and back again, and

Coyote taught the People how to gather Salmon in seine nets spun of Spruce roots by the mouth of the river and in intricate weirs, mazes, baskets, and traps in the narrower, quieter areas. From above the rapids, the People built stages and speared or netted the leaping Salmon.

These People are called Chinookan, and for them, this being is named. Another name, King, refers to the fact that they are the largest of the Salmon family and the *Oncorhynchus* (hooked jaw) genus. Chinook is commonly three feet long and weighs about the same as a Human leg but has been seen even larger.

Like other Salmon, Chinook goes through a physiological and morphological change called smoltification before heading to sea. Born in freshwater, Chinook smolts in Eastern Rivers and lives there for about half a year until the time for migration to the ocean nears. Then, these incredible beings lose the dark bars along their flanks and begin to acquire a dark back, a light belly, and an overall silvery color typical to their ocean-living cousins. They seek deep pools, they avoid light, and their gills and kidneys begin to change to adapt to saltwater. Young Chinook hangs out in tidal creeks and estuaries, feeding on small fish, insects, crustaceans, and mollusks until they gradually move into deeper, saltier water, and then the ocean.

Chinook spends an average of three to four years in the ocean before again changing their appearance and physiology. Bucks become evergreen with rose-pink flanks, their backs grow humps, and their jaws grow hooks with sharp teeth.

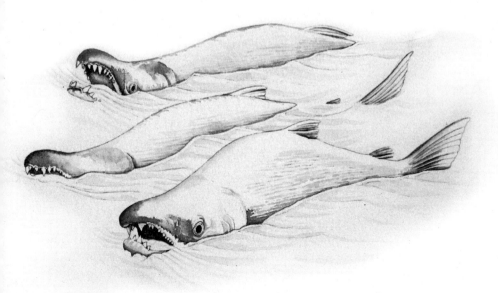

Hens, too, turn a rosy pink and deep green, but a lighter shade with a brassy sheen. Both begin the upstream journey, neither eating but using their fat stores for the trip and eventual reproduction. Chinook will make this journey but once, dying upon laying or fertilizing eggs. (In contrast, Steelhead may make this miraculous change as many as four times!)

Chinook in Columbia River tributaries is officially endangered. A century's worth of overfishing, dam construction, and pollution have threatened Chinook in other regions too. Nevertheless, Chinook remains powerful in Cascadia— not only culturally and through their connection with the tribes but also for what Chinook reveals about the river's health. Tribal fisheries, alongside other organizations, are deeply invested in restoring the traditional runs of Chinook. This will no doubt benefit all beings and please Coyote as well.

SHERMAN ALEXIE
Migration, 1902

The salmon swim
so thick in this river

that Grandmother walks
across the water

on the bridge
of their spines.

Caddisfly
(*Trichoptera* spp.)

They are case-building, net-spinning, tube-making, trumpet-netting, and more—each different species, but all Caddisfly! Each of the thousands of different species of Caddisfly goes through complete metamorphosis, like Butterfly or

Dragonfly. Caddisfly larvae, which live in water, all have bodies like Caterpillar and a hardened head, simple eyes, and a pale, soft belly. This being is segmented, and from each segment sprouts a segmented leg—and here is where differences start to show. The legs may have sharp tips, hooks, or rows of hairs or bristles (setae), and these differences are some of what separates one kind of Caddisfly from another.

The various tools on Caddisfly's legs are used to gather food and move and collect building materials. To protect their soft belly and provide a safe place to retreat, Caddisfly makes a case. Caddisfly, you see, has the fantastic ability to produce a silken thread (spun by glands on the floor of their mouth), and each species makes a unique case. Some cases are built of small rocks and sand, some are like longhouses made of twigs and stems, and others are reinforced with bark, leaves, seeds, and mollusk shells. Here Caddisfly will stay as larva for most of their life, often one or two years. As Caddisfly grows, more material is added to the front of their tubes (repairs are constantly being made). Caddisfly can even turn around in the tube and trim the rear to keep it from dragging.

Caddisfly grows from larva to pupa, when they grow wings and fly. Above water, brown-and-gray Caddisfly lives for about a month, feeding on nectar at night and being fed upon by Bat, for whom they are an essential food source. Caddisfly will mate, and the female will lay a gelatinous mass of eggs that hatch in a few weeks, beginning the cycle again, building a beautiful home and proving themselves champions of underwater architecture.

NOAH DAVIS

Caddisfly (*Trichoptera* spp.)

Here in the willow,

    above the shovel-skulled trout
    who waits to dig through the dust of our falling,

we cling to limbs
    drying our newly shelled wings

        that quiver,
        morning caught in aspen leaves,

    before we fly

    and join ourselves with the river

    to loosen our pearled children
        off our bellies,

        then lift

    to keep ourselves out of the trout's mouth

    a moment longer.

White Sturgeon

(Acipenser transmontanus)

Beauty comes in many forms in Eastern Rivers. From red spawning Chinook to budding Black Cottonwood, beings we have come to know well. But there is beauty in mystery, too, and indeed, the most mysterious fish in Cascadia's Eastern Rivers is White Sturgeon. Since the time of dinosaurs some seventy million years ago, White Sturgeon has remained essentially unchanged. According to Stó:lō oral tradition, this being was created when a young woman was cast into the river.

This impressive being glints like a new dime; they have dark eyes and whiskers, lines of ridges run down their sides like a perfect mountain range, and half-moon gills rise on their cheeks. Sturgeon's underside is a vulnerable white, and their chin is pocked with taste buds. Under the skin, plated like that of an alligator, is knowledge of a life we don't know much about.

White Sturgeon, your Latin name, *Acipenser transmontanus*, translates to "Sturgeon beyond the mountains." We know, White Sturgeon, that you feed on mollusks and Salmon. We know you can live to be one hundred years old. We know you spawn in freshwater and even exist in landlocked rivers, yet some of you take voyages to the sea. We know that you inspire contemporary Stó:lō artwork, linking past, present, and future generations. And White Sturgeon, we know those future generations are in peril. We know that dams are not good for you and that fishing can wear you down, injure you so that even if caught and released, you become vulnerable and weak. We know your decline will echo throughout the ecosystem and upset the already delicate balance.

A beautiful mystery you are, White Sturgeon. A mystery worth protecting for future generations to explore.

BRIAN DOYLE

from "The Creature Beyond the Mountains," in *One Long River of Song*

There are fish in the rivers of Cascadia that are bigger and heavier than the biggest bears. To haul these fish out of the Columbia River, men once used horses and oxen. These creatures are so enormous and so protected by bony armor that no one picks on them, so they grow to be more than a hundred years old, maybe two hundred years old; no one knows. Sometimes in winter, they gather in immense roiling balls in the river, maybe for heat, maybe for town meetings, maybe for wild sex; no one knows. A ball of more than sixty thousand of them recently rolled up against the bottom of a dam in the Columbia, causing a nervous United States Army Corps of Engineers to send a small submarine down to check on the dam. They eat fish, clams, rocks, fishing reels, shoes, snails, beer bottles, lamprey, eggs, insects, fishing lures, cannon-balls, cats, ducks, crabs, basketballs, squirrels, and many younger members of their species; essentially, they eat whatever they want. People have fished for them using whole chickens as bait, with hooks the size of your hand. They like to follow motorboats, for reasons no one knows. As with human beings, the males wish to spawn in their early teens, but the females wait until their twenties. The females then produce epic rafts of eggs, 3 or 4 million at a time, from ovaries that can weigh more than two hundred pounds. On average three of those eggs will grow to be mature fish. Some of the fish that have been caught have been fifteen feet long and weighed fifteen hundred pounds. There are stories of fish more than twenty feet long and two thousand pounds. A fish that long would be taller than three Shaquille O'Neals and heavier than six. There is a persistent legend in southwest Washington State that somewhere in the water near Mount Saint Helens is the biggest fish of this kind that anyone has ever seen or heard about or imagined, a fish so big that when it surfaces it is occasionally mistaken for a whale, but this is the same region of the wild and wondrous world where Sasquatch is thought to most likely live, so you wonder.

Idaho Giant Salamander

(Dicamptodon aterrimus)

Not all giants are giant. Behold Idaho Giant Salamander—the smallest of the amphibian "giants" in the family *Dicamptodontidae*. Idaho Giant Salamander is perhaps a little shorter and stouter than their giant cousins and is about the length of a pencil and the weight of three of them. They are found only in central Idaho (where, thanks to then junior high student Ilah Hickman, they are the official state amphibian!) and two places in western Montana—you can't find them anywhere else on the planet.

Idaho Giant Salamander goes through three stages: First is the larval stage, when they sport gills and live entirely underwater in nooks and crannies made by rocks and fallen trees. In the second stage, the Giant is called a paedomorph and looks like an adult but stays in their aquatic home. In the third stage, Idaho Giant Salamander moves to land, becoming gill-less. Terrestrial adults range from gray to brown with a beautiful copper pattern that looks like a topographical map of the Bitterroot Mountains. These colors fade along their sides, becoming pale pink to tan on the Giant's belly.

Young Idaho Giant Salamander shares their cold mountain streams with the usual host of invertebrates such as Caddisfly, Stonefly, and Mayfly larvae, as well as Crayfish, all of which Salamander eats. Rocky Mountain Tailed Frog is commonly found in streams occupied by Giant, who makes a meal of Frog's tadpoles. Ashore, adult Giant can eat beings as large as Shrew, Mouse, and small Snakes, along with other Salamanders. Basically, they will eat anything that they can catch. And Idaho Giant Salamander shows up on other beings' menus as well, such as Garter Snake, Weasel, Water Shrew, and various fish like Bull Trout and Steelhead, to name a few. To defend themselves against predators, Idaho Giant has a few strong defenses: toxic secretion from their skin, warning postures, a bark (not unlike Steller's Jay's call), and they will bite. Is their bark worse than their bite? Well, Idaho Giant Salamander's bite can easily break the skin of a Human, so be warned!

ROB TAYLOR

Idaho Giant Salamander

> Homage is, perhaps, simply appropriation with the current reversed;
> "here," we say to the thing, "is a tribute from our culture, in which
> having a face is the premier sign of status."
>
> —Don McKay

One day the water
of Lake Coeur d'Alene
will flow backwards
like a wind-carried ribbon
up the Bitterroots.

I Google your scant facts
imagine your 'bark'
the relief shrews must feel
when it's only a wolf—

you snake-eaten
eater of snakes.

One day the water
of Lake Coeur d'Alene
will flow backwards
and carry you up into
the lightest blue eddying pools.

You breathe through toxic
leopard skin. You eat whatever
you catch. Your bite's
drawn human blood—

why do I tell you
what you've already tasted?

One day the water
of Lake Coeur d'Alene
will pounce on its name-
bearing basin
then slink away

and 10,000 feet
in the grey, mottled sky
only your face
will remain.

Western Ridged Mussel

(Gonidea angulata)

Vulnerable. Imperiled. These are now the words most commonly associated with Western Ridged Mussel. Recent efforts have been made to list this being as endangered because their habitat—mostly cold streams and rivers—has decreased. Many rivers, like the Snake, have been altered by dams, which causes changes in water temperature and sediment deposits. Hydraulic and gravel gold mining have also damaged the habitat that homes this being.

Western Ridged Mussel once flourished in Cascadia and was an important food source for Native people, including the Nimíipuu, who call this being Seewi's. The tribes traditionally boiled or dried Ridged Mussel in the fall and used them over winter to supplement their food supply. Shells were used for jewelry, beads, ornaments, and ceremonies. Today, instead of harvesting, the Nez Perce fisheries and other tribes work to protect and conserve this unique and important being.

Put your hands in prayer and place them in the river. This is the way and shape of Western Ridged Mussel. The shell, about half the length of a dollar bill and covered by a fine, skin-like layer that works much like the screen protector on your cell phone, is yellowish brown or black. The inside is usually white but can be salmon-colored or pale blue. The shell protects the bivalve within as Ridged Mussel, in turn, protects the river, cleaning pollutants from the water as they feed.

Freshwater mussels like Western Ridged eat plankton. Slow growers, they live long lives of twenty to thirty years. To reproduce, a female releases packets (conglutinates) of fertilized juveniles who hitchhike on the gills of host fish for a few weeks or months before dropping off to settle and join existing mussel beds or begin a new one.

Gently open and close your hands in the water. Let the river flow through them, and maybe send some love along to this being, that we may act soon enough to help them repopulate and protect our rivers.

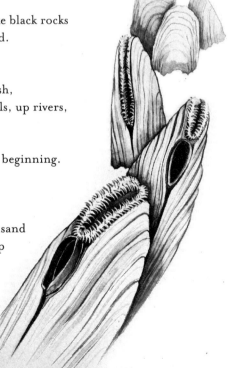

RICK BAROT

Hidden

One way of being hidden
is to be in plain sight, looking like black rocks
among other rocks in a streambed.

Another way is to be small,
latch on to the fins and gills of fish,
and travel up rapids and waterfalls, up rivers,

across lakes, then let go,
away from the home that is every beginning.
Still another way is to live

so long you outlive counting,
like the pine twisted into its thousand
years, like the cousin species deep
   in the silt

of its two centuries. Another way
of being hidden is to be a speck
in the vibrating web of water and earth,

to be quiet and rare, the gold
of broken places, continuing in the fire, rain,
snow, light, and pollen

that keep their touch on those broken places.
One more way of being hidden
is to close so completely you contain

the world's dreaming, the skies
of that sleep glowing like nacre: faintly blue,
as though it were water,

faintly pink, the eyeshadow of spring.

American Dipper

(Cinclus mexicanus)

Take an afternoon picnic to your favorite stream or river. Find a bridge or cliffy place, somewhere with an overhang. These places are perfect for Dipper's nest, which is mounded and round like a Hobbit hole and often the size of a soccer ball. Look for the gray, smoky being who may be doing any number of the following: dancing, twitching, preening, bobbing—or swimming! North America's only true aquatic songbird, they are known as Water Ouzel to some. To others, they are Trout with Feathers. The Yupik name for Dipper is Puyuqumaar(aq), which loosely translates as "the little bird that looks like smoke." The scientific name means "a kind of bird from Mexico," though few Ouzels migrate, and their range to the south is much less extensive than in Cascadia. The Iñupiat

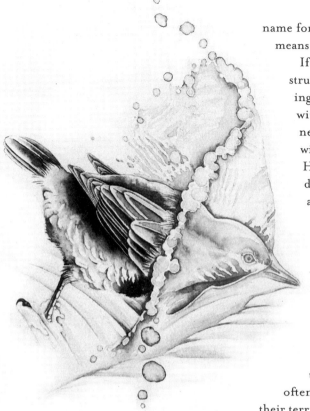

name for the bird, Arnaq kiviruq, means "woman sinking."

If Dipper is singing and strutting, you may be witnessing courtship, which begins with a male stretching his neck upward, bill vertical, wings drooping and spread. He then swaggers and sings directly in front of a female, a bubbling, Wren-like voice that rises above even the roar of nearby rapids. Sometimes both male and female perform together, finishing with a hop and a chest bump. Dipper mates for life but likes solitude; after the chicks fledge, parents often divide their brood and their territory and part ways.

Maybe Dipper is preening, which they do often and for long periods. Dipper's dense, soft coat of feathers is heavily waterproofed (their preen gland is ten times the size of any other songbird's). It may be late summer, and if so, Dipper is molting, shedding, and replacing wing and tail feathers all at once—temporarily flightless.

Maybe Dipper is feeding, catching an insect midair or plucking a bug off the stream bank. Or maybe they are chasing their favorite foods, like Water Beetle and Minnow, underwater—Dipper *is* like a Trout with feathers! Dipper often feeds by swimming on top of quick-moving water like a duck and dipping their head to catch their prey. Even more impressive, Dipper can dive (as much as twenty feet) to the bottom and walk there by wrapping their toes around rocks. While underwater, special muscles in their eyes constrict for better vision, and the scales on their nostrils close.

If Dipper is twitching and stretching wings, rapidly bobbing up and down some forty to sixty times per minute—well, your guess is as good as any! Some think this is a display of physical fitness, others think it is a dance to deter predators, and yet some others believe it is Dipper-to-Dipper signaling. If disturbed, Dipper blinks their white-feathered eyelids, perhaps a warning to their nearby mate.

Whatever Dipper is doing is bound to be fantastic, and no day is ever wasted (as Dipper knows) along an Eastern River!

GARY SNYDER

from "Little Songs for Gaia"

trout-of-the-air, ouzel,
bouncing, dipping, on a round rock
round as the hump of snow-on-grass beside it
between the icy banks, the running stream:
and into running stream
right in!

you   fly

Red-Osier Dogwood

(*Cornus sericea*)

Red-osier Dogwood leaning toward a stream makes one think that spawning Kokanee Salmon borrowed their bark and fallen leaves as an autumnal disguise. Standing as tall as a mailbox or growing as high as nine feet, Red-osier (French for "red willowy shoot") is beloved streamside and also as an urban garden plant.

Recognize this being by their flat, umbrellalike clusters of four- or five-petaled white flowers and prominent veins that gently curve to trace the shape of each leaf margin. The branches of Red-osier, even in winter, stay a warm, passionate red. The most reliable way to identify any Dogwood is to carefully break the leafstalk (petiole) and slowly pull each half apart to reveal the stringy white inside. Dogwood pith is unusual in its rubbery elasticity, which allows it to be pulled like cotton candy (though it is less sweet or brightly colored).

Red-osier Dogwood is one of several beings Indigenous people refer to as Kinnikinnick for its use as a tobacco substitute. The inner bark of young stems is split and scraped into threads and toasted over a fire, then mixed with tobacco. Edible plant enthusiast H. D. Harrington writes that Red-osier "is said to be aromatic and pungent, giving a narcotic effect approaching stupefaction."

Red-osier Dogwood is used for basketry, wicker furniture, farm implements, and weaving shuttles. Lovely wreaths—circular or heart-shaped—are made of Dogwood's bright red twigs. The word Dogwood, in fact, is a corruption of the Scandinavian term *dag*, meaning "skewer"—the hardened sticks are wonderful for roasting meat. Although the word has nothing to do with our canine companions, it still allows for the clever botanical joke, always worth repeating: "How do you tell it is a Dogwood? By their bark, of course."

MATT RADER

Red-Osier Dogwood

Lo, in the cave
of fragrance and sun,
I was

of a sudden naked
before myself
and the many

thousands
of candleflames
dappling

the red-osier dogwood
in its altar
of being. No one

laughed. Except
the elderberry
and the goat's beard

and the flickering
creek that held
no reflection,

but continued
to give itself
away without

hesitation. How
do I clean
this mirror

of running water?
I asked the congregation
which was

the sky in its blue-
white vestments
of oxygen,

which was the red-
osier dogwood,
its ministry of silence.

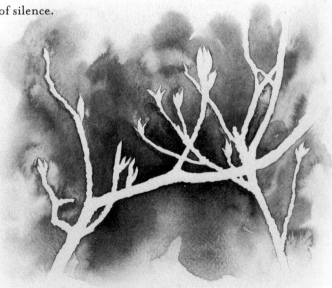

Black Cottonwood

(Populus trichocarpa)

Meet friendly, social, beautiful Black Cottonwood. One of the first smells of spring along Eastern Rivers is that of the sticky resin on Black Cottonwood's leaf buds—a pleasant, balsamic fragrance. Cottonwood is a delight for the eyes as well: standing about one hundred feet tall and sporting a black coat of bark, heart-shaped leaves, and flowers that, though inconspicuous, develop into red catkins that later burst with fluff that floats down from above during spring and early summer like a warm-season snowfall, seed by cottony seed. Though not as showy as the leaves of their famous (but less common in Cascadia) relative Quaking Aspen, Black Cottonwood's leaves turn a beautiful yellow in autumn.

Black Cottonwood is hardy, fast-growing (growing at a rate of five feet per year), and relatively short-lived, though some have been known to live for up to four hundred years. Black Cottonwood is a pioneer species, meaning it is one of the first beings to initiate an ecological community where currently no other exists, such as in places disturbed by floodwaters, and Black Cottonwood thrives in environments with recurring floods. Without disturbance, Cottonwood is replaced by other species on upland sites.

Trichocarpa means "hairy-fruited," referring to the cottony fluff that helps disperse the minute seeds over long distances. The Spanish name for

Cottonwood is álamo, and this name has lent itself to some famous places in America. Other names are Balm of Gilead, Bam, Tacamahac, or Heartleaf Balsam Poplar.

Black Cottonwood resin has been used for centuries for its medicinal qualities. Some of the books on your bookshelf were likely made from Cottonwood, as are many objects: contemporary plywood, as well as canoes, ropes, baskets, and fish traps crafted by Native people. Owl, Osprey, and other birds perch or make homes in Cottonwood, and ground-dwelling beings seek shelter in Cottonwood's shade. Indeed, Black Cottonwood is a being that has so much to give, including a nice place to lean and rest on an Eastern River walk.

CHRIS DOMBROWSKI

Cottonwoods

Through the coulee a river of cottonwoods runs.
In winter the river runs dry, all but a trickle.

But autumn the water's golden and its running
drowns out even the real river's running.

You can breathe inside this water, too, and let
its conflagration raze the brain's old homestead.

It's just yellow leaves, though, their stems' ends
aphid-bulbed, freckled and edged with brown.

A long time ago when God was reading the earth
the angels interrupted, pleading for another galaxy.

He made this stand his bookmark. Some frigid nights
you can almost hear the dusty spine unfolding.

Columbia Desert Parsley

(Lomatium columbianum)

"I have something to teach you" is something that Native people have heard for years from many beings. Indigenous languages, cultures, and spirituality are tied to the natural environment. The relationship sustained between the beings, Human and non, is essential to the health of both. One being critical in all aspects of that relationship and to many tribes throughout Cascadia is Cous, or Cous Cous (an anglicized version of Qawsqáws, the Umatilla word for this being), also known as Columbia Desert Parsley.

Early season hikers along Eastern Rivers delight in seeing and smelling this stout, fragrant plant, also known as Spring Gold. We are greeted by a being barely knee-high, a stocky soul with arms extending from the earth as if offering a bouquet in rays pinkish and lightly purplish—the color of amethyst and some types of wine. These blooms arise from taproots that allow this being to thrive on the dry, rocky slopes, making this display seem like a bright call, saying, "Here, I have something for you."

Along with the joy of seeing beautiful Desert Parsley are the gifts Native people and others know the roots hold. For centuries, people Indigenous to Cascadia have held a thanksgiving to celebrate the onset of the harvest of Cous, and it is easy to understand why. Cous Cous roots resemble small Sweet Potatoes and can be eaten raw in spring. Desert Parsley is

often ground into meal for finger cakes or dried whole—eaten this way, the root tastes like stale biscuits, hinting toward the name Biscuitroot. An infusion of the root is used to quell symptoms of the flu and colds; mashed and applied as a poultice, Desert Parsley draws out infection or helps heal Horse's saddle sores. Warm Springs people use the paste to process buckskin, and others work it into their hair as a tonic against dandruff.

In so many ways, Qawsqáws may be trying to show us that culture is tied deeply to the land through the foods we harvest and celebrate; by extending beauty outward, others might see the beauty and value we keep underneath. Qi'ce'yew'yew', Qawsqáws! Thank you, Cous!

CHRISTIANNE BALK

Taproot

I think of the desert parsley's
seared stalks covered with bumblebees

in the early summer, shrinking
slowly in the heat to a mound

of barely visible leaves, brown
and tangled on the dusty ground.

The thick root taps through volcanic
rock with its own pulse, iambic

in my dreams, each tendril ticking
a path into the rubbled earth

to rest in the darkness, circling
slightly at the tip like a fern.

Asleep, it's easy to forget
today's thick, broad, shimmering net

of a record 110.
We'll still be here, hollow stems hum,

urging me to resist succumbing
to my species' windswept numbing

hope that our world will not ignite.
Still, I can't forget the bobwhite

pair's soft calls last night, *ty-ty-ty*
as they searched for one another

in the gorge's dry grass cover
or the gray-purple hovering

of the parsley in May, lining
both sides of the trail, billowing.

Chukar

(Alectoris chukar)

In Eastern Indian mythology, Chukar is a symbol of deep love. In the history of Cascadia, Chukar is a relative newcomer who was first brought to North America from Pakistan in the late 1800s as a game bird, and has become a familiar voice in the Eastern Rivers community.

Chukar got their name from their song: *Chuck-chuck-chuck-chukar!* They sing to welcome the morning sun: *Squee.* They sing to wish it goodnight in the evening. They sing *wheetu* before (and often during) flight. They may even sing *chukara-chukara-chukara*, to rally their covey, alerting each other to a coming storm or predator.

Find Chukar hanging out with Desert Parsley (whose seed, along with leaves, berries, and insects, they love to eat) and dashing through Sage. *Dashing* is pre-cisely the right word, for Chukar was born to run. Though Chukar adults are capable in the air, their real strength is held on the ground. Hatchlings are unable to fly at all. Instead, they use a technique known as wing-assisted incline running. Young Chukar, all orange legs and granite-colored feathers, turns uphill and starts running and flapping. Though this may seem comical and somewhat endearing, it is also a lesson in the evolution in flight. Two theories exist: birds learned flight "tree down" or "ground up." Chukar assures some scientists that ground up is the way ancestors learned to fly, as running while flapping was a faster way to scramble up steep inclines. Though the jury is still out, Chukar doesn't seem to be changing style. This hardy, hard-to-find being can easily outrun a hunter.

The rocky slopes, canyons, and otherwise arid regions that Chukar calls home require Chukar to take advantage of all water sources. They've been known to go into mine shafts, sometimes ten feet belowground, seeking a sustaining drink. To see Chukar is to see a Quail-like being with orange-brown and slate upperparts and breast, black-and-rufous-barred white flanks, and a white face with a deep black eyeline. Chukar's bill and legs are the color of sunsets.

Though we lack their speed and beautiful plumage, we can try on some of Chukar life. Outstretch your arms, and flap as you run uphill, duck through Sage and around boulders, sing *wheetu*, and know that you, too, have celebrated the Chuk-Chuk-Chukar!

PRAGEETA SHARMA

Bird-Eye View

for Bakirathi Mani

I find my kinship with a Chukar, a steadfast walker like myself.
I'm thinking of her and how we tend
to our loved ones, as they hurtle out of time.
For my flight I'm only now committing to driving,
to get him to the hospital.
I'm not straying too far from water, finding
him the nourishment to fight this rare cancer.
I have learned the inset of emancipation,
and how to fight the insuperable pain of unbelonging

and being unforgiven in certain communities.
A Chukar will emigrate to the air with chatter,
or a cry for protection, and yet have the clarity
to stay strong in this face.
I too, with my South Asian origin,
came west and stayed put,
Montana and now further west to California.
Looking up from the ground, the freckled plains,
sprite mountains of dry earth.
We are both red-legged partridges
feeling out all the migrational mantras.
I'm trying to heal him from illness's grip.
I try to say my father's mantra but it's a mouthful
and it's fifteen minutes long. In our scrub, he and I consider
both our health and surroundings,
our apparent fact of faith needed, and how this imperial world
with its incessant and "disorienting" Big Pharma, clinical trials,
hospitals with "hope" brimming over in branding,
won't give me any respite images with which to identify.
Stay steadfast to the winged one and how it practices
a running hop to nest tending, with pinyon and keeping.

Bushy-Tailed Woodrat

(Neotoma cinerea)

Being a Bushy-tailed Woodrat (or Pack Rat by another name) gets a bad rap but is actually pretty awesome. You can collect sticks and bones and pine cones, bits of rope and leather, feathers, Owl pellets, paper, and anything else you find interesting. As Pack Rat, you will stack these treasures and then, well . . . piss on them, both marking your territory and, once the urine crystalizes, fortifying the walls of your hidden home with cement-like strength.

Scientists studying Pack Rat homes have learned much about history. In southcentral Idaho, at the City of Rocks, middens date back forty-five thousand years. The contents of these middens create a picture of local ecology, past and present, and even give clues about the role wildfire has played over time.

Your house, Woodrat, may be in a Human-made place. It may be in a cave or rockslide or a similar crevice. You'll be called Bushy-tailed by some, and then, by others who know you well, a Trade Rat, for sometimes as you carry a treasure home, a better one presents itself, and you trade. What findings aren't used in homebuilding are eaten. On the menu will be plant parts: Pine's needles and cones, leaves, fungi, and all sorts of fruits and berries. One southeastern Idaho study found that you may enjoy Cactus, Grasses, Vetch, Juniper Berries, and Sagebrush too. Throw in Spider, Centipede, and maybe even Scorpion, and you have a regular Pack Rat buffet! Conversely, Pack Rat can be pretty tasty to some others. Because they tend to like the nightlife, Woodrat shows up on the menus of Weasel, Fox, Bobcat, Coyote, and most significantly, Spotted Owl.

Pack Rat weighs about the same as a full can of beer, is about the same size, and is covered in brown to gray fur with a streak of white underbelly from chin to bottle-brush tail (hence "bushy-tailed"). Pack Rat is promiscuous: both males and females prefer the company of many others for breeding—a conclusion drawn not through observation but due to overlapping ranges. A litter of as many as six pups, pinkies, or kits are common, and mom can get pregnant again in six hours. Being a Pack Rat means having big families—up to three litters each year.

So, as you add another trinket to your treasure trove, think of Pack Rat's discerning eye.

JANE WONG

FIRST

I was born in the year of
                    the wood rat, the first
in the zodiac. At the hospital,
                    my mother held me up, eyes
whirling a planet into being.
                    I did not cry. I did not blink.
Some golden hunger stirred
                    within me, thunderous. My mother
told the nurses: *she knows*
                    too much. The bushy-tailed
wood rat is born with its eyes
                    shut. Fifteen days later,
the coldest fog licks its eyes
                    clean. A group of wood rats is
sometimes called a swarm
                    or a plague. I think about what we
fear, what we will ourselves
                    to fear. The stink of worry lines
for whatever dwells deeper
                    than we can see. Fear of dirt, disease,
something coming in we
                    want out. Wood rats in your car
engine, in your attic, in
                    the soft wooden folds of night.

During the pandemic, were

                you afraid of me? Did you want me

out? Such hate makes me

                heart sick, slumped in the bluest

bathwater. Wood rats drum

                their feet when alarmed. Beat of

my heart, thumping, trilling

                earthy measures. According to the zodiac,

wood rats are charming,

                quick witted, clairvoyant. Also,

survivors. Let us tell you

                a future then. In the future, our nests

will shimmer with so much

                gleaming gold, you will finally see

what has been here all

                along, first.

Shrub-Steppe

Art by Emily Poole

Perhaps a light rain has just moved through morning skies. You close your eyes and take a deep breath, smelling the unique mix of wet rock, Bunchgrass, dust, Lupine, Desert Parsley, and everywhere, the distinctive bites of Sagebrush. In this wet light, you can almost feel the pores of stones opening.

These moments are especially precious for their rarity. A steppe is a large area of unforested grassland, and Cascadia's Shrub-Steppe receives less than ten inches of rain during a typical year. But truly, this is a land of contrasts. A hundred-degree day is followed by a cold night, and the next afternoon might gush with thunder showers. In summer, the wind blows hot and dusty, while winter's freezing gales swirl with snow.

This near-desert might appear lifeless and uniform, but as spring arrives, melting snow gives way to an incredible display of wildflowers: lemon dabs of Sagebrush Buttercup, pale pinks of Prairie Star, purples and golds of Lupine and Balsamroot, creamy white to rose of Bitterroot, fire-orange Globe Mallow, and every shade in between in Phlox, Wild Onion, Larkspur, and Scarlet Gilia.

As he shares stories of the time before European settlement, Okanagan tribal member Len Marchand says that "grasses were belly high to a horse back then." But in the last two centuries, the Human impact has been massive. A combination of clearing for agriculture, grazing (overgrazing), Human-caused wildfires, motorized recreation, invasive species, and road building for oil, gas, and wind exploration has left only about 40 percent of this special biome intact.

The mostly treeless Shrub-Steppe affords expansive views across rolling hills, flats, and basaltic canyons. Even so, you might hear the clear whistles and a flutelike song before you see Western Meadowlark perched high on a bare and twisting trunk of Big Sagebrush, bill opening with each liquid note. Listen also for the rustle of grasses as Pygmy Short-horned Lizard crawls in search of ants. And in the night, if you're lucky, you might hear the shrill yips and cries of Coyote shivering the air and remember something you may have almost forgotten about wildness.

TAMI HAALAND

Goldeye, Vole

I say sweep of prairie
or curve of sandstone,

but it doesn't come close
to this language of dry wind

and deer prints, blue racer
and sage, its punctuation

white quartz and bone.
I learned mounds of

mayflowers, needle grass
on ankles, the occasional

sweet pea before I knew
words like perspective or

travesty or the permanence
of loss. My tongue spoke

obsidian, red agate,
arrowhead. I stepped

through tipi rings, leaped
buffalo grass and puff ball

to petrified clam.
Jaw bone of fox, flint,

blue lichen, gayfeather,
goldeye, vole—speak to me

my prairie darling, sing me
that song you know.

Coyote

(Canis latrans)

The variousness of Coyote lives everywhere in this being. Look for them trotting across a road or clearing, wearing any of their amazing array of colors, which includes butterscotch, buff, brownish-yellow, black, brown, gray, rust, and cinnamon. Though you might hear them at any time of the day, Coyote is typically more vocal at night. And you might be hearing one or five—it's often hard to say. Though their Latin name means "barking dog," they communicate all kinds of information about potential dangers, intentions, food, and proximity through woofs, growls, barks, bark-howls, whines, yips, and howls. They even make a yip-howl, or greeting song, when reuniting with each other.

You might also come across signs of Coyote's variety in their tracks. Depending on the circumstances, their clawed prints might reveal a trot, a walk, an extended gallop, or a bound. Coyote will stalk Mouse, Vole, Columbia Basin Pygmy Rabbit, and others, then pounce. We most often know Coyote by sound and sign, which they leave for us to interpret.

Coyote's diet is amazingly variable and helps explain why this being is such a survivor. Coyote will eat almost anything they can get their teeth into: berries, mushrooms, Grasshopper, rodents, Grass, Snake, Salmon, Deer. And orchard windfalls. Daniel Mathews, author of *Cascadia Revealed*, reports that on a trail near Mosier, Oregon, he encountered scats that were as black as Bear's and full of cherry pits.

Though Coyote was once most at home in landscapes such as the Shrub-Steppe and has even been called Prairie Wolf and Brush Wolf, they now inhabit most communities of Cascadia. Highly adaptable, they have thrived in areas significantly altered by Human development. Still, you may not see them. Coyote has a natural wariness of Humans and is genius at living invisibly right under our noses.

Coyote even inhabits our voices in different ways. In general, many people on the more urban west side of the Cascade Range tend to say "Kai-yo-tee" with the stress on "yo," and people on the more rural east side tend to say "Kai-yote" with the stress on "kai."

Coyote has long engaged our fascination. Indigenous people have many stories featuring Coyote as a trickster, sometimes helping a tribe, sometimes hurting it, often as a teacher disguised as a buffoon. In some stories, Coyote is devious, lustful, and greedy. In others, Coyote is the creator who helps people learn the proper rituals and techniques to catch Salmon.

You may have noticed that Dog seems to read an invisible book of the world through their nose. This is true of Coyote, too, and probably more so. Their book might even have pop-ups or slide-outs! They can smell another animal from a mile or two away or even your passage from days earlier. If you come across the twisted, tubelike shapes of Coyote scat,

take note of its location. Is it in the middle of a trail? This is no accident. It is more like a billboard whose big letters are written in the font of odor: "Coyote was here!"

Coyote's enduring survivorship is in part due to their innate population control. When food is scarce and Coyotes are ubiquitous, a high percentage of the females won't go into heat. However, whenever their numbers are low, their reproduction increases dramatically. This is a fact often poorly understood by Humans involved in pest eradication projects in Cascadia.

AL REMPEL

Afternoon Coyote

this afternoon coyote
is in the ditch
I can see by his coat
he's blending in well
with these fields in fall
stalks broken off
yellow & gold
he's in there listening
for mice & voles
listening to the whole world
as it blows across
like lips to a reed
when a child
takes a deep breath
coyote listens
to the human hubbub
west of the ditch
semis, distant planes
and me
letting the car coast
to look down at him
my daughter unaware
happy with new earbuds
you see
east of here there's nothing
but trees & bush & lakes
and the odd logging road
he's listening to that too
the racket of sandhill cranes
and the peep-whistles
geese make
shuffling into their vee

Greater Sage-Grouse

(Centrocercus urophasianus)

During most of the year, you might have a difficult time finding Greater Sage-grouse. Though Cascadia's Shrub-steppe is the only place in the world they can be found, they tend to be nearly invisible, thanks to their speckled brown-and-gray plumage.

But in spring they gather to strut, dance, and breed in leks, or dancing grounds, on clearings like grassy swales or ridgetops. Some say disco will never die, and this being seems to agree. What happens at these leks is one of the strangest and most spectacular displays in Cascadia. Keeping their starburst tails erect behind them, the male Sage-grouse struts and shuffles as they gulp up to a gallon of air into yellowish air sacs that jiggle on their chest like two bulbous water balloons filled to bursting. They jerk their head as they expel air, letting out a series of noises that might make you giggle: a hollow, flexible tube whirled and whiffling through the air; Sasquatch's chortle; or a room of students doing finger-mouth pops. Added to these vocalizations are some coos, whistles, and huffs, while wing and neck feathers combine to make a swish. All these movements are choreographed, and the complex array of sounds are timed to seduce the gathered and watching females.

Lekking sites are often used year after year. Other than these forays into such clearings, Greater Sage-grouse stays close to Big Sagebrush, which provides them cover, nesting habitat, and their primary source of food. In fact, their stomachs have evolved over time to better digest those pungent leaves.

CORRIE WILLIAMSON
Sage Grouse: A Prayer

Let us agree at least on this: it is not above a bird
to hold a sacred map in the mind. It is not below

a bird to nest tucked to earth, ceilinged by fragrant
sage whose double roots have dual plans: a layer

of veined lace at the surface, that drinks sudden
rain, and the deep taproot that holds and seeks, holds

and gathers. Suede-leaf eaters, the female gray
and essential as grass, the male with his throne

of feathered spines, drums in the great sagging
feathered breast, they return year after year

to the lek to dance. Return to the shadow of the oil
derrick and its plunging black ever-lapping tongue.

Return to land slicked over by asphalt or raised up
and rowed by the plow, shorn clean by tooth

and hoof's slow grind. Let me keep the sage hen lodged,
lodestone-like, in my brain, trying to see it this way:

that the body offers itself to song, on land unparsable
from the dance, life beginning as thunder in the throat.

Columbia Basin Pygmy Rabbit

(Brachylagus idahoensis)

The world's smallest rabbit might also be considered the world's cutest. Columbia Basin Pygmy Rabbit can fit in the palm of your hand—soft, gray fur; short, round ears; and eyes like drops of obsidian peering into yours.

Like Greater Sage-grouse, they rely on Big Sagebrush for most of their food, as well as for cover to keep them hidden from Weasel, Coyote, and other predators. Unlike other Rabbits, who use existing burrows created by other beings, Pygmy Rabbit digs their own in loose sandy soil. Once their burrow is created, they become the ultimate homebodies and range only up to about three hundred feet away from one of their four or five burrow entrances for the rest of their life.

Columbia Basin Pygmy Rabbit is mostly crepuscular, meaning they are most active during dawn and dusk when dim light gives them the best chance to stay hidden while foraging or socializing. They can have several litters during the spring and summer, filling their burrows with tiny, squirming kits.

As much of the Shrub-steppe has been lost or fragmented due to Human activity, Columbia Pygmy Rabbit's population has declined to near extinction. In 2001, only sixteen remained in Washington, but with help from caring Humans, the wild population is showing signs of recovery.

During winter months, in search of food, Pygmy Rabbit tunnels from their burrows to nearby plants. The next time you gaze out across a snow-covered Shrub-steppe, imagine all the life going on below.

XAVIER CAVAZOS
Columbia Basin Pygmy Rabbit

when i dream
                    fuego

is a bobcat's
open mouth—an owl's

turning eye-gaze

            when fuego dreams
raven   weasel and even i

are called by name
kindle kindle

kindling

Big Sagebrush
(Artemisia tridentata)

Of all the plant beings in Cascadia, Big Sagebrush has had some of the greatest number of uses for Indigenous people. The leaves are used medicinally for many ailments, including in a tea for colds. They are also used as a natural fumigant and insect repellent. When dried and bundled together, they make smudges for cleansing and healing ceremonies. Sagebrush wood has long been used for cookfires, and the stringy bark woven into ropes and baskets. Among the world's oldest-known footwear are a pair of sandals made from the shredded bark of Sagebrush. Named for the place of their discovery in Oregon, the Fort Rock sandals are over nine thousand years old.

So much about Big Sagebrush says they belong right where they are, on the dry side of Cascadia. Their marvelous adaptations to their near-desert landscape include a pelt of fine pale gray hairs that protect their leaves from water loss by reflecting sunlight even as two kinds of roots take in water: shallow roots grow widely to capture rain and snowmelt near the surface, and thicker, longer ones reach down to deeper water. And that frequent and insistent wind blowing through your hair? That's what carries this being's pollen after the small golden-yellow flowers bloom in late summer and early fall.

One of the ways Big Sagebrush proliferates is by shedding some leaves that release compounds to the soil that hinder the growth of other sage-land beings, such as Bunchgrass. This allows Big Sagebrush to become well established.

Humans are not the only beings in Cascadia who rely on Big Sagebrush. Their leaves provide essential cover and food for Columbia Basin Pygmy Rabbit, Greater Sage-grouse, and Hera Buckmoth. Big Sagebrush is such a ubiquitous being of Cascadia's arid plains that the Shrub-steppe is sometimes referred to as the Sagebrush Grassland. This being is so aromatic that you may smell their sharp scent before you see their gray-green, three-toothed leaves. Slow growers, Big Sagebrush might take a hundred years to reach six feet in height.

URSULA K. LE GUIN

Lesser Senses

Thinking of beauty
as sight we keep forgetting
     the warmth of the fire
in the brightness of firelight,
in the graceful ripples the grace

    of water to thirst,
Soft as air, the touch of fur
     on the touching hand
is as beautiful surely
as the curve of the cat's leap.

    No keener beauty
than a dry branch of sagebrush,
     the harsh, poignant scent
bringing the silent desert
distances back to the heart.

Hera Buckmoth

(Hemileuca hera)

Like Greater Sage-grouse and Columbia Basin Pygmy Rabbit, Hera Buckmoth relies heavily on Big Sagebrush for food. In caterpillar form, as they dine on the pale green leaves of Big Sagebrush, they cluster together on a single branch like fuzzy, purplish-black beaded necklaces. When you come across Hera Buckmoth in this form, be careful. If you want to touch them, it would be best to extend a finger and let one crawl on if they choose. Avoid picking them up, as their bodies are covered in silver hairs that sting like Nettle.

After they emerge from their pupal state, they don't need leaves or anything else to eat. In their adult form, winging over the Shrub-steppe, they do not even have mouthparts. With an average life span of about two weeks, they are able to live off food stored in their bodies from when they were wriggling caterpillars.

Hera Buckmoth, also called Sagebrush Moth and Sagebrush Sheep Moth, is active during the day. Their flight is seemingly erratic and unpredictable, as if they can't make up their mind. Look for them in mid-July to late September. You'll know you've found them if you see white wings with bold black lines, as if a page from an artist's sketchbook has fluttered to life.

EVER JONES
Moth

Its wings don't ground into dust, nor do they signal
another ending. That is up to us, our rippled fingertips

smoothing the contours that flutter away
from our wish. The wings' scales are tiny windows,

cathedrals of solar dust sealed into letters
that contain all of our questions: why are we here?

where do we go when we die? are we really so alone?
The moth collides endlessly with the moon, we see

its celestial weaving with immeasurable fragility,
and we feel night exposed for the first time again:

chafing pine needles erasing all we thought we knew
of this life, the owl screeching the universe's original

vowel. When the earth is no longer ours, the letters
will slide open easily as a palm cupping water

or a moth revolving around a porch light pouring
fine dust into a thirsty mouth that calls everything loss.

Columbia Spotted Frog

(Rana luteiventris)

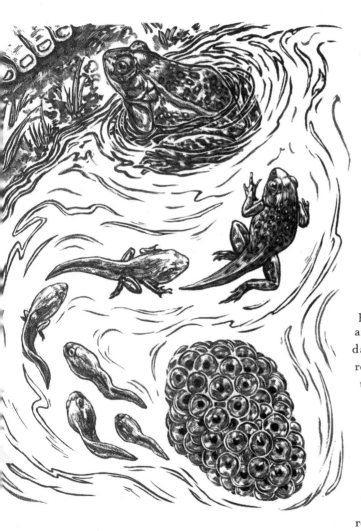

If you find yourself near a pond, lake, or slow-moving stream in late winter or early spring, you might hear a low knocking sound. This isn't Edgar Allan Poe's Raven about to tell you "Nevermore," but Columbia Spotted Frog calling to attract a mate. This olive-green to light brown being gets their name from the black spots that dapple their back and legs, and the edges of their dark, upturned eyes reveal chartreuse flecks that glitter like a fire opal.

Once a pair has mated, the female lays an egg mass that fills with water to about the size of a grapefruit and resembles a gelatinous cloud with a thousand black eyes peering every which way. In fact, she can lay up to 1,300 eggs.

During the winter, Columbia Spotted Frog goes into a sluggish state, moving in slow motion through the water. When temperatures plunge below zero,

Spotted Frog survives only because the high amount of sugar in their blood acts as a natural antifreeze. Amazingly, even if their breathing and heart stop, they will rejuvenate when the temperatures warm.

If their water source dries up, this being will migrate. Imagine them springing through the Shrub-steppe in search of a new pond. What a sight that would be!

JILL MCCABE JOHNSON

Tadpoles

With our toes touching the lake's edge
we saw a simmer of frog eggs
floating just beneath the undulating water.

Every day something new as the sacs
pulsed up from muddy dregs
just beneath the undulating water.

Mouths agog they siphoned great gulps
and swam the algae bed
where our toes touched the lake's edge.

Translucent tails shaped into pollywogs.
Their gills quivered. Their bodies spread
just beneath the undulating water.

What started as gelatinous globs
morphed and sprouted uncertain legs
where our toes touched the lake's edge.

Agog ourselves—me eleven, you twelve—
we barely believed our own legs could bud or fledge
but our toes touched at the lake's edge
just beneath the undulating water.

Cryptobiotic Soil

There are many reasons to tread with care in the Shrub-steppe. One of them is Cryptobiotic Soil, whose name means "hidden life." If you are lucky enough to encounter this being, which is typically darker than the surrounding soil and bumpy looking, kneel next to it—carefully!—for a close look and imagine the wonder of seeing a thousand-year-old Sitka Spruce in Cascadia's Temperate Rainforest. This elder being you are in the company of might be five times as ancient. Maybe more.

Cryptobiotic Soil, also known as Cryptogamic Crust and Biological Soil Crust, is as vulnerable as they are venerable. One errant foot- or hoof-step may take a century to repair. A special collective of lichens, cyanobacteria, mosses, fungi, and algae, Cryptobiotic Crust is vitally important in that they add nutrients to the soil and protect it from erosion. Imagine what all that prairie wind would do were it not for the anchoring grace of this being.

CMARIE FUHRMAN

Cryptobiotic Sonnet

The ashes of my beloved tasted like nothing
and swallowing them didn't bring him back.
They still feel warm, my mother said, as we fed him to the river.

He and I were pregnant then, but I bled the unknowable into soil.
There were no songs. I often walk the desert looking
for proof of my ancestors. I once found a Clovis point
unbroken by years, cattle hooves, or floods, an icicle
with an amber heart and tip dipped in blood.
I felt only its primeval edge when I pressed it to my tongue.
I buried the artifice in soil whose name means hidden life.
An ancient skin which binds together the dead
in layers to hold new lives. I'll be dead
before the scar I made heals by the beautiful work of rot,
which I carry now beneath my fingernails like ten black and
    waning moons.

Giant Palouse Earthworm

(Driloleirus americanus)

One of the more mysterious beings of Cascadia, Giant Palouse Earthworm, has
proved nearly as elusive as Bigfoot. First described in European American cul-
ture in 1897 by Frank Smith and later feared extinct, they were found again by
eminent mother-son Earthworm scientists Dorothy McKey-Fender and William
Fender in 1978. This being then went mostly underground until the first decade
of the twenty-first century, when University of Idaho researchers successfully
went in search of them.

    The individuals they found in 2010 averaged eight or nine inches long, but
early reports spoke of much larger ones being common—if not the ten feet of
an Australian variety or the three feet of their Willamette Valley relative. Their
reputed lily-like scent and spitting habit, described by sodbusters when Giant
Palouse Earthworm was common in the Palouse, have not been observed in the
few latter-day specimens, which may have been juveniles. These beings range
from the typical pinkish-brown worm color to chalk-white albino.

    Agriculture in the rich loess soils of the Palouse and nearby Shrub-steppe has
greatly reduced their habitat and presumed population. Happily, however, the

recent sightings confirm the resilience of this dramatic Earthworm, which lives in vertical burrows that can extend fifteen feet below the surface. They, along with other Earthworms, whom Aristotle referred to as "the intestines of the earth," are vitally important to the health of soil. As they eat plant litter, they help recycle nutrients for use by other beings. Their castings (waste) enrich the soil, and their tunnels help water and oxygen spread more easily.

Giant Palouse Earthworm, like some other beings in this field guide, is endemic to the region, meaning Cascadia is the only place on the planet you will have the opportunity to encounter them.

ROBERT MICHAEL PYLE

"Rare Worm Doesn't Spit or Smell Sweet"

Thus spake *USA Today* when
the Palouse Giant Earthworm
turned up again after twenty years
of absence. Well, not really *absence*.
They were down there all along,
relaxing into their flaccid longitude,
deep underground. Their cousins,
the Oregon Giant Earthworms, had
been missing even longer.

Old lore said the Palouse Giant
Earthworm smells like lilies. Old
lore said it spits, and stretches
up to six feet long. Not so,
said *USA Today*—these were only
foot-longs, no spit, no sweet scent.
Kind of like finding Bigfoot, and he's
only five-foot-ten, with 9B trotters.

I don't know about the spitting. But
what if you were lost for twenty years,
then found, and weren't the same
as everyone expected? What if
they all found out
you don't smell like lilies
after all?

Pygmy Short-Horned Lizard

(Phrynosoma douglasii)

You will have to be sharp-eyed to spy the grays and browns of sand, soil, and stone worn by Pygmy Short-horned Lizard, especially when they freeze in place to avoid detection or shimmy into sand to escape the heat.

The adults are only about two to three inches long and have small nubs (or horns) pointed outward from the back of their smallish head and a round, flattened, spiky body edged by pointy scales.

Like other reptiles, they are ectothermic (cold-blooded), relying on the external environment to regulate their body temperature. Unlike most reptiles, however, who lay eggs, these females give birth to live young. Imagine holding seven tiny dragons, each as big as the tip of your pinkie, and you'll understand why you might call this being magical. These little ones exist solely on a diet of

Ant, so wherever they are, an anthill or three will be close by.

The only place on the planet you will find this being is in Cascadia. Sadly, they have been extirpated from their former range in British Columbia but can still be found in other parts of the Shrub-steppe, and there are even some who live in the mountains where, as they hibernate under four to five inches of sand, they freeze solid like an ice pop, only to thaw in spring and crawl forth into the light.

DORIANNE LAUX

Pygmy Short-Horned Lizard

Flat-bodied with a bluish underbelly
I loved to rub until her eyes
slowly closed, or his eyes, whatever it was.
We called them horny toads,
scooped from the sun-beaten
canyon floor, caught asleep
under the sagebrush shade.
They were more docile than the sleek,
slippery lizards, always squirming
through our fingers, feeling
for a way out. But the horny toads
seemed content as kittens,
would purr if they could.
I'd stroke the skin
between their ancient
triceratops heads, touch
a finger to the horned tips

and never break the skin.
I liked how they popped up on all fours
like a dog, looking for ants, then
flattened themselves to ground,
blending into the grainy tans
of sandy soil. I kept one in a shoebox
under my bed for days, feeding it
flies, a blue bottlecap of water
tucked in one corner, a bed
of newspaper ripped in strips,
headlines torn in half, then torn
again. It was the shredded world
she lived in, a mayhem of tiny letters
she couldn't read, but even I,
a child, could see I had to give her up
to the dangers and cruelties,
the mess we'd made of it,
and let her go back to her home
under the high-tension towers
that buzzed through the canyon,
the smashed beer bottles
and crushed tin cans, plastic bags
struggling in windy branches
like trapped birds. And if he or she
could live there and thrive,
so could I. She never once
spit blood from her eyes.
Never ran. Only walked slowly
from my open palm and stood
above her shadow
on the cracked earth,
turning to stare at me
for what seemed like a long time,
before unhurriedly turning away.

Montane

Art by Claire Emery

It is the place dreams go to play. Where granite springs are the beginnings of mighty rivers. It is the high place, one of mountain peaks, where Mountain Goat looks like a cloud on a precipice and Larch sings the coming of autumn as golden arrows pointing toward sky. Here, summer is short and winter is harsh with beauty framed in cold and snowpack. And though we Humans may not be in attendance for the deepest days of winter, many beings have adapted and thrived in the Montane, from Canada Jay's down, which allows her to sit on her eggs in the subzero, to the sleekness of Subalpine Fir's limbs that hold little snow. This place of nodding Glacier Lily and bursting Beargrass combines absolute beauty with determination and survival.

Take a hike up your favorite trail into the Montane community. You'll be 5,000 or as much as 10,800 feet above the Salish Sea. Bring a tasty lunch, and don't be surprised when Marmot and Canada Jay hit you up for a taste (but don't give in!). Walk along a stream and look for ephemeral Trout. Sit beside Fir and Larch as they sough you their secrets, then lie back, close your eyes, and listen to the sound of Nutcracker. Send up prayers for the beings, such as Whitebark Pine, whose lives are threatened—and while you are at it, thank the stars above (for if you stay the night, you will see trillions of them) for your time in the Montane.

ROBERT BRINGHURST

Song of the Summit

The difference is nothing you can see—only
the dressed edge of the air
over those stones, and the air goes

deeper into the lung, like a long fang,
clean as magnesium. Breathing
always hollows out a basin,

leaving nothing in the blood
except an empty
cup, usable for drinking

anything the mind finds—bitter
light or bright darkness or the cold
corner of immeasurable distance.

This is what remains: the pitted blood
out looking for the vein,
tasting of the tempered tooth and the vanished flame.

Glacier Lily

Erythronium grandiflorum

As sure as longer days and receding snow mark the beginning of spring, so does
the bursting yellow bloom of glorious Glacier Lily. Maybe because they are shy,
or maybe because spring snow might crush their six long stamens were their
bloom open to sky, but Glacier Lily bows to the earth. As do we for a closer look
and grateful greeting to this being.

You can chase spring up the mountain with Glacier Lily. It is as if pulling back the snow releases them to leap up from the earth for a few short days and reminds us how to love the color yellow. Call them Trout Lily, Yellow Avalanche Lily, or Snow Lily. Call them Dogtooth Violet, Fawn Lily, or Adder's Tongue. This bright being will still rise. And Bear will be glad! Both Black and Brown Bear love Glacier Lily as an early spring wake-up snack. And they're not the only ones—Native people and others boil and eat or dry the corm (enlarged stem tissue) for a midwinter snack. Bighorn Sheep, Elk, Deer, and Mountain Goat, however, are happy to take them raw.

How about a cool botanical fact? Glacier Lily has tepals, which occur when sepals (modified leaves) and petals are identical to each other. Maybe Glacier Lily is neither bowing nor shy. Maybe this confident spring being is nodding *yes*, like we are, to how wondrous they truly are.

ROBERT WRIGLEY

Glacier Lily

For its face is downcast always,
being both showy and shy, the sky
one day gray and dispensing snow,
the next day cloudless and perfectly blue

until, two weeks into its blooming
it is nearly blown, each of six yellow petals
bent back, white stamens and red anthers
yearning toward the ground it never

looked up from, and why it is I kneel and lift
by a sepal's slender bulge this one
in its late sullenness, to speak directly
into its bashful ear, my gratitude and love.

Westslope Cutthroat Trout

(Oncorhynchus clarkii lewisi)

To hold Westslope Cutthroat Trout in your hands is to hold a dream of clear, fast water; winters in deep lakes; and the secrets of headwaters where this being often lives. Perhaps this is whom Trout Lily is named for; their spring spawning is a gift for predators and those of us who spend long afternoons lying on the shores of perennial streams with the hope of glimpsing a spawning Westslope.

And to see one is fortunate indeed. The introduction of Kokanee, Lake Trout, and Whitefish into Cascadia has been great for sport fishing but disastrous for Westslope—their numbers have decreased by 90 percent or more. And it's not just the competition; livestock grazing, agriculture, logging, road building, mining, and dam construction reduce the number of spawning Cutthroat each year. In fact, this being—who can live in rivers or lakes or migrate between both—inhabits only 59 percent of their historical range.

Westslope Cutthroat makes up in splendor what they lack in size; in fact, a Westslope over five pounds is extremely rare. Not a pescatarian like other trout, this being prefers a diet of aquatic invertebrates (think Worms and bugs). One of the wonders of the Westslope is the glorious color they display as a juvenile: belly a sunset blush of crimson transitioning into an upside-down sunrise that spills into a chartreuse meadow dappled with black spots ("rose-moles all in stipple," as Gerard Manley Hopkins writes). Oh, Westslope Cutthroat, we will never get enough of you.

ANDREW C. GOTTLIEB

The Walking Gods

The weight of the descending flow—cold, heavy,
dedicated to places downstream—confronts you
while you stare alone for giant cutthroat,
mythic, in the deepest pools.

There are gods in these woods, walking slopes
and meadows, the weight of seasoned legs
plunging spongy hole to hole.

A river never forgives, never compromises
its vision. The biggest boulders thunder
as they trundle on the bottom.

Deep in the old growth, there's a presence,
a recent breath, the deepest scent on rocks
left traced by the navigation of mosses.

A walking stick and a steady step prevent accidental
drowning. The river's intimate tug presses
its indifferent love like a rope. Elsewhere, the tall gods
bustle. One stubborn bole leans over
like the oldest, strictest teacher.

Rocky Mountain Snail

(Oreohelix strigosa)

Look down at the trail. The forest floor. Turn over a leaf, perhaps. Do you see
a slow-moving being? That's Rocky Mountain Snail. You'll know them by the
shell, the earthy color and relaxing spirals, and the fact that a nickel could hide
them. Get on your knees and greet Snail. Once they get comfortable, the head
will emerge. Now you can examine the ocular and olfactory tentacles as they see
and smell you. With just one foot on the ground, Snail trolls the forest floor
searching for detritus. This busy omnivorous scraper (Snail eating is called
scraping) isn't a picky eater; they'll rasp through the waste of any organic nature.
They are, after all, professionals in the field of decay.

Snail works in this way: slow and solo. Snail takes up to a week, moving
constantly, to go about a half mile. And perhaps because they have little time

to waste on the frivolity of mating, when two Snails meet, each can leave the union fertilized by the other and ready to lay eggs since they are hermaphrodites. As for homemaking? No annual nest or den for them; they pack their homes along with them as they travel.

All that toil can prove for naught if Thrush spies and makes a supper of Snail. But if they avoid their many predators, Snail can live for years (as many as five) before shrugging off their mortal (calcium carbonate) coil. And when they do, gather up that shell. Blow into it for the whistle it makes. Hold it in your hand to remind you to slow down and to watch where you step.

STACY BOE MILLER

Treatment of Uncertainty

You called it
hunting.

Hunting, the children
said, tucking vials in their
pockets to fill
with snails. Together

we tore quiet
bodies from the base
of trees, watched
as they curled back

from air. *Oreohelix*
you told them.
Oreohelix said our children,
and dumped them on the table
where they dried forgotten.
Occasionally one escaped, and I

found it by following—I'm sorry

I couldn't stay,
sorry I stayed
so long, the way
a forgotten body
dries to almost

nothing, the way
escape can leave
an obvious path.

The title of this poem, "Treatment of Uncertainty," comes from "*Oreohelix*
strigosa cooperi (Cooper's Rocky Mountain Snail): A Technical Conservation
Assessment," prepared for the USDA Forest Service, Rocky Mountain Region,
Species Conservation Project, by Tamara Anderson, PhD.

Beargrass

(Xerophyllum tenax)

Beargrass is the raciest plant in the Montane community. Showy, certainly, with
tall white stalks streaking into the summer sky, but also exquisitely feminine. Many
have said that to look down at blooming Beargrass is to see a white breast and nip-
ple. Seems apropos. This being, with a once-in-a-lifetime bloom stalk that holds
up to four hundred small milky flowers, feeds hundreds of forest insects—even

though they only bloom for a mere five or so days. Perhaps Beargrass should also be called Mothergrass, as mothering is an obvious trait of this being. People have long used Beargrass fiber for clothing and the roasted rhizomes for food, and Eastern Plains Tribes use the roots to treat sprains.

Beargrass is not an actual Grass but in fact a type of Lily. The leaves are fodder for Bighorn Sheep, Deer, Elk, and Mountain Goat. And though this being has been given many names, from Soap Grass to Basket Grass, to describe their many uses, the favorite moniker of the Montane remains Beargrass, for Brown Bear has been known to bring these leaves into their winter dens.

When we see these beings on rocky slopes, dry ridges, or in open coniferous woods, and when they survive moderate fire and grow back quickly to help prevent soil erosion and regenerate a site, maybe this breast of a bloom is reminding us of the many ways this plant is, in fact, a mother, and to give her some love right back.

JENNIFER PERRINE

Forgive Me

How many times did I see your arching
fountains of olive blades before I knew

your name? Even then, how long did it take
before I recognized what a mistake

it is to describe you with words given
to us by men on an expedition

who saw only your resemblance to their
experience? They had not learned enough

to know your tufts were not grass at all. How
often had I witnessed you in this form—

tussocks tenacious enough to endure
drought and frost—before I found myself struck

by luck: a whole meadow of your many
bodies, tall stalks rising into clusters

of cream flowers blooming from the bottom
up? Even now, I cannot detail each

way I perceived you: pale breasts with tightly
budded nipples, mounds of marshmallow fluff,

cotton swabs, fields of froth, fireworks fizzling
as they burst, haute couture of delicate

lacework. Each likeness falls short, does not praise
how you're the first to arrive after fire,

how your rhizomes survive mudslides to sprout
bounties of green shoots, how you wait years for

just the right amount of rain to blossom,
to adorn some unsuspecting clearing

with your brash display. How often will I
pass through the same stretch and never again

catch—no, be caught by—such exuberance?
I still come across your seas of verdant

puffs, let them brush my knees. Now, I call you
quip-quip, a term whose exact sense I can't trace

but on its face suggests the joke's on me,
wishing for what's past, stumbling on wonder

once and believing I can make it last.

Hoary Marmot

(Marmota caligata)

They are sometimes called Whistle Pig. You know why if you've heard them
shriek, this rotund being sunning on a rock, the largest of the Squirrel family.
No matter their name, this being's life looks pretty ideal from where we stand.
Marmot spends half of the morning lying around on warm rocks and the rest
of the day eating, and then they retire to their burrow for their evening rest.

But Marmot's whistle is more than a tune. Hoary Marmot whistles to scare
off predators such as Coyote, Eagle, and Fox. Hoary Marmot is named for
their pelt. *Hoary* means "aged gray or white" and speaks to the silvery fur of
this being, particularly around the head and shoulders. The rest of Marmot is
reddish-brown-bodied and black-footed. In fact, *caligata* means "booted." Lil-
looet and Nuxalk people value this being for both fur and meat. Traditionally,
four tribal groups—Nootka, Kwakwaka'wakw, Tsimshian, and Tlingit—hunt
Hoary Marmot, but southcentral Washington and northcentral Oregon Natives
do not, for fear of eating Marmot's whistle will cause them to go mad.

Hoary Marmot is characteristically charismatic. More sumo wrestler than
distance runner, sometimes Marmot will spar for hours, standing on back legs,
grasping forepaws, and merely pushing against one another. Which, by the way,
they do for fun. Those living around Humans are not shy about approaching
for a treat. They do best on a diet of green plants and seeds, though, so keep
your sandwich for yourself.

Marmot mating brings about two to four pups and happens just after they
emerge from the burrows where they have stayed for as many as eight months,
living off the fat layer they accumulated before winter. When food is plentiful,

Hoary Marmot lives in colonies with a dominant male attending mating duties. When times are lean, one male and one female alone birth and raise their brood.

Marmot often benefits other beings in their community. Abandoned holes become homes for other small mammals, and in moderation, their digging and defecation loosens, aerates, and improves the soil. So don't let their siren scare *you* off. These wilderness whistlers may be reminding you to pay attention—or just to stretch out across the warm rocks and take a nap.

DEREK SHEFFIELD

How We Look

Fur-fat and stock-still in the trail
they appear to be looking
into a mythic sky, posed
for a feral portrait, or a wish
to draw us closer before they turn
and level a frontal marmot scrutiny.
The way their noses aim askance
says they're not here. Or we
are gone. Or we are here

but they're not sure.
Upright on boulders, they are ready
to tumble at the shrill signal
if we become, in a blink,
by sneeze or shuffle, believable.
Our pack-heavy shapes, gathered
in their sky, look up
to Shuksan: how distant

and present it juts, how sharp
a lookout, clarity
we envy through tilted glass
until from every nowhere
the whiteout. When the peak
disappears, we turn and labor
down the moraine, switch-
backing like mules silently spaced
in the falling snow.

While we drive our miles and climb
to bright rooms, they settle
below in a general huddle,
slowing for their long dream.
Between one flake
and the infinite next, one pulse beat
and the second, our burdened forms
waver and loom, weave and are gone.

Ice Worm

(Mesenchytraeus solifugus)

Rollicking as his poem is, Robert Service didn't have it quite right. Ice Worm is not a bilious blue but a silky, deep brown-black. Ice Worm is not four inches long but less than an inch. But . . . a Worm that lives exclusively in and around glacial ice? Worms that would die of heat if they rested in your palm? Yes. Ice Worm is real and really more amazing than could be imagined. Even Barman Bill would have to admit this truth.

Ice Worm actually looks quite a bit like the familiar wrigglers in your compost bin, feeding and crawling like Earthworm but smaller and skinnier (even threadlike)—and Ice Worm lives entirely on and through ice rather than soil. In fact, they will not be found far from glacial ice. Ice Worm needs to be not too hot (not over 40 degrees Fahrenheit), not too cold (not under 20 degrees Fahrenheit), but *just* right. Given those conditions, Ice Worm lives between five and ten years. And there can be a huge number of them if conditions are right. Researchers working on Mount Rainier estimate up to five billion Ice Worms can be on a single glacier there.

In summer, Ice Worm will scrunch under the ice or roll in slushy melt to stay cool on sunny days (the Latin name *solifugus* means "sun-avoider"), emerging at dusk to feed on algae, pollen grains, and bacteria. This is convenient for Ice Worm, for dusk is when their predators, Snow Bunting and other birds, are most often sleeping. What about winter? Humans think of ice as an extreme environment, but ice actually moderates intense swings of temperature. If Ice Worm burrows down, they can find a nice, comfy 32 degrees Fahrenheit again. In fact, Ice Worm can move easily on and through ice thanks to the small, hooked hairs (called setae) on their undersides that help them get a grip.

Ice Worm officially entered the scientific records via a discovery in the heart of Cascadia: Glacier Bay's Muir Glacier. Since that discovery in 1887, Ice Worm has been found in glaciers and perennial snowfields elsewhere in Cascadia, and similar beings are reported in other icy regions that glint near temperate areas, such as Patagonia, but you won't find Ice Worm in the Rockies or British Columbia's Interior. If you happen to be in Cordova, Alaska, in January or February, you can join in on the Ice Worm parade, tail hunt, and more during their annual Iceworm Festival.

What about reproduction? For now, Ice Worm is keeping that part of their life, along with many other details, private, thank you very much.

ROBERT SERVICE

from "The Ballad of the Ice-Worm Cocktail"

But sadly still was Barman Bill, then sighed as one bereft:
"There's been a run on cocktails, Boss; there ain't an ice-worm left.
Yet wait . . . By gosh! it seems to me that some of extra size
Were picked and put away to show the scientific guys."
Then deeply in a drawer he sought, and there he found a jar,
The which with due and proper pride he put upon the bar;
And in it, wreathed in queasy rings, or rolled into a ball,
A score of grey and greasy things, were drowned in alcohol.
Their bellies were a bilious blue, their eyes a bulbous red;
Their backs were grey, and gross were they, and hideous of head.
And when with gusto and a fork the barman speared one out,
It must have gone four inches from its tail-tip to its snout.
Cried Deacon White with deep delight: "Say, isn't that a beaut?"
"I think it is," sniffed Major Brown, "a most disgustin' brute.
Its very sight gives me the pip. I'll bet my bally hat,
You're only spoofin' me, old chap. You'll never swallow that."

Mountain Goat

(Oreamnos americanus)

All fluff and bright white, they cling to the edge of a precipice like a snagged cloud, causing us to hold our breath even as they maneuver deftly with one or two kids in tow. Mountain Goat dons a coat that grows double layers in winter and is shed in summer. This jettisoned fur has long been collected for ceremony and woven into Chilkat blankets admired internationally for their beauty and uniqueness. In the Montane, it is said that to find a tuft of Goat fur is to have luck on the mountain.

Nannies and billies and kids they are, but Goat they really are not. *Oreamnos americanus* is more closely related to an antelope. A ruminator, like Cows and Bison, this herbivore (who favors Moss, Lichen, and twigs), makes a cud to chew, regurgitate, and chew again—as if life on the edge has filled Mountain Goat with ennui.

Mountain Goat is not particularly large but often is the largest mammal at high Cascadian altitudes. Qosalat, as known to Nimiipuu, are just over three feet at the shoulder with long, dense bodies, weighing in between one hundred and three hundred pounds. The two straight horns on both sexes are fanciable, but they are not mere ornamentation. Sharp, pointed, and up to a foot long, they hold Goat's age in their rings and are used to defend personal space.

What must it be like to live out your life on the edge of a cliff? To blend with the snow in winter and the clouds in summer? We may never have this experience, but if you're lucky enough to spot Mountain Goat or clutch a tuft of their white fur, you'll be that much closer to knowing.

GABRIELLE BATES

A backward looping arrow

appears on the screen
and I touch it.
The mountain goat

is back in her matted wool coat,
and the early spring snow
is snow again, everywhere.

I watch her spinning, bucking
movements, the more-and-more
cast rags of fleece

until the white at her feet
is water and all the winter
growth is off. The arrow

appears again. It hunts itself
back to the beginning
and I am—what?—

its servant? Its god?
I touch it again
under the bus shelter.

Again on the bus.
Only the fact of mediation is human:
the frame. This video

of a mountain goat and her new kid,
too new to even know winter,
mimicking her motions—

her pale shadow.
I try to look at them as them
but I feel allegory

straining to be born
in the holes
behind my eyes, something

about emptiness. Inheritance.
A self-shaped burden.
The end of a cold season.

Canada Jay

(Perisoreus canadensis)

Cha-cha-cah-cah, whee-ooh! Better hide your picnic—there's a Camp Robber near!
Not a very affectionate name for quite a lovely bird, but Camp Robber does
seem fitting for this being who thrives in places where Humans leave (or offer)
snacks. Actually, Canada Jay (or Gray Jay or Whisky Jack) thrives in any location
where fungi, small rodents, eggs, fruit, berries, and insects can be readily found.

Related to Crow, Raven, and Magpie, Gray Jay has a few tricks tucked under
their wing. If they've had their fill, they'll carry leftover food in their black feet,
then use their sticky spit to glue their cache in tree bark or other hiding spots
high above the snowpack. Such clever stowage allows Gray Jay to stay in the
Montane through winter.

When snow is high, night is long, and temperatures drop as low as 20 below,
Canada Jay is incubating eggs for the first (and only) brood they'll raise all year.
Fortunately, Canada Jay has incredibly thick, fluffy plumage, which they will puff

up in cold weather, making a kind of downy snow pants to keep their naked legs and feet warm. Even Jay's nostrils are covered with feathers.

Canada Jay lives and forages together in family groups. The adults, as one of their common name indicates, are gray, about the size of Robin, and weigh the same as two AA batteries. Big for a songbird, small for a Jay, but still quite the eater, this being needs about forty-seven calories a day. If Canada Jay were Human-sized, that would be a whopping 47,000 calories! No wonder this being wants to be invited to your picnic.

JOE WILKINS

My Son Asks for the Story About When We Were Birds

When we were birds,
we veered & wheeled, we flapped & looped—

it's true, we flew. When we were birds,
we dined on tiny silver fish
& the watery hearts
of flowers. When we were birds

we sistered the dragonfly,
brothered the night-wise bat,

& sometimes when we were birds

we rose as high as we could go—
light cold & strange—

& when we opened our beaked mouths
sundown poured like wine
down our throats.

When we were birds
we worshipped trees, rivers, mountains,

sage knots, rain, gizzard rocks, grub-shot dung piles,

& like all good beasts & wise green things
the mothering sun. We had many gods
when we were birds,

& each in her own way
was good to us, even winter fog,

which found us huddling
in salal or silk tassel,
singing low, sweet songs & closing
our blood-rich eyes & sleeping
the troubled sleep of birds. Yes,

even when we were birds
we were sometimes troubled & tired,

sad for no reason,

& so pretended we were not birds
& fell like stones—

the earth hurtling up to meet us,
our trussed bones readying
to be shattered, our unusually large hearts
pounding for nothing—

yet at the last minute we would flap
& lift, & as we flew, shudderingly away,

we told ourselves that this falling—

we would remember. We thought
we would always
be birds. We didn't know.

We didn't know
we could love one another

with such ferocity. That we should.

Alpine Larch

(Larix lyallii)

Look for this golden candle flame of a tree as the harbinger of autumn in late September and early October. Larch has pulled energy from their green needles all spring and summer, which soon will turn yellow and fall. Larch, one of a handful of deciduous conifers in the world, uses this shedding strategy to survive grueling winters and deep snow—needle regeneration also makes *Larix lyallii* resilient to the challenges of fire and insects.

Larch isn't just autumn punctuation among their evergreen neighbors. As snows recede, we breathlessly await the chartreuse green of Larch that lets those in the higher altitudes know spring is arriving. Larch is a joy to meet on the trail. Their circular clusters of needles brush your face, soft and welcoming. Their

wide canopy shields many beings during a summer rain. Take your rest against the thick bark of this Montane forest being and know that you are leaning also against galactan, a natural sugar that resembles bitter honey and can be used in medicinals and as baking powder.

Should the wind come up, you'll be in for a breathtaking show. Tall, lanky Larch is flexible and will bend and sway, sometimes nearly touching the ground. As you walk through a grove, try to find the tallest of these beings and wonder if it beats the tallest on record, which stands at just over 126 feet at (of course) Larch Lake, Washington. Regardless of the height, give Larch a big hug; this tree teaches us so much about being flexible, resilient, and adaptable.

CMARIE FUHRMAN

Prophecy

The White Man will never be alone.
Let him be just and deal kindly with my people,
for the dead are not powerless.
                                        —Chief Seattle

> Coyote knows what she is doing.
> Transmigrating souls
>
> of the real people
> into Larch. You must know, too,
> because every autumn
>
> Larch celebrate their abundance
> with potlatch
> and give away their summer gold.
> When you see
>
> the bare limbs and spine
> you will also see the real people,
> to which Coyote taught
>
> that survival comes
> in shades of brown.

Clark's Nutcracker

(Nucifraga columbiana)

Clark's Nutcracker doesn't have any true songs. Instead, they have a repertoire of calls ranging from a rasping, metallic *kraak-kraak* that keeps them in touch with other Nutcrackers to an actual squall when disturbed. They even croak. But this beautiful black-and-gray bird who flashes white in tail and wing calls a little differently to family, using a low, melodious song that rises in pitch and sounds a bit like a Human baby gurgling and cooing.

Nucifraga columbiana, or Nutcracker of the Columbia, is one of very few members of the corvid (or Crow) family in which the male shares incubation duties with his mate. This incredible being uses a daggerlike bill to dig into Pine cones and pull out large seeds, which they stash in a pouch under their tongue until they can store them in the cracks of bark or in little trenches they dig with their bills.

Not only does Clark's Nutcracker depend on Pine seeds, but Pine has been changed by their relationship with Nutcracker. Pinyon and Limber Pines, among others, depend on Nutcracker to disperse their seeds. Over time, this relationship has changed the trees' seeds, cones, and even overall shape in comparison to pine species who rely on the wind to disperse their seeds.

Perhaps the most critical relationship Nutcrackers have is with Whitebark Pine (whose seed, ounce for ounce, has more calories than chocolate!). Whitebark is in decline due to Mountain Pine Beetle infection, blister rust, and the long-term effects of fire suppression. Clark's Nutcracker is integral to the restoration of Whitebark Pine. Whitebark needs Nutcracker to cache seeds in excess (more than they'll ever eat) for healthy stands to regenerate. Without the Whitebark, the Nutcracker loses a vital food source and may no longer nest in areas where the tree is a primary source of life.

We believe, as Robin Wall Kimmerer writes, that "names are the way we humans build relationship, not only with each other but with the living world." Many believe the time has come to rename this amazing being to better reflect the relationship Nutcracker has with fellow beings and not the relationship it never had with a history that regarded beings only in the ways they may glorify a single Human.

ALEXANDRA TEAGUE

First Seeing Clark's Nutcrackers: June 2020

Shoshone County, Idaho

We'd driven to a mountain named Grandmother to be alone in
fields of bear grass with our fears. We'd brought binoculars to
bring the world close without touching it. We were just starting
to suspect for years we'd been like children playing with bin-
oculars the wrong way round: tunneling everything to one dis-
tant spot called the future. Playing pin-the-treasure on every
map we had to survive here. Between Douglas firs, nutcrack-
ers *kraaked* and rode the updrafts, their tails fanning like flying
pianos with too few black keys. Their beaks' jet trowels, *the orig-
inal jaws of life*, could pry open the tightest cones of whitebark
pines. In one summer, we read, one bird could stash 80,000
seeds in mounds of two or three; then precisely remember
months later those tens of thousands of caches under snow-
drift and deadfall. The land shedding seasons and details,
adding saplings and squirrels and heather, like those word
problems we never thought we'd really need. We were start-
ing to suspect knowledge was never a single compact apple. We
were starting to wish we hadn't just copied from the answer
key. *How to Stay Alive in the Woods* said, *There is just one method to keep
from getting lost, and that is to stay found.* Like most tautologies, the
distance between a thing and itself only grew farther as we tried
to speak of it. *Stocked-grocery-store*
      family-at-holidays
      faces-with-two-whole-halves
people-not-dying-or-fewer. What we thought were trees swept by
fire on the ridge, their trunks blanched ashy, were whitebark
pines killed by beetles and blister-rust. *A ghost forest.* Only the
caches the nutcrackers fail to find may grow more trees. Imag-
ine mapping more than your own survival. Knowing, months
before, how to pry and fly and hide one seed, then another seed.

Subalpine Fir

(Abies lasiocarpa)

Straight, tall arrows. Steeple-like, Pino real Blanco de las Sierras, or Subalpine Fir, keeps their branches close and offers a single crown. To some, they seem the perfect Christmas tree. To others, like Cascade Pine Squirrel and Richardson's Grouse, the seeds are an essential food source. But it is less important how you see this being so long as you do pay them a visit.

The purplish cones of this beautiful tree stand upright on the branches that hold them out—as hands extending a gift. Their trunk looks like the legs of Elephant, rough and grayish, flaking or blistering from resin as they get old. And

they do! The eldest Subalpine Fir had nearly five hundred rings—five centuries of life. Subalpine Fir can reach 150 feet (three times the height of the Hollywood sign) but usually only reaches sixty to one hundred. In their natural subalpine habitat, they are often dwarfed by wind and snow and may only grow one foot in fifteen years.

Subalpine Fir spends most of the year in the deep snows that grace these high Montane places. When weighted down to the ground with snow, the lowest branches sometimes take root, forming new shoots and creating krummholz (which means "crooked wood" in German). In the Cascadian Montane, when we speak of krummholz, we're talking about the matted, dwarfed trees that circle the tops of some mountains, separating lower-elevation, upright forests from tundra. Subalpine Fir inspires us with their tenacity in the face of harsh conditions—they grow at altitudes up to twelve thousand feet. They can withstand consistent winds and temperatures down to −20 degrees Fahrenheit. What beauty and strength in the face of what may seem adversity!

KIM STAFFORD

Lessons from a Tree

Seed split. Root sprout. Leaf bud.
Delve deep. Hold fast. Reach far.
Sway. Lean. Bow. Loom.

Climb high. Stand tall. Last long.
Grow. Thicken. Billow. Shade. Sow seed.

Rise by pluck, child of luck,
lightning-struck survivor.

Burn. Bleed. Heal. Remember. Testify.
Nest. Host. Guard. Honor.

Fall. Settle. Slump.
Surrender. Offer. Enrich.

Be duff. Enough.

Post-Volcanic Succession

Loowit—
Mount St. Helens

Art by Travis London

May 18 is Cascadia Day. It is the day many Humans in Cascadia celebrate their bioregion. It is also the day that, in 1980 at 8:32 a.m., the eruption of Mount St. Helens sent superheated rock, organic material, ash, and hot gases at speeds of up to four hundred miles an hour across the land. This pyroclastic flow blew at twice the speed of the highest winds ever recorded, with a temperature of almost 700 degrees Fahrenheit. In an instant, the mountain lost 1,300 feet of elevation, and all the blasted material of the north side obliterated more than 150 square miles of old-growth forest. Many thousands of trees, shrubs, and grasses; more than one thousand Elk and two hundred Black Bear; millions of birds and smaller mammals, amphibians, reptiles, and insects; and fifty-seven Humans were gone—incinerated, pummeled, buried in ash. The same ash would, in the coming days, blanket much of Cascadia and lift as high as fifteen miles into the atmosphere as it traveled around the globe.

This is the most destructive and deadliest volcanic eruption in the recent history of our region. And yet, if we take a longer view and try to see through time in Cascadia's eyes, we understand that such disturbances are an integral part of the story. Just in the last four thousand years, from Mount Baker to Lassen Peak, there have been over sixty-five eruptions in the Cascade Range. If you are ever fortunate enough to visit Crater Lake in Oregon, one of the wonders of the world, you will be standing on what's left of Mount Mazama, whose eruption altered much of Cascadia 7,700 years ago.

So what is the real story then, if not one of devastation? The lesson the most active volcano in Cascadia has to teach might be better understood by the people who have lived for so long in her shadow. The Cowlitz know her as Lawetlat'la, and the Klickitat call her Louwala-Clough, meaning "Smoking Mountain." In a story from the Puyallup Tribe, she is called Loowit, which is the short form of Loowitlatkla ("Lady of Fire"), and she is a faithful source of the fire Humans use to stay warm, cook food, and shape tools and the land.

As scientists flew over Loowit in the days immediately following the eruption, they saw a moonscape—a sterilized, ashen land littered with the bleached trunks of thousands of trees like so many bones. They believed that recovery would take a long, long time, but their research over the last forty-two years has yielded many epiphanies and astonishments. Thanks to the biological legacies of plants, animals, seeds, and spores that survived underground or beneath snowbanks, Loowit's beings are recovering more quickly than anticipated. In one such story, Lupine added nutrients to an ashy soil that Gopher mixed well enough to support new plants, such as Scarlet Paintbrush, who attracted Elk, whose hooves broke up the ash and mixed their droppings with the soil, droppings that contained seeds and fungal spores leading to more plants, more animals, more life.

Life is finding a way. This is one of Loowit's lessons. And there are more to come as apex predators such as Black Bear and Cougar return. How will they affect this resilient community as they become part of it?

Louwala-Clough is still sending plumes of steam into the sky. Take the time, when you can, to tread these slopes. Feel the soft ash crumble in your hands, hold up a chunk of pumice light as a handful of feathers, and see this place of resilience with your own eyes. You will find yourself in a gray land going green.

JOHN DANIEL

To Mt. St. Helens

You were the perfect one,
the saint of symmetry.
We glanced at your benign
bright face, and you shined back
your blessing, you smiled
peacefully upon us.
We didn't much believe

your smoke and stir, we thought
your restiveness would pass—
and then you shuddered hard
and blasted yourself across
four states, engulfed a lake,
gorged rivers with gray mud,
flattened entire forests
and whatever lives they held
in your searing smother.
Your evenness and grace
exploded twelve miles high,
then showered down as grit
on our trim lawns and gardens—
and there you slouch, smudged
and gaping, spewing smoke,
resting in your rubble.
You did it, Mt. St. Helens.
As all of us looked on
you stormed in solitude,
you shrugged and shook aside
what we called beautiful
as if none of us were here,
no animals, no trees,
no life at all outside
your ancient fiery joy—
I admired you, mountain,
but I never loved you until now.

Prairie Lupine

(Lupinus lepidus var. *lobii)*

If you come upon Prairie Lupine after a recent rain or heavy dew, bend down and see how (amazingly) the individual leaflets are, together, able to hold a glistening drop of water. Some of us have long called these little miracles mountain diamonds.

Beyond such beauty, this flower holds the secret to resilience. Prairie Lupine was the first plant scientists discovered in the ash-scape of post-eruption Loowit. Think of the incredible regrowth that began when an individual Lupine was able to grow in that sterilized ash, fix nitrogen, and then, as the plant died, add even more nutrients to the soil. Four years after that first Lupine flowered, scientists counted sixteen thousand individuals nearby. And three years after that, thirty-five thousand. Now, there are untold numbers of Lupine painting the gray slopes of Loowit with great splashes of purple and blue. This keystone species has helped create the soil that has allowed so many more plant beings to take root across the otherwise stark and sweeping Pumice Plain.

In addition to their ability to add nutrients into the soil, Prairie Lupine has other superpowers. They can self-pollinate. Pretty handy in the post-apocalyptic landscape where much of the 2009 movie *The Road* was filmed. You may have heard that one of the ways to ameliorate the heat of climate change is to paint rooftops white. Prairie

Lupine figured this out long ago. The shiny silky hairs that cover their leaves reflect the sun. They are also able to turn their leaves toward the morning and evening sun and away from noon's bright glare, thus allowing themselves to photosynthesize at cooler times of the day. Attend, attend . . . we have so much to learn from Lupine.

ELIZABETH AOKI

Prairie Lupine

Imagine if your body required all your skin scored/
scarred/broken so that a new you could burst out green.

Imagine eating ash like porridge, liquid smoke like caviar.
Stretching your toes in the now-cooled pyroclastic flows

leftover from when Mt. St. Helens blew her top. Stop
to think how you came from a single seed of thought,

rolling in a gully-washer down to where you could plant
yourself deep, great-grandmother of them all, microbes helping

keep the sweet sweet nitrogen bathing your roots.
You fought to hold every pearl of dirt you could clutch

til all your daughters grew, a lace of lupine in a circle
around your singular wildflower head. Wasn't easy,

though others would say your comeback was foregone.
Elk scat. / Deer mice. / Toadlets climbing out of burrows.

Four years later, they count 16,000 purpling heads nodding for joy.
You had to believe in the future before it could arrive.

Northern Pocket Gopher

(Thomomys talpoides)

Perhaps you, like other gardeners in Cascadia, have happened to see the frilly top of Carrot in one of your rows trembling on a calm, windless day—then, like that, it's gone, sucked into the ground. Yep, that's Northern Pocket Gopher. While some vegetable lovers and overly meticulous lawn keepers might see them as pests, more than one scientist has called them the heroes of Mount St. Helens.

Northern Pocket Gopher, with big protruding front teeth, powerful front claws, and heavy shoulders, is perfectly adapted to dig, dig, dig. When they dig with their teeth, they close their lips to keep dirt out. And that's what they were doing three days after that incredible blast in 1980: digging. Scientists flying over the gray world of the blast zone were astonished to see, here and there, signs of life in the little mounds of dirt Gopher makes while creating their burrow tunnels. And as they dug, they churned old, buried forest soil into the newly made ash, allowing seedlings to make contact with mycorrhizal spores, which began everything.

There's a marvelous word used to describe the fact that these beings spend almost their entire lives underground digging: *fossorial*. Because they were in burrows as much as six feet underground, Northern Pocket Gopher became a living fossil, if you will— one of the few survivors of Loowit's eruption. Can you imagine what that massive blast, the equivalent of about twenty-five atomic bombs, must have sounded like? Felt like?

The two exceptions to their fossorial nature include popping out for a quick bit of mating and the time that comes when a mother feels her pups are old enough to be booted from her burrow. Northern Pocket

Gopher spends most of their life alone, but they have been known to share burrows with Mouse, Skunk, Rabbit, Ground Squirrel, Lizard, Toad, and Snake. Another heroic trait for those other few survivors or newcomers to a blasted land.

LAURA READ

Northern Pocket Gopher

I believe in the resurrection
of the body because every Sunday
I sat patiently in my pew
and watched a priest hold up a small circle
of unleavened bread and proclaim,
This is my body, I give it up for you.
He did not mean his own body, of course,
which was hidden beneath so much
purple or gold. Bolts of fabric.
I love the word bolt with fabric, don't you?
I love it when the women at JoAnn
take the bolt you hand them
and unfold it and unfold it until you
tell them to stop. I don't want them to stop
unfolding. To get out their large scissors.
I want the fabric to be continuous.
The way I want the body. For example,
I only start to believe someone is dead
if they've been dead for years. And mostly
not even then. This is what I like about you,
Northern Pocket Gopher.
I have never actually seen you in person,
but that doesn't mean that I won't.
I like pockets in general, they're a novelty
for women, you know,
who are always exclaiming about a dress,
It has pockets! because for centuries
no one believed
we might want to carry something.

I can tell you we do.
I thought the pocket was the place
in the dirt you poked through,
or a pocket in time where your life and mine
could finally intersect,
but in fact, the pockets are your cheeks
that you stuff with food like a man
who doesn't know where his next meal
is coming from. Just try telling you
you can't take it with you.
Whenever my mother told a story
about my father,
I tried to be quiet enough
that she wouldn't get distracted
but not so quiet
that she would notice her spell.
One I especially liked was The Dinner Party.
Someone brought a pineapple.
They were walking up the steps of the porch
when my dad opened the door and exclaimed,
Thank you! Jane never lets me have pineapple!
It's like a photograph people sigh
when they see and say,
Well, that really captures him.

Sitka Willow

(Salix sitchensis)

When you meet Sitka Willow, reach out and stroke a leaf to know why this being
is also called Satin, Velvet, and Silky Willow. Those words perfectly describe
the feeling of touching the undersides of the leaves, which are covered in soft
hairs. Those leaves, with their broad, rounded ends, shine dark green above

and whitish below. When the wind blows, they put on quite a show, flashing their bicolor beauty.

After Prairie Lupine and others helped make new soil from the ash around Mount St. Helens, Sitka Willow took hold and started thriving in riparian areas. As they became established along streams, they provided food for Elk and Beaver and shelter for birds.

Sitka Willow can grow as high as a three-story house, but in the story of Loowit's regrowth to date, a species of invasive weevil is keeping them much smaller, thus preventing them from providing a more substantial starter kit for the kind of forest community that lived at Mount St. Helens before the 1980 eruption.

Native people have long relied on Sitka Willow and other willows. The shoots are especially popular in basket weaving, and the bark can be chewed to relieve headaches and other pain. Aspirin, in fact, is derived from a substance (salicin) in Willow.

CHARLES GOODRICH

Bellies Full of Sand

Sitka Willow (Salix sitchensis)

They'll thwack you in the face
and thicket your path

but I've always admired willows,
stitching river banks together,
straining floodwaters,
leaning lithely
out over the current.

Until one summer beside the Willamette,
while my small son waded in an eddy,
I noticed a young gravel bar
just risen up
out of the water

and the willows were on it already
like vultures on a carcass
snaking their roots into the sand
sucking minerals
from the cobbles.

"We've got to go," I told my son.
He shook his head, waded deeper.
I tugged him out of the water
and carried him
unhappily home.

Because I'd underimagined willows,
how brilliantly ambitious they are,
colonizing every fresh island,
voraciously filling their bellies,
propelled by an urge to turn sand
into leaves, enamored of the sun,
indifferent to us.

Elk

(Cervus canadensis)

One of the most surreal sounds you will ever hear in Cascadia is the bugling of
bull Elk. The song begins low and throaty and gradually rises to a hollow squeal.
Once you hear it, you will never forget it, especially if you hear it at night when

Cervus Elaphus

Elk

it seems that the very spirit of wildness, at once thrilling and haunting, has taken corporeal form.

Every fall, during the rut, bull Elk engages in an extravagant courtship ritual as he tries to ward off other bulls while attracting cows to his harem. As you might suspect, the massive antlers are heavily involved as Elk thrashes against trees, bushes, the ground, and competitors. Behind those antlers are a thousand pounds of dark brown neck and tan body. Just imagine the shock of two sets of those antlers clashing together!

Another way a bull tries try to attract cows in rut is by scratching out a depression, or wallow, peeing in it, and then rolling around to try and coat their hide in the smell of their own urine. Maybe give that some thought the next time you splash on your aftershave or perfume.

Before Europeans arrived, there were great herds of Elk throughout the continent, second only in number to herds of Bison. Their numbers quickly dwindled as they were slaughtered by commercial hunters to feed logging camps and burgeoning towns, and later shot by ranchers to reduce competition with Cattle for grazing land. The Elk living in Cascadia today are the descendants of those who found refuge in remote mountains and forests.

Amazingly, within days of Loowit's 1980 eruption, Elk was stepping through the ash in search of food. As they did, they sped up the revegetation process. In some places where they stepped, such as hillsides, their hoofprints loosened the ash and led to erosion, which allowed buried plants to sprout. In other places, their hoofprints became places where windblown seeds collected and sprouted. Spores of mycorrhizal fungi and seeds of other plants they had ingested were deposited through their scat. The travels of this being spread life in their wake.

KEETJE KUIPERS

The elk my father shot

is an imagined butterfly of flesh—
thin cannon bones pinning back its winged hide

like a boxed *anartia amathea
amathea*, all white speckled gristle

and silver tendon seam—when he calls me
from the mountaintop and leaves his breathless

message (afraid, at last, of what he's done)
telling of the bow, the arrow, his tin

pan trembling heart and shaking arm, quiet
so as not to scare away the grazing

ghost he's made, as if this yearly taking
of a life were a talisman carried

in his pocket beside the knife, a charm
against entropy, his own brittle bones.

Pearly Everlasting

(Anaphalis margaritacea)

Wind played an important role in the early succession (the changing of the land and plant and animal communities through time) that occurred after Loowit blew. One of the beings that drifted in and stayed was Pearly Everlasting, whose seeds are light and easily carried by the wind. Along with Prairie Lupine, Pearly Everlasting, whose flowers look like a collection of rounded white buttons with yellow centers, was one of the first beings to take root in that seemingly sterilized place. Imagine rolling hills of gray pumice and ash dabbed here and there with green stems, green lance-shaped leaves, and waist-high blooms.

This being is indeed everlasting in a couple of ways. After their flowers bloom in the summer, they can last until the first snows of winter. Also, the white bracts (leaves) that surround the yellow disk make this being ideal for dried flower arrangements, keeping their just-bloomed appearance for months. And as we tell you this, we want you to be aware that picking is not permitted in some places, such as most parks. In these areas, you might recall this catchy advice: "Spare a flower, share a flower." We also encourage you, in the spirit of the "Honorable Harvest" described by Robin Wall Kimmerer, to "ask permission of the ones whose lives you seek" and "abide by the answer." Think not just about what you can take from a place,

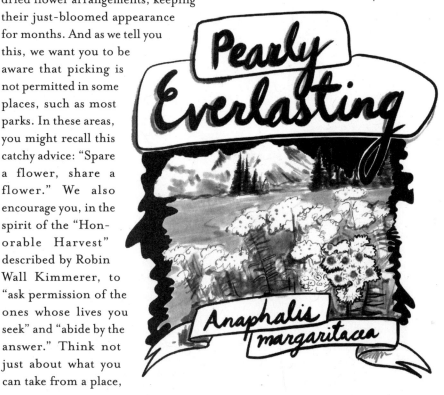

but what you can give. These are the questions we all must be asking ourselves: How can we reciprocate? How can we help restore balance?

Native people have many uses for Pearly Everlasting. The Kwakwaka'wakw dry them and then mix them with Yellow-cedar pitch to make a poultice, and the Nlaka'pamux use them in a medicine for influenza.

JEAN-PAUL PECQUEUR

On Naming Wildflowers

When the body slips the bonds of sense, the spirit seeks its familiars. Dusty maidens spreading groundsmoke. Prairie smoke. With frosted paintbrush and yellow rattle. Coltsfoot in fairy slipper. In northern suncup sky pilot. Smooth hawksbeard and rough cat's-ear. Baby stars, baby blue-eyes, in cream cups and self-heal. Expanding traveler's joy, memorializing each reunion with its proper name. Sea-watch. Fetid adders tongue. Pearly everlasting.

Oregon Junco

(*Junco hyemalis oreganus*)

Just about any stroll through a forest in Cascadia will include a glimpse of Oregon Junco, a ubiquitous member of the Sparrow family. You will often see them flying up from the ground where they had been foraging until you walked up. The way they pump their tail feathers in flight makes them easy to identify, as this action makes their white outer feathers clearly visible.

Junco has a sharply defined dark hood, a light brown back, a white belly, and a pale, pointed bill. Instead of walking or strutting when on the ground, they tend to hop, scratch, and peck in a kind of Junco break-dance as they forage for seeds.

Since Oregon Junco is one of fifteen different subspecies of Dark-Eyed Junco, many birders are content to use the latter term. However, in an attempt to be as precise as we can and to represent Cascadia's true diversity, we like the name Oregon Junco. It's also good to keep in mind that between new information (from field or lab) and cultural changes, naming can be in constant flux, like a river.

Oregon Junco in Cascadia mostly migrates vertically, rather than north–south, and is equally at home in subalpine and coastal environments. They spend summers in the forests covering mountain slopes up to eleven thousand feet and then spread out across the lowlands for the winter. Females select the

nest site, which is usually in a nook or depression on a slope or rock face, in dense brush, or beneath the roots of upturned trees. And, of course, there was plenty of real estate in the upturned trees at Mount St. Helens.

Because Junco typically nests on the ground instead of in trees, they were one of the first birds to return to Loowit after the eruption. Late winter snowbanks had provided refuge for tree saplings and shrubs and other plants, and these habitats offered enough plant diversity for Junco to take up residence. After Loowit's immense shrug and deafening roar, there was silence and ash and steam. And then wind. And then the long musical trill of Oregon Junco.

WILLIAM STAFFORD

Juncos

> They operate from elsewhere,
> some hall in the mountains—
> quick visit, gone.
> Specialists on branch ends,
> craft union. I like their
> clean little coveralls.

Western Thatching Ant

(Formica obscuripes)

The first dark patches you might see emerging from Cascadia's spring snows will often be the mounds made by Western Thatching Ant. These solar-heated nests are commonly about a foot tall and about three feet in diameter, comparable perhaps to the first small pile of leaves you might rake together in October. If you do some searching online, however, you might find the footage of an enormous one in the Columbia River Gorge, which looks to be about as tall as an SUV. As you may have guessed, these mounds are made of thatch—small twigs, bits of Grass, leaves, and plant stems—which acts as an effective insulation to regulate

Western Thatching Ant

formica obscuripes

the temperature and humidity in Ant's nurseries below.

It turns out that Humans are not the only animals who trim the vegetation around their homes. Western Thatching Ant has three different castes of workers devoted to maintaining their mound, and one of those castes is responsible for cutting (biting) down plants and Grasses that grow in and around their dwelling. This prevents shade from cooling the nurseries below optimal temperatures.

Western Thatching Ant is often black and red, but some in the same colony can be all black. Most colonies number between seventeen thousand and forty thousand, but one in the Blue Mountains of Oregon had over fifty-six million members. This is a case in which several neighboring nests belong to the same colony (polydromy).

After Loowit's eruption, Western Thatching Ant was an important pioneer being. As they flew into the blast zone in their winged form and established new colonies, their nests became what Mount St. Helens ecologist Charlie Crisafulli has described as "islands of fertility." Crisafulli, who has given most of his life to researching Loowit's regrowth, says that he nearly had to break the *y*-axis to measure the level of nutrients at these nest sites. Western Thatching Ant proved to be incredibly successful at concentrating the scant resources of a wider area to enrich the soil more quickly and to a higher degree than other keystone beings such as Lupine, Alder, Elk, and Beaver. And even as we type these words, this process continues.

If you ever see Crow or Jay or another bird standing or lying on a mound, there's a good chance they are taking an Ant "shower." We aren't sure exactly why they do this, but we have a couple of ideas. One postulates that the formic acid released when Ant bites may kill various pests such as bacteria, mites, and fungi. The other possible explanation is that Ant is more palatable *after* they have emptied their sac of formic acid. This is only one of many mysteries held by Cascadia's beings. Ornithology (the study of birds) has long relied on citizen science. Maybe you have a role to play in the lore of our bioregion.

MATTHEW NIENOW

Harvesting the Verb

The world for us is meat to gather
and store in a maze of nests and tunnels,

safe under the soft dome of our needle

thatch, a muted brown so like the bare
earth below salal and trailing blackberry,

below the curving stems of calendula

upon which, in summer, we farm
our sweet aphids—and though the source

of our common name is the appearance

of our home, we know ourselves by
what we do, by how, in droves, we move

across the land harvesting the verb left

in every fallen life. We cannot help but be
on purpose in our work, culling, making

use of what the ground provides. We,

a multitude of one mind, have no need
for leisure, no word for waste.

Green Alder

(Alnus viridis ssp. *crispa)*

You will know Green Alder by their leaves, which have fine teeth along their edges, their characteristic dangling spikes of flower clusters (catkins), and their cute cones, which look like miniaturized versions of Ponderosa Pine cones.

Green Alder can appear shrub-like or grow as tall as a basketball hoop, depending on conditions. Another common name for them and their close kin, Sitka Alder, is Slide Alder. They grow very well in the chutes left by snow and rockslides, aided in this ability no doubt by their exceedingly pliable trunks.

Like Prairie Lupine, Green Alder has aided the regrowth at Mount St. Helens since they, too, are able to take nitrogen out of the atmosphere and fix it into their roots and surrounding soil. As Alder has made the land more nutrient

rich, other beings such as Green Corn Lily, Mertens' Sedge, and Black Cottonwood have been able to grow in the areas most impacted by the eruption.

Indigenous people have many uses for Green Alder. It is a choice wood for smoking fish. Juice scraped from the bark can be applied to the skin to relieve itching from rash. And if you are ever out on a hike and a few days away from your last good wash, you might like to know that Green Alder can be cut and worn for their sticky, sweet-smelling scent.

PETER TROWER

The Alders

The alders are the reoccupiers—
they come easily
and quick into skinned land
rising like an ambush
on raked ridges—
Jabbing like whiskers up through the washedout
faces of neverused roads.

The alders are the forestfixers
bandaging brown wounds
with applegreen sashes—
filling for the fallen
firs—
jostling up by the stumps
of grandfather cedars—
leaning slim to the wind
by logjammed
loggerleft streams.

The alders are the encroachers
seizing ground the greater trees owned
once
but no more.

It is the time of the alders
they come
like a bright upstart army
crowding the deadwood spaces
reaching
at last for the hand of the whole
unshadowed sun.

Willamette Valley

Art by Jillian Barthold

Another August sunset and a sky the deep red of pomegranate juice. Driving along a two-lane country road through miles of fields, you roll down your window and the warm air rushing into your car holds the aromatic, distinct scent of Mint. There's nothing like it at harvest time when tubs of freshly cut leaves and stems are hauled to stills where they are steamed to produce barrel after barrel of extremely potent oil, a drop of which may very well have gone into your toothpaste.

This is the Willamette Valley, a place of incredible fertility and growth where a cool, moist climate and rich soil make for some of the most productive agriculture in Cascadia. Listen for the *chok-chok* as gigantic sprinklers send long pulses of water arcing through the air to shower down on all sorts of crops. In addition to Mint, you'll find vegetables, nurseries, tree fruits (especially Hazelnut), Christmas trees, Grass seed, Wheat, and many kinds of berries. We contend that the sweet, juicy, sun-warmed black Blackberry you pick here is the best on the planet. And have you tasted Marionberry cobbler? Tayberry jam? Yum! More recent crops include hops (for all those Cascadian microbreweries), cannabis for CBD oil and hemp, and wine grapes. Almost twenty thousand acres of vineyards support over five hundred wineries, making the Willamette Valley for many synonymous with wine country (Pinot Noir, anyone?).

There's a story underneath all this green and growing, of course. It goes back to the end of the last ice age when ice dams formed to create a body of water called Lake Missoula and then broke to send megafloods rushing up to one thousand feet deep down the Columbia

River and on into the Willamette Valley where, thanks to mountain ranges to the west, south, and east, Lake Allison was formed. Stretching from Portland all the way to Eugene, this lake was as deep as four hundred feet above sea level. Lake Allison formed and drained, then formed and drained again and again until around thirteen thousand years ago. When the last iteration of Lake Allison finally drained away, it left an incredibly rich, silty soil about two hundred feet deep.

The Willamette Valley was the primary destination for wagon trains of emigrants traveling the Oregon Trail in the nineteenth century. Before their arrival, the Kalapuya, Molala, and Chinook tribes inhabited this region alone, and as settlers arrived, that sovereignty was broken, yet their connection and presence remain. When the First People were the only Humans here, the Willamette Valley was filled with wetlands and gallery forests along the length of the Willamette River and tall grasslands broken up by groves of Douglas-fir and Oregon White Oak. People shaped these groves, using fire to manage growth, keeping shading forests at bay and encouraging open grasslands, including great patches of Camas.

In Canada, Oregon White Oak is typically called Garry Oak. And indeed, the Willamette Valley is remarkably similar ecologically to the Garry Oak ecosystems of southern Vancouver Island and the southern Gulf Islands, which is considered one of the most endangered ecosystems in Canada.

Despite the more than one million acres devoted to modern agriculture, you will find traces of the valley known by the first Humans. Look for it in patches of bluish-violet blooms in wet meadows the plow blades missed. Look for it in the groves of trees surviving on steep terrain and along property lines. Its song still plays in the wind through their limbs and the *dee-dee-dee* of Chickadee's bright call.

LEX RUNCIMAN

Green

Lebanon to Hebo, Iron Mountain
        to Mary's Peak, over the rumpled
sheet of this valley, color begins—
        rose of Nootka Roses, white petals
of blackberries, mountain ash,
        camas blue and red currant red
to make the brown dirt, the sillion
        of plowed fields, browner,
not flat but fertile, the nativity of color.

And by late spring in this valley,
            what the world wants in its visible way
to say before it goes torrid, limp and drought-
            weary, the message I miss in distraction
every year, is green. Green of marshes shrinking.
            Duck feathers, the iridescent greens.
The slick sheen of the tops of cottonwood leaves
            and the matte silver of their undersides
as they semaphore on and off in wind,
            black and pewter in moonlight.

Yellow-green of willows, alders,
            the sterner iron of oak leaves
and the pliable flags of maples, black
            firs, their new tassels, the outsides
and the insides. New wheat or foxglove,
            vanilla leaf, whatever it means,
grand fir or red cedar—whatever it means
            is green, whatever it means.

Common Camas

(Camassia quamash)

Beneath the striking blue-violet flowers of Camas lies one of the most prized vegetable foods for Native people of Oregon, Washington, and British Columbia who have long harvested the bulbs. In terms of trade volume, in fact, this food has been second only to Salmon, sometimes making up to half of the diet of a tribe.

Where Camas grows in moist meadows, a family will mark out and maintain a patch year-round for generations, keeping it free of weeds and periodically burning it. As they tend their patch, families are especially focused on eradicating any Death Camas, a lookalike whose bulbs are deadly poisonous and will kill Humans and other animals due to a high alkaloid content. The best time to tell these two plants apart is when they are blooming. Death Camas has a creamy-white flower.

Native women in particular have tended the family Camas patch. The harvest is quite an event and may take weeks and require temporary shelters. Traditional harvesters dig out the bulbs using fire-hardened sticks or Deer antlers, keeping only the larger bulbs and tucking the smaller ones back into the earth for the next year's harvest. In this way, about fifty pounds of bulbs can be collected in a day. The bulbs are then steamed in large pits for up to three days. During this process, the plant's complex carbohydrates break down into sugar fructose. This means what you might think it means: the cooked bulbs are delicious. When they are warm, wrote the Scottish botanist David Douglas, they taste like baked Pear. After cooking, the bulbs can also be dried and ground into a meal that, when mixed with water, makes excellent pancake batter. Another use for the meal is to mix it with water and shape it into large bricks to be cooked and stored for later use.

Camas is not nearly as abundant now as it was before Europeans arrived. Meriwether Lewis's journal entries give us some sense of what we have lost because of contemporary agriculture and urban sprawl when he compares a meadow full of Camas in bloom to "lakes of fine clear water."

In a rare act of recognition for the important relationship between Indigenous people and Camas, this being's Latin species name is *quamash*, which is the Nimiipuu word for "Common Camas."

BETH PIATOTE

qémes

After World War II, advances in astrophysics allowed humans to see their planet from space. In 1972, the Apollo 17 took the most famous photograph of Earth, the blue planet. It might be fair to say that since the mid-twentieth century, humans have seen things that were never within their visual grasp before. But do we have better dreams? Have we seen better things? I think I would give up my fridge magnet of Planet Earth, every glimpse of snowy mountain folds from the window of a plane, the glittering view of Paris from the Eiffel Tower on New Year's Eve—I would give up all of these things to see what our ancestors saw, to dream their vivid dreams, to come over a mountain with my mothers and sisters and suddenly see, in the wide open, an enormous blue meadow of blooming camas, an endless, unbroken field of periwinkle, lake, and lapis that today you could barely imagine, a land breathing and rolling with blue, a land so beautiful that you would wonder how to find your voice, find your offering, draw out a song on your breath and press the strength of your body to the earth, into the earth, into the deep wild blue.

Western Pond Turtle

(Actinemys marmorata)

Basking in the sun on a log or rock just above the surface of a pond or river is how you will most likely encounter Western Pond Turtle. If you can approach stealthily, unobserved, you will get to see the tectonic-plate-like pattern of their dark (brownish to olive-green) shell and the intricate patterns of lines and dots on their head. Once you are observed, however, Western Pond Turtle will slip into the water with a soft plop and swim for cover.

In addition to ponds and rivers, they like lakes, creeks, marshes, and irrigation ditches that offer plenty of vegetation for eating and spots on which to bask for several hours each day. These perches can be in high demand and lead to territorial disputes in which one Turtle tries to scare off another by opening their mouth to expose their yellow and pinkish lining, perhaps as if to say, "Don't make me bite you!"

Like other reptiles, Western Pond Turtle is ectothermic (cold-blooded) and needs the sun to raise their body temperature. In addition to heat, UV rays help keep them healthy and regulate their moods. Many a Human on the west side of the Cascades during our famously gray winters can definitely relate.

After mating in April and May, females clamber onto land, dig a nest in a place with full sun not too far from the water, and lay between two and eleven eggs. Their eggs are about the size of a quarter and are ovular, like giant white vitamins. When they manage to dig their way to the surface, hatchlings, about as big as your child's palm, with big, cute, dark-pupiled eyes, rely on instinct to find their way to water.

Pond Turtle numbers have dropped dramatically over the last century due to loss of habitat (especially wetlands), invasive plants such as Reed Canarygrass overwhelming nesting sites, and competition and disease from invasive Turtles, especially Red-eared Slider. Invasive Bullfrog has also reduced their

population by preying on hatchlings. Their range used to stretch from British Columbia to Mexico, but they have been extirpated from Canada, and the populations that remain in Cascadia are isolated. Organizations such as the Oregon Zoo are participating in the Western Pond Turtle Recovery Project, rearing Turtles until they are ready to be released in the wild with a much better chance for survival. Projects focused on wetland preservation and restoration are underway too.

Western Pond Turtle's name in Northeastern Pomo is kʰá:wanaka and the Lushootseed know them as ʔaləšək. But what do they call themselves, you might wonder? And so do we.

DEBORAH A. MIRANDA

The Hatchling

It's an old tale: young girl flees a house made of anger,
takes refuge amongst mosquitoes and stinging nettles

down by a little pond with no name. It's not her skin that hurts.
Dragonflies skim on stained-glass wings, bees heavy with delight

whisper praise into blossoms. Cedar waxwings coax the girl
into a lush thicket surrounded by swaying alders.

Salmonberries fall into her hand at a touch: sweet roe,
fat suns. One by one, novas burst, form the phoenix of her tongue.

The girl swallows mystery like mother's milk, slides down
the slick bank of trilliums, pure white flags that never say surrender.

Black with volcanic ash, earth smudges her hands, knees, catches
her in a nest of bleeding hearts and resurrection. Breathless

at pond's edge, she looks up into a sky encircled by sharp pines.
An eagle spirals slow as smoke—hangs on an updraft—

folds wings tight, dives straight toward the still water at her feet.
She thinks it will pull up, she thinks it will drown, she thinks

you aren't made for this—

the curved bill splits the surface, huge body plunges into darkness,
yellow talons follow. The girl leans over, peers beneath, *into,*

sees shadow wings beating, beating upwards from the depths,
closer—scales replace feathers, closer still—webbing stretches

between black claws, beak shrinks into short jade curve—a soaring
body hunches into stone-like shell—and gleaming pond turtle emerges

where eagle fell. Paddles to the opposite shore. Crawls out. Looks back
over a hard gray shoulder. *Pay attention*, says turtle, eyes clear as rain.

Leaves behind a new story, forged from the carapace of transformation.

Thimbleberry

(Rubus parviflorus)

According to Daniel Mathews in his essential field guide, *Cascadia Revealed*, a great
controversy exists about the palatability of Thimbleberry versus Salmonberry.
He is most definitively of the "thimbleberry cult," writing that he finds a good
Thimbleberry to be the "most exquisite berry flavor on earth." We invite you
to taste these berries for yourself and, if you feel strongly about the issue, share
your gustatory convictions with Mr. Mathews!

Of course, Native people have long enjoyed both berries, often eating them
with Salmon; their sharp tang tempers Salmon's rich flavor. Kwakwaka'wakw
collect Thimbleberry when they are young, firm, and pink and store them
in bags made of cedar bark to ripen. When ready, they are de-stemmed and
eaten or dried. Nuxalk people consider Thimbleberry inferior to Raspberry

and Blackcap, so when they add dried Thimbleberry to cakes, they mix the three berries together. In addition to the berries, Native people eat the young, peeled shoots of Thimbleberry. The Nuu-chah-nulth have been known to collect the shoots in bulk. In the language of the Concow tribe, this being is known as wä-sā'.

Thimbleberry, which can grow to between two and ten feet in height, has delicate white flowers and berries that look like shallow, velvety, rounded raspberries. The plate-sized, maple-like leaves are exceedingly soft and fuzzy—and why some in Cascadia think of Thimbleberry as "Toilet Paper Bush."

Since the core stays behind when the berry is picked, the hollow berry resembles a thimble, which may have been what gave this being their name. Many beings live in close relationship with Thimbleberry. Birds and Bear eat the fruit, while Black-tailed Deer browses the young leaves and stems. The flowers are important to native pollinators, such as Bee, and Yellow-banded Day Sphinx relies on this being as a nectar source and host for their young.

KATHLEEN FLENNIKEN

Thimbleberry

One taste

and the rest
is what came after.
Little berry,

you're the flavor
of my best,
most necessary

kiss. Fit
for a tongue tip,
exactly.

You were nothing
until I picked
you once.

How long
do we willingly
live without?

How hungry
would I be if
I'd kept walking?

Cougar

(Puma concolor)

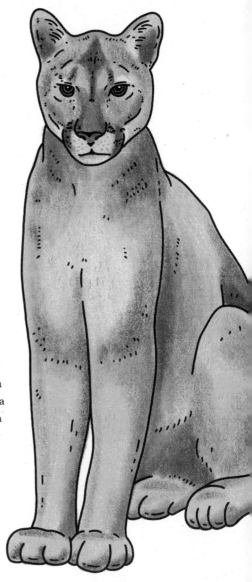

You can spend a lifetime exploring Cascadia's wilder regions without seeing so much as a paw print from this being, and though you may never see Cougar, who is also known as Mountain Lion, Puma, Catamount, and Ghost Cat, you have almost certainly been seen by Cougar. In fact, Cougar has been known to follow a solitary hiker for days without ever being spotted.

If you are one of the fortunate few Humans to catch a glimpse of Cougar, you will see a long, slender being as tall as a kitchen counter and as long as a park bench with ruddy brown fur and a long, thick tail. Despite one of their names, they don't roar like a lion. Cougar is typically silent and only rarely purrs, chirps, yowls, or screeches. That woman screaming bloody murder in the woods? She could be a female Cougar sounding her eerie scream, telling any males in hearing distance that she's ready to mate.

More and more, as Human's range continues to expand into Cougar's range, the news contains stories that would paint Cougar as a threat. But the statistical reality is that there is on average only one fatal attack on a Human per year in North America. This number is far less than the number of fatal Dog attacks every year. And the ecological reality is that Cascadia needs Cougar. Although they feed on all sorts of animals, from Cricket to Porcupine, Cougar's favorite prey is Elk and, especially, Deer. After they locate deer by sight or smell, they will approach very slowly, sometimes freezing for a few minutes as if to pass for a log; once they are within about thirty feet, they take bounding leaps and bite their prey on the nape of the neck, sometimes severing the spinal cord. Amazingly, Cougar can leap as high as twenty feet and as far as forty feet! This predation thins Deer and Elk herds of weaker members, some of whom may be diseased, and it keeps these hooved grazers moving through their range, preventing overbrowsing that can seriously degrade the health and diversity of a plant community.

Cougar is an apex predator, and their essential presence touches everything in an ecosystem, including, as in the case of the wolves of Yellowstone National Park, the very course of the rivers.

PATRICK LANE

Cougar Men

They came out of the hills with their arms
hanging in fists. Across the fenders and the hood
the cougars rested their long yellow, the male
with his eyes closed, not staring at whatever was left,
and the female's open, her lips pulled back over
the teeth, the long ones broken off at the base
by what must have been a stone, flakes of quartz
glinting on her torn tongue. The hounds
tied to the door handles with short ropes
raged at the air, one thin bitch tearing at the end
of a tail, the hair stripping off into her mouth
and her spitting, leaping again at what was dead.
The people came to the station in twos and threes
from the bars across the street, men mostly,

but women too, some with children. One was me,
a small boy with white hair as if I'd grown old
before my time. I reached for a head
and when no one stopped me, touched
my finger to the female's eye, the ball sinking
in. When I pulled away, the ball stayed as it was,
a cup now, holding the light of the autumn sun.
A bottle of whiskey was broken open
and the men took it in their fists and drank, wiping
their mouths with their wrists. *Don't get too close,*
boy, a man said, and kicked the bitch in the ribs—
her falling under the other dogs and rising again,
slavering, her high wail wet among the pack. The crowd
passed the long teeth among them and then, because
there was nothing else to do, returned to the bars
and streets, women pulling their children by the arms.
The cougar men tied the dogs into the truck box
and pulled away from the station,
the tails of the cougars dragging in the dust.
Then the street was empty, the sun
caught in the tired elms. It was Thursday, I think,
though I cannot be sure. It was a long time ago.
Those dogs and men are dead now, gone to bone,
but that eye I touched still holds the light
in what little is left of me in those far hills.

Douglas-Fir

(Pseudotsuga menziesii)

If you are fortunate enough to encounter a giant Douglas-fir such as Doerner
Fir in Coos County, Oregon, who is 327 feet tall and between 450 and 500
years old, place your palms against the thick dark brown bark and let your eyes
follow deep grooves up and up. You might think you are seeing through a dream

or maybe a Hayao Miyazaki film into a world of clean gigantic limbs perfectly spaced for climbing, as if inviting you to come on up and see the view.

"Who *are* you?" wondered just about every European as they first met Douglas-fir, including the Scottish botanist David Douglas, who popularized this being for cultivation in Europe. Based on observable characteristics and using standard classifications, European naturalists tried on the name Oregon Pine, but that didn't quite fit, nor did Yew-leafed-fir, Douglas Spruce, or False Hemlock (though this one survives in the first part of the Latin name). Eventually Douglas-fir won out. The hyphen isn't always present, but it should be, for it denotes that this being is not a true fir like Grand, Noble, and Pacific Silver. The cones of these firs stand upright and come apart after the seeds ripen, whereas the cones of Douglas-fir dangle and remain intact. When you come across one such cone, look for the characteristic three-pointed bract that resembles the two hind legs and tail of a minuscule Mouse trying to slip under a woody scale. There's an old story, in fact, that seems to have Indigenous roots. Once there was a great forest fire. When Mouse realized they could not outrun the flames, they asked the trees for help. Western Redcedar, Bigleaf Maple, and other trees were unable to help. The giant Douglas-fir, however, offered protection. They told Mouse to climb up their thick, fire-resistant trunks and hide under the scales of their cones for safety. By taking shelter inside the cones, Mouse survived the great fire. And even today, you can see their tail sticking out from beneath the scales of the cones. Another way to identify this being is by the way Douglas-fir's inch-long, green needles grow from all sides of their branchlets like the bristles of a bottlebrush.

Douglas-fir is the most abundant and ubiquitous tree in Cascadia. They are able to grow almost anywhere, filling different ecological roles depending on where they are. They are strong, and they grow fast and straight. And they might be a candidate for our planet's tallest tree. Records from the early logging industry indicate that there were individuals cut down that were as tall as 415 feet, over 100 feet taller than the Statue of Liberty. In the early days of Cascadia's logging, Douglas-fir was prized, but as the stock of old-growth individuals dwindled, the industry moved on.

Native people have long had many uses for Douglas-fir. In addition to chewing the sap, they have made all sorts of implements from the wood, including Salmon weirs, harpoon barbs and shafts, dip-net poles, and spear handles. The pitch is used for caulking canoes and making a medicinal salve for wounds and skin irritations.

SHANKAR NARAYAN

Tree of the Moon

A HAIBUN

On the third moon mission, an astronaut who was a fireman
in Cascadia brought a pouch of Douglas-fir seeds. 360 feet of
Saturn bathed the gantry in white fire, thrusting the module
up through earth's thin skin of air, beyond the stratosphere.
Through five days of flight, the seeds collided and trembled
like molecules in a hot liquid. But inside they were still—
their nature patience until the right moment. Some believe
Douglas-firs once reached 450 feet, the tallest beings that have
ever lived. Only scattered survivors of the great fellings now
hint at those titans' might.

The seeds circled the moon 34 times and returned to earth.
They had traveled a million miles. As human beings will, a
man nearly ended everything by spilling the seeds into a vacu-
um. But they survived, pushing up unlikely sprouts. One came
back to Cascadia, planted in a carefully designed government
plaza by some fine examples of large-scale brutalism.

Betrayed by his pancreas, the fireman died. The tree out-stripped the bureaucrats' vision—through decades it thrust upward and upward, into twilights of deep indigo as only Cascadia's gods can create, indigo over a fraying mantle of evergreen. Its roots cracked the carefully designed sidewalk. The bureaucrats, unable to process imperatives of accidental precious things, rushed to defend the plaza with its 24-hour traffic. They ordered the tree felled.

Soon there will be no being on earth who has traveled to the moon. One day no being will believe such a thing was ever possible.

Inside my right lung
the red fir grows
a desertful of stars

Chestnut-Backed Chickadee

(Poecile rufescens)

Walking through a stand of trees, perhaps Douglas-fir, you might hear the thin, high, scratchy *chick-a-dee, chick-a-dee* of, you guessed it, Chestnut-backed Chickadee. This being seems to always be happily exploring a tangle of brush, peering into nooks, scrutinizing tree cones, and constantly chattering about all of these things and more.

Like Black-capped and Mountain Chickadee, this bird has bold black and white markings on their head, but in this being's case, their nut-brown back and flanks blend perfectly with the bark of the conifer trees they frequent and help distinguish them from their Cascadian cousins.

If you are ever feeling down, look for a flock of these beings. It's really hard to feel anything but perky and optimistic when in the midst of their ceaseless flutters and *dee-dee*s. The tiny industry of Chestnut-backed Chickadee seems utterly boundless. And Humans, many of whom put out feeders to attract them, aren't the only ones who like to socialize with them. You will often see their roving flocks, which tend to be comprised of up to ten members, mixed with other birds such as Nuthatch, Goldfinch, Creeper and Junco. It appears that these other birds are fluent in Chickadee and rely on their communications, especially their warning calls, so they can spend more energy on searching for food and less on watching for predators.

All the busyness of Chestnut-backed Chickadee is of course not just about cheering us up. The individuals in Cascadia's northerly regions can store about eighty thousand seeds in one season to help them survive a snowy winter. Instead of keeping these seeds in one place, they keep them in thousands of places, anywhere a seed will fit: tapped into the base of a cluster of tree needles, tucked into a bark crevice, and so on. Incredibly, through the long and cold winter,

Chickadee can remember where each morsel is stored. What's more, they know which ones are more nutritious and which ones have already been eaten.

Though almost half their diet does consist of seeds, Chestnut-backed Chickadee eats plenty of insects and other animals. In fact, in the first seven to ten days after their eggs hatch, the parents search especially for Spider to feed their young. Spiders contain an amino acid called taurine, which is necessary for brain development. After the Spider course is done, the parents feed their nestlings mostly small Caterpillars; in one day, they can collect over a thousand.

LYANDA FERN LYNN HAUPT

Cedar Bird of Life

Neck aching, arched to see your tiny tree-cave nest high in the snag, I have one question: *Why do you exist?* There are many chickadee species, more than most humans know or could dream. Why another in this Cascadian place, just here? Surely the ubiquitous black-capped has all chickadee matters under control. I have come to understand one thing at least: You are not a *chestnut*-backed chickadee. A color from a standardized nomenclature for a forest bird where chestnuts do not grow?

I have been watching you. Your mate helped to choose this nest, but it is you, the female, who gathers threads of bark to blanket the cavity. Together you glean the evergreens in the deepest forest for nourishment: cedar, fir, hemlock, spruce. A singular bark-ochre color feathers your back, yes, and your flanks, and your overtail. It wanders in tiny passages onto your breast. Your color is Cedar. Western red here in Cascadia, tree of life. You are Cedar Chickadee.

And here is the path into my inquiry.

My vision blurs around you, perched there in feathers and branches, until you are surrounded by a cloud of your ancestors, not Cedar yet, following the edge of the receding Pleistocene glacier north, and west, and north again, into emerging forests, making homes and lives in the canopy. While other chickadees seek an easier life—one with more light, less moss, fewer ferns, lighter rains, you nourish yourself and your young upon this forest, and the forest upon your work, your lives,

your deaths, until you grow into one another—color, feather, bark, flight. Though I have walked among this bird-forest my whole life I have never found one of your tiny bodies, so quickly are you gathered into moss and soil and cedar again. You exist because the forest exists, and this forest because of you.

Steelhead

(Oncorhynchus mykiss)

It's impossible to write about Steelhead without also writing about Rainbow Trout. They are the same being, mostly. That is to say that their genetic makeup identifies them as *Oncorhynchus mykiss*, but whereas Rainbow Trout stays in freshwater lakes and streams, Steelhead is anadromous, meaning that they, like their Salmon kin, swim to the sea for a part of their lives. To make this happen, their bodies go through an incredible metamorphosis that allows them to breathe saltwater for one to four years before they transform again and breathe freshwater as they return to their natal streams to spawn. Unlike their Salmon kin, Steelhead do not die after spawning. As they travel upstream, they continue to feed on many beings, including insects such as Caddisfly. This characteristic, coupled with the fact that the food-rich world of the ocean has helped them grow much bigger than Rainbow Trout (up to forty-five inches long and fifty-five pounds), makes them a revered being among anglers who keep the locations of their

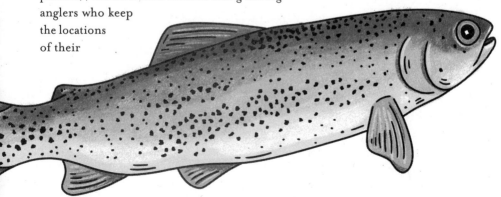

favorite riffles a secret. Some of these riffles are located along the Willamette River, which has traditionally held one of Oregon's richest runs of summer Steelhead.

Though their colors vary, with sea-run fish being mostly silver, spawning adults have a beautiful reddish-pinkish band (the rainbow from Trout's name) that runs the length of their sides. Young Steelhead, like others in the Salmon family, have dark, oval spots along their lateral line that are called parr marks. Speaking of lateral lines, did you know that fish "hear" through their skin? Their neuromast cells, strung out along their flanks and visible as tiny dots, help fish sense movement, vibration, and pressure gradients.

Steelhead, like their Salmon kin, is endangered. Their populations have been much diminished in the last 150 years: dams, overlogging, overfishing, pollution, loss of wetlands, low water levels, and most recently, warming, have contributed to the decline. When water temperatures reach above 70 degrees Fahrenheit, there isn't as much oxygen in the water for the fish to breathe. In extreme events like the heat dome of the summer of 2021, fish become incredibly stressed and begin to suffocate.

Because we know what's killing Steelhead, we know what to do to save this beautiful, vibrant being. In 2020, a federal judge ordered the US Army Corps of Engineers to take immediate action to improve fish passage at dams in the Willamette basin. As of the writing of this book, we are still waiting to learn more about those recovery efforts. We can tell you about the two dams on the Elwha River on the Olympic Peninsula of Washington that were removed in 2013 and 2015. Less than a decade later, Steelhead, nearly extirpated by the dams, have already returned in numbers that most researchers predicted they wouldn't see for one hundred to three hundred years. As it did after the glaciers' retreat, as it did after the eruption of Mount St. Helens, life is finding a way.

RICHARD BRAUTIGAN

from *Trout Fishing in America*

> I threw out a salmon egg and let it drift down over that rock and WHAM! a good hit! and I had the fish on and it ran hard downstream, cutting at an angle and staying deep and really coming on hard, solid and uncompromising, and then the fish jumped and for a second I thought it was a frog. I'd never seen a fish like that before.

God-damn! What the hell!

The fish ran deep again and I could feel its life energy scream-ing back up the line to my hand. The line felt like sound. It was like an ambulance siren coming straight at me, red light flash-ing, and then going away again and then taking to the air and becoming an air-raid siren.

The fish jumped a few more times and it still looked like a frog, but it didn't have any legs. Then the fish grew tired and sloppy, and I swung and splashed it up the surface of the creek and into my net.

The fish was a twelve-inch rainbow trout with a huge hump on its back. A hunchback trout. The first I'd ever seen. The hump was probably due to an injury that occurred when the trout was young. Maybe a horse stepped on it or a tree fell over in a storm or its mother spawned where they were building a bridge.

There was a fine thing about that trout. I only wish I could have made a death mask of him. Not of his body though, but of his energy. I don't know if anyone would have understood his body. I put it in my creel.

Later in the afternoon when the telephone booths began to grow dark at the edges, I punched out of the creek and went home. I had that hunchback trout for dinner. Wrapped in cornmeal and fried in butter, its hump tasted sweet as the kisses of Esmeralda.

Sharp-Tailed Snake

(Contia tenuis)

Many of us on the west side of the Cascades grew up singing "Rain, Rain, Go Away," but Sharp-tailed Snake was singing another song entirely. The gorgeously pitter-pattering days of October through May are when you are most likely to encounter this being in a forest or grassy meadow when they venture out to hunt their favorite prey: Slug. Sharp-tailed Snake appears to be well adapted for their food. The sharp tail of their name is a long, pointed scale, which some researchers believe helps them stabilize their prey as they eat it. They also have needlelike teeth that help them grip the slimy squishiness of their go-to meal.

Don't be too surprised if you have never encountered Sharp-tailed Snake. This being typically spends the warmer months staying cool and moist in underground burrows excavated when the soil is wet. And even when they are aboveground, they are notoriously secretive, using whatever is around them as cover—bark, logs, leaves, and rocks. This helps them avoid being eaten by Steller's Jay and other birds, small mammals, and other Snakes. There is even one documented case of Brook Trout eating Sharp-tailed Snake.

Even though they tend to be secretive, so much so that their population can be difficult to determine, Sharp-tailed Snake is also often described as being gregarious—in spots offering good cover, you might find several of them sheltering together.

The lucky few Cascadians who have seen Sharp-tailed Snake have seen a being about eight to twelve inches long whose smooth upper scales shine like a ribbon of burnt umber. The bottom scales are variously paler and bear a series of black bars. As far as we know, their populations are spotty in northern Cascadia but increase as you travel south.

JOSHUA MCKINNEY

In Paradise

The perception of beauty is a moral test. —Thoreau

          have you availed
yourself of spring meadows

                 their lush grasses green   and wild
     flowers

           and tarried there rolling
some large stone aside   to find
      the sharp-tailed snake   *Contia tenuis*   which otherwise
     spends its life   in seclusion

             and have you   gently
   lifted one
        and have you seen
its rosy dorsal hue   the sheen
     of its scales   the contrasting
   cream of its belly

           and have you felt it   quicken
    the heat of your warm-
blooded hand passing into it

           and have you observed
    at the end of   its tail
          the sharp spine
the function of which is not fully understood

and have you looked

                                     long into the tiny eye
          a darkness without reflection

                               and have you smelled
        the bitter scent it secretes
its sole defense   though feeble
            against you

and did you release it   back
                    to cool earth   to shade
        beneath the stone
                and turning homeward   feel
its motion still
        in your empty hand
      feel it truly   a living thing?

no?

good god man

Pacific Yew

(Taxus brevifolia)

Scraggly, gangly, scrubby. These might be some of the words that come to your mind when encountering this sprawling, many-branched, shrub-like tree. But this is no Charlie Brown Christmas tree. This is Pacific Yew, one of the more legendary beings of Cascadia. Aside from their scragginess, look for grass-green needles that come to a fine point. Though arrowed, they are not prickly like Spruce but soft like Larch. Their trunks are reminiscent of Madrona's, covered with papery scales that peel away to reveal a reddish to purple layer of new bark.

Yew is unique among Cascadia's conifers in that they are an understory specialist. They like moist, mature forests and grow well in the shade of tall Douglas-fir and Western Hemlock. Yew can be found in their shrubby form and also in their taller one in which they tower over a hiker, reaching five to thirteen times a Human's height.

Yew has long been a legendary being among Native people. Because this wood is extremely hard yet still limber, Yew is the choice wood for bows. In fact, in some Native languages, Yew's name is "bow plant." W̱SÁNEĆ mold their bows to the proper curvature by first steaming them inside a stalk of Bull Kelp. Paddles, wedges, clubs, digging sticks, spears, adze handles, harpoon shafts, dip-net frames, bark scrapers, snowshoe frames, drum frames, dishes, spoons, bowls, fire tongs, and combs also come from Yew.

If you come across Pacific Yew in late summer, you will notice what look like tiny, translucent, red fairy goblets. These aren't berries but arils (seed coverings) that taste, according to at least one account, like mild cherry Jell-O. But it's probably best *not* to find out for yourself because Yew's seeds are poisonous and can cause cardiac arrest. Cascadia doesn't have many berries, or berrylike things, that are toxic to Humans, but when in doubt, stay away from the smooth red ones. (Yeah, we mean you, Baneberry.)

For all the poison in their seeds, Yew is, paradoxically, also legendary as the original source of Taxol, a drug used to treat cancer. In the 1990s, thousands of trees throughout Cascadia died when foragers stripped their bark. Just when it looked like this slow-growing being might be in trouble, pharmaceutical companies, understanding that their source for Taxol was finite and growing ever more so, created a synthesized form of the drug, so our beautiful Yew still thrives in their home-woods. Seek them.

W. TODD KANEKO

Pacific Yew

for my father

Wherever I close my eyes I can see
you and the old yew tree, roots still
exhuming thick marrow from where

your ghost has laid its bones deep
beneath island soil. My house is in Michigan
where my son says he hates cancer

for killing you and so many people we love.
Your house overlooks Puget Sound, shore
held fast by the forest's anchors and grief

is a word we use to describe that
distance between tendrils of poison
ivy creeping through my neighborhood

and the old yew tree, wished upside down
by my son, its boughs now burrowing into
the ground for berries, roots into the sky

and so many ancestors billowing forth
in beautiful plumes: his grandmother,
my grandfathers, our old uncles and aunties—

and you wearing your down vest and
sly mustache. I can bring your knife, my son
my knife; and we can meet you by that old yew

overhanging your driveway. Together,
we can carve our initials into its trunk
so no one forgets who lives there.

Oregon Spotted Frog

(Rana pretiosa)

In the early spring, near Cascadia's rivers, lakes, ponds, and wetlands, you might just be fortunate enough to hear a series of short, rapid croaks, almost like the knocking of a distant Woodpecker. This is Oregon Spotted Frog, specifically the males who are singing to either attract a mate or mark their territory.

This being, about the size of your palm, gets their name from dark, ragged spots that cover their body. Younger Frogs can be brown or olive green, but as Oregon Spotted Frog grows older, they become reddish brown and can even turn brick red. There's something incredibly cute about the way their chartreuse-flecked eyes sink out of sight when they blink.

Oregon Spotted Frog is the most aquatic Frog in Cascadia. They spend their whole life cycle in water, and they need shallow bodies of water that have an abundance of floating plants, which allow them to warm themselves in the sun and hide from predators. Tragically, over the last century, as more and more wetlands in the Willamette Valley and elsewhere in Cascadia have been drained and turned into fields for agriculture and as more of our region's rivers have

been corralled for irrigation, Oregon Spotted Frog has lost about 90 percent of their range, making them the most vulnerable Frog in our region. In 2011, they were the first being ever to be emergency-listed as an endangered species in Canada, and in 2014, they were listed as threatened under the Endangered Species Act in the US. Other factors that have contributed to their decline include the spread of invasive, non-native beings. Reed Canarygrass grows so densely that they eliminate sites suitable for egg laying, and Bullfrog both eats Spotted Frog and outcompetes them. Since these listings, there have been efforts by various people and agencies to balance the water needs of agriculture with those of the ecosystem, because all involved understand that, in the end, the two are intertwined inextricably.

If you do some searching online, you can find some marvelous footage concerning efforts to save these beings from extirpation in the Deschutes River basin. There, you will see images of Oregon Spotted Frog parents lying below their egg masses—and the sight is nothing short of sublime. There they are, peering up through a gelatinous, greenish cloud dotted with a galaxy of small velvet-black spheres as a water-lensed light suffuses the whole scene, a glimpse, perhaps, of something like the origin of life on our planet.

MICHAEL MCGRIFF

Animal Theory along the Marys River

I write *The sun calcifies along the ridge*, but maybe I mean
I've awakened into the prime of my own mediocrity.
Sound travels far here. A cultivator tine hits red clay a few acres
    downriver,
or maybe it's the carrion snap of a crow pulling a coyote's tendon
over a kind of hollow instrument the low moon has made of us
    all . . .
Farm kids whisper over a tent of sticks, a book of matches, a
    clump of hair . . .
A question I refused to listen to, once, in a moment of conse-
    quence,
finally reaches me—that, too, is a sound I've learned to ignore,
like a wall clock or the coarse paper the dead fold into ridiculous
    swans . . .

Who am I to write *The sun calcifies along the ridge*? King-Fucking-
   Nobody,
that's who. But it's not so bad to enter one's irrelevancy, to
   become
a kind of mannered longhand, an abacus, the return spring
in a rotary dial . . . What's certain is that we live in an age of
   certainty.
My qualifications for this life include replacing the real with
   anything
but the real. The apogee of a star searching for still water. A
   pillow filled
with blue down and regret. A list in search of items is all I am
when sitting among sourcane along the riverbank. I tilt my
   crown of roots.
I become a thrush, a dirigible, an apple. I'm now an animal that
   eats gravel
to break down the food in its gut. Why know the names of things
when you can imagine that the Oregon spotted frog
means *memory eater* in Latin? Dear Landscape, Dear Life in Bold
   Letters,
why has my friend been forced to kill, breaking down doors at
   given sets
of coordinates in a country whose name has made a career of
   being butchered
on public television? Forgive me, whoever you are, I know it's
   inconvenient
to think about the poor and their tasks. My task?—to brood and
   wander,
and why should you care? I'm talking with friends and the air's
   finally cool
and the river's music has dampened. I started with *The sun calcifies
along the ridge*, but really I meant *I love the world most when animals serve
as mere ornamentation*. They froth at the ends of their chains and
   bang
their bone plates against the unmarked crates in my heart. The
   wind is green.
Larval husks rattle in the wheeling air. I am home. I have every-
   thing

I've ever wanted or mourned. I take my assigned seat in the
  order of the evening.
A frog plays a bit role with its small complaint—and what I ad-
  mire most
is that it remains a thing I've never seen, even though, without
  thinking, I polish it
to an unnatural shine with all the rags and ash that fall
from the moon-bleached and darkening trees as a few feet from
  us all
a single mooring cleat holds the universe in its place.

Outer Coast

Art by Raya Friday

Once you venture beyond the protected waters of the Salish Sea, you'll find another world waiting. Some familiar beings might accompany you—Sea Otter, Killer Whale, Tufted Puffin—but offshore you'll be influenced more by the Kuroshio Current coming across the Pacific from Japan and the California Current flowing down from Alaska than by shorebound Cascadia.

Look out at the horizon. Keep a sharp eye. You never know whom you might find: Short-tailed Albatross, Northern Elephant Seal, Pink-footed Shearwater, Sperm Whale—so much is possible in the cosmopolitan Pacific Ocean, where beings travel with ease across Human-drawn borders of nations and time zones. You are as likely to see a "vagrant" from the far western Pacific as a nearshore local taking a trip out into the depths. Either way, one of the formative essences of Cascadia is our oceanic connection to the North Pacific's wild waters and distant lands, be they Russia, Japan, Hawaii, or the Philippines. In the open ocean, we all touch one another's shores.

Indeed, Cascadia's Human cultures are part of this rich exchange and have been for millennia—from the arrival of the First People across Beringia many thousands of years ago to Spanish colonial forays up California's coast in the 1500s to the Russian fur traders drawn by reports from Vitus Bering's voyages in the 1700s. Coastal people like the Makah learned to build watercraft that can manage the Pacific's waters, enabling them to make the migration of Gray Whale part of their community, and other oceanic bounty nurtured the rich cultures developed on Cascadia's Outer Coast.

More recent people arriving from across the ocean—Chinese, Japanese, Vietnamese, Cambodian, Samoan, and more—have continued that trans-Pacific sense of self that is unique to Cascadia. Here, we touch an ocean that binds together all of who we are—storytellers, homemakers, scientists, thinkers, traders, gatherers, and sometimes exploiters—it is at this coastal seam that future meets past, where we may dream into what may be if we recognize and honor what links us all, all of us who live alongside Sea Otter, Pacific Octopus, and other Outer Coast beings who have lived here long before Humans even took breath on this earth.

ELIZABETH BRADFIELD

from Deliquescence

—*The liquid resulting from the process of deliquescing*

Dawn on the bow. Or some hour early enough to be,
for at least a while, alone. Firm horizon denied by mist. Prow

rocking forward into swell.

Sky becomes water, water, sky. And I . . .

dissolve   *dwindle*
disband   *disperse*   *dissipate*
become delinquent to the self

This water. This water. This
cloud light liquid shiftless resistance this

rendering of all we might become.

Tufted Puffin

(Fratercula cirrhata)

Puffin. Tufted Puffin! This gorgeous, orange-footed, hatchet-billed, chunky-bodied bird captivates nearly everyone who sees them. A charismatic member of the alcid family (which includes Murre, Guillemot, and Murrelet), Puffin is, let's admit it, a showstopper.

In Cascadia, both Horned and Tufted Puffin thrive and breed; Tufted Puffin is the larger of the two, the one with a dark chest. In winter, Tufted Puffin is subdued, but come breeding, both males and females go wild! Sun-yellow feathers trail from their brows like bicycle streamers, their cheeks flash bright white, and a green-yellow sheath bulks up their already impressive bill. The annually shed sheaths of Puffin bills (as well as the bills themselves) are an important element of blankets, rattles, and other traditional regalia in Cascadia.

Tufted Puffin thrives at sea, spending most of the year offshore and only coming ashore in the breeding season to nest. You can find Tufted Puffin from the Aleutian Islands to Southern California. Like many oceanic birds, Puffin is long-lived (over twenty years), maintains long-term pair bonds (the same couple comes together, often in the same spot, year after year to breed), and shares parenting duties (both male and female incubate, brood, and feed their chicks). Tufted Puffin

digs a deep burrow for a nest and lays only one egg a year (many songbirds lay multiple eggs multiple times a year). Puffin parents spend considerable time and energy getting their single chick ready for fledging, putting all their eggs, so to speak, in one annual basket.

When a Puffin chick fledges, they do so decisively: they flap off to sea and won't come back to land for three to four years, when they themselves are ready to breed. Imagine launching yourself from a cozy burrow into the unfamiliar air and sea with no training, no guiding hand. Then you fly and dive, foraging in wild waters until, years later, you are ready to return to a spot you only knew for a couple of months in your chick-hood and find a mate to pair with for the rest of your life.

ANASTACIA-RENEÉ

Birdwatching

after talking to my
bright-eyed-hoodied
children about flight

two chesty crests
beak: one. by. one by. one.
(puffins)
roosting (safely)
below my caged window
mother puffin masked
like the superhero
they once knew her (to be)
how mother puffin leapt off
the page & spun (puffins)
tales of the day's work

& mother puffin a bird with
slow-moving eyes
feather to stay alive

(puffins)
each sing
a bright orange
one popsicle & one sunset
watch them soar
from mothers puffinry
an extended lifespan
& hope
when (puffins) return
all three still squawking

Spotted Ratfish

(Hydrolagus colliei)

"The spotted ratfish . . . is a chimaera"—so begins the 2021 Wikipedia entry for this being. No, not a female fire-breathing lion/goat/serpent, but an ancient subset of the cartilaginous fishes (sharks, rays, and skates) that have come to differ in interesting and subtle ways since they split four hundred million years ago into their own taxonomic population. Ratfish is an exception to most deep-dwelling chimaeras in that they live in relatively shallow waters, though it's still rare to see one at the surface.

Have you caught Ratfish on the end of your line? You'll know by the bronze flank spotted with white dots, the pointy nose that is Ratlike and Rabbitlike at once, the large dark eyes, and the relatively oversized pectoral fins. Watch the spine! While not lethal to Humans, the venomous spike at the leading edge of Ratfish's dorsal fin (a vital defense against Harbor Seal and other predators) can really hurt. Why the name "Ratfish"? It's their unique tail, which tapers nearly to a point, ratlike.

Spotted Ratfish finds food by smell as they swim above the seafloor. Clams and Crabs are favorites. The egg laying of Spotted Ratfish is protracted and complicated, and it takes about a year for the young to hatch from their egg cases, which look like Banana Slug–sized lawn darts the color of old oak leaves with a bold stripe down the center. There are many gorgeously strange beings in the oceans of Cascadia, and Spotted Ratfish is a glorious one.

SIERRA NELSON

Spotted Ratfish

Like the rabbits that have graced my garden all spring,
they come gliding up from the depths to greet divers,
little water hares, rabbit-faced, with luminous
green eyes reflecting light with tapetum lucidum,
now barrel rolling, pectoral wings'
languid flap, mousy-brown
with hues of gold green blue
and iridescent fawn speckles.
Cartilaginous, especially fond of crunching
crustaceans and slow mollusks, can sting
in self defense with a venomous spine.
I remember my first time seeing one
at the aquarium, glimmering surreptitiously
in a dark tank on the way to the bigger
attractions—*Who is that?*
Is there something you
don't know
about yourself

but you
do know,
somewhere,
back 400
million years
ago? The
ratfish knows
and doesn't
mind: waits
for your
whalefall
with elec-
tro-
re-
cep-
tion.

Dungeness Crab

(Metacarcinus magister)

Any Human-told story of Dungeness Crab must begin with yum—Yum! Human, Seal, Sea Lion, Sea Otter, and more love to feast on this being. Sweeter and more delicate than Atlantic Lobster, King Crab, or Blue Crab (at least as tested by one editor), Dungeness Crab is a delicious denizen of Cascadia.

This iconic crab feeds largely on small Clams, which they open by chipping away with their large pincers (look for Dungeness sign on shells in the wrack line). Dungeness will also eat Shrimp, Worms, fish, and more. While Dungeness Crab can live and are often commercially caught in rather deep water (up to three hundred feet), they may also be found burrowing themselves in shallow, low-tide-exposed Eelgrass, only their eyestalks and antennae poking above the sand. Is that a Dungeness you've seen along the shore or hauled up in your pot? The shell will be some shade from reddish-brown to purple and will stretch a handspan across (6.25 inches for a legal-sized Dungeness); the

tips of the foreclaws will be paler than their base and will have toothlike ridges on their outer edge.

How does a creature grow within armor? Like all Crabs, Dungeness grows in stages punctuated by molts. Because Crabs can't increase the size of their outer shells, they must find another way to get larger, so they back out of their shell, inflate their soft body, then harden up a new protective coat. The process takes a few days. Is the shell at your feet "shed" or "dead"? Give it a sniff. Molted shells have no stink to them. When young and growing quickly, Dungeness molts up to six times a year. Once they are about three years old, they dial it back to one annual molt per year (Dungeness usually lives about ten years).

Equally challenging for any Crab is how to mate while dressed in armor. In spring, a male Dungeness will seek a female who is about to molt, then hold on tight until she does, when he can give her his spermatophores. Afterward, he keeps hold of her, offering his own shell as protection until hers hardens. In fall, she will release her eggs, fertilize them with the stored sperm, and tuck them under a flap on her belly until they hatch, drift, and metamorphose from zoea to megalops to Crab.

RACHEL EDELMAN

Dungeness

Beneath what I see is what I know.

When the dark sinks in,
drop a lantern off the dock.

What gathers looks, at first, like specks of dust,
then moths at a porch light in summer.

Stay put. Pass a bottle. The great beneath
keeps rising to the beacon,

brine breathing around us like a lung.
Disc of carapace. Fleck of claw.

A crab's shell starts out too soft
to be protection.

Think of the depth it sinks to,
fresh from the molt,

to bury itself in the sand.
I know how it feels

to realize I've bricked my own dungeon.

Heermann's Gull

(Larus heermanni)

There's an old naturalist joke: "What do you call a seagull when it's in a bay?" Answer: a bagel. This points, of course, to the underappreciated nature of gulls in general. Not all gulls are alike. In Cascadia, we have Herring Gull, Glaucous-winged Gull, Bonaparte's Gull, Mew Gull, Black-legged Kittiwake, and more. Each has different plumage, life history, and calls, and Heermann's Gull is distinctive among them for many reasons.

First, their beauty—for they are magnificently beautiful. Heermann's Gull has a subtle cloudy-gray breast, a bright white head, and charcoal wings (juveniles are all storm-dark). Their bill is startling crimson with a neat black tip. Next, their movements: while most birds in Cascadia breed in the northern summer then migrate south for the winter, Heermann's Gull does the opposite, breeding in Baja California (mostly on Isla Raza), where they lay eggs on the ground in a scrape, then migrating up along the shoreline to spend the fall off the coast of Washington and British Columbia. Listen for their laughing, Kooka-burra-like call, *Whooo, ha-ha-ha-ha-ha.* And then greet them: *Hello! Welcome!*

Heermann's Gull can be a kleptoparasite, stealing food from other birds rather than hunting fish themselves. Nearshore, they also take the eggs of Tern. Attending Heermann's Gull and learning their nuances is akin to attending Cascadia itself. A labor of love.

With Seagulls

The wind today contains some errant sea breeze,
redolent of the fifth day of our honeymoon
when we bought a pail and shovel

at a hardware store.
I'm pondering the sci-fi novel you described
over fish and chips barely mentioning

the characters, since love
and human frailty are secondary
to black hole transport and the problems

of colonizing the ring around a moon.
Then you segued to the data center at work
and my mind defragged for a while.

In one of the chambers of your heart
a seagull is always riding a thermal,
genius of the physics of the wing.

In my family growing up, seagulls
were considered rude opportunists
with vacant looks and dirty minds.

I forget for years at a time
how far you and I have traveled,
then a seagull drops down for a French fry

and there you are, holding so still,
the transaction between you is personal,
and delicate, like when two married people
start liking each other again.

Tomcod / Bocaccio

(Sebastes paucispinis)

Tomcod is a name used for two very different fish, but the one we're talking about here is of the rockfish (*Sebastes*) variety. Some call them Salmon Grouper, Salmon Rockfish, Slimy, Red Snapper, or Bocaccio. *Bocaccio* means "mouth" in Italian, and like most rockfishes, Tomcod does have a large mouth (and eyes). They are rusty orange and mottled, and adults reach about the length of a Human arm.

Fish in the *Sebastes* genus generally are long-lived, and Tomcod is no exception, living (we think!) fifty years or so. Females only begin reproducing at twenty years of age, which makes Tomcod very susceptible to overfishing in regions where there is a commercial harvest. Enough of the youngsters must be preserved to grow into reproductive vigor for the population as a whole to thrive.

Rockfish are unusual in that, rather than releasing their eggs to the sea, females hold them internally and give birth to live young. As a young larva,

Rockfish eats whatever drifts by them and can fit in their small mouth. Once large enough, they begin eating fish and squid. Don't be shocked, but Rockfish like best of all to eat Rockfish!

Tomcod is generally the name used for younger fish, which are more easily and often caught, as they live in shallower Kelp forests. Since 1990, there has been a precipitous decline in Bocaccio numbers in British Columbia, where they are listed as endangered. Puget Sound's population was overfished, and today neither commercial nor recreational catches are permitted; Bocaccio in this population is listed as endangered. Offshore of Oregon, though, in wild Pacific waters, Tomcod still thrives.

FRANCES A. McCUE

Tom Cod

A Cod is not a Cod
If he's a Tom.
Cod is a misnomer
since he's actually
a fledgling
Rockfish,
Juvenile *Bocaccio*,
Who could grow
to be a *Big Mouth*
darter in the deep—
and then, perhaps,
at thirty or forty,
a sanguine moon
held up in the gillnet,
then crated into
the freezer truck,
laid flat on the ice-bed
at the market
where a man will
shovel ice chips.
Colder, colder.

Or, if the ocean were our indoors,
    willowy seagrass our décor—
        a baby fish, Tom Cod in the creche,
    swimming under platforms by the oil jets.
            He will grow and leave the shallows
relishing the sunken chill of colder
                depths. He'd get out; he'd escape.

But that is just a wish.
No place is cold enough.
As a poet, I too craft a net.
All this slanty rhyme and
holes in the meter somehow
weave and snare a small
and unsuspecting fish.
Oh to dismantle all of it!

Giant Pacific Octopus

(Enteroctopus dofleini)

The legends and stories are vast and true. Octopus shape-shifts, changes color and texture, plays Houdini as they escape and move between tanks in aquaria under the cover of night. Octopus can open jars, and Pacific Octopus is the largest of all the known octopuses. Eight arms, three hearts, nine brains (one in their head and one in each arm), 280 exquisitely sensitive suckers. Yes. And yes. And more. And back into deep time—the oldest-known fossil of Octopus dates back some 296 million years.

    Found throughout the North Pacific from Japan to Mexico, this cephalopod, while legendary, lives only about five years in the wild. It's hard for Humans to understand an intelligence so vastly different than our own. Octopus can stretch to span over twenty feet, which is a stretch greater than Giraffe is tall, and can squeeze through any space larger than their beak, which is inside their bodies

and about the size of a quarter. Read more. Learn more. You'll be even more amazed.

You may or may not want to take parenting tips from Octopus, though. Female Pacific Octopus attaches eggs (thousands) to the ceiling of her den. For six months or so, she stays with them, fasting, guarding, blowing water across them to make sure they have rich, clean water. When they hatch, she dies. To be fair, we should also say that male Octopus stops eating and dies even more quickly: just after mating.

In Haida and Tlingit cultures, Pacific Octopus is sometimes referred to as "Devil Fish," and has an important role as a destructive and seductive creature. There's a spot on Prince of Wales Island, in Southeast Alaska, named Devilfish Bay. We can't tell you the story here, as such stories are owned by individuals and can't be retold without permission, but seek out someone who might share the story with you, and know that this being has been recognized for centuries for their shape-shifting, powerful nature.

SHANKAR NARAYAN

Love Letter from Immigrant to Octopus

We are impossible creatures
five octopus lifetimes into this country, impossible
to unfamiliar tongues—enter-
octopus *dofleini*, Shankar Rajamani. Enter, god

with infinite arms, mesmerize past ironic borders to
    America's dark
waters where we den and hide from ice-
cold predators, eyes huge and omnivorous
for things just beyond our grasping, stealing

colors of our captors. We are lovers loving to death,
then feeding our bodies to each other, to something larger
than our lives, like your parents working sweatshop
jobs for so many lifetimes for the small miracle of you. Sacri-
    fice the body

and move on. Master your disguise, ink wisely, obfuscate
when necessary to survive, curiosity immune to catastrophe.
    How can we be still
when the wild world beckons just beyond that glass
border? Octopus, I feel

the art of your escape, unstoppable
no matter how small the opening, compress the mortal
body to the size of a hungry mouth—
the only solid thing you own—swallow the pulse and go. This is
    what freedom

is—taste its eightfold embrace, dozens of suckers,
thousands of hooks, meaning hang onto what you love
with everything you've got. And when what you love
is a distant sea the grey skies keep drizzling into—remember all
    oceans are yours

and the limb you dip in the Duwamish
is already touching Mumbai. In the end become our own
parachutes unfurling into a Milky Way of inconceivable ap-
    pendages, defy
the odds and thrive, dwarf to world-swallowing god

in three paces. Nurture our hidden weapons—the poison
turning blue rings in your throat, a secret apocalypse
to be unleashed with divine grace, a dance that ignites the
    cosmos. Open
your arms, leave them all stunned. Touch

the vein just under the skin
of your white lover's wrist, already turning
colors you've never seen. Feel her blood pulse
blue. Feel coral borders, galaxies collapsing. Who knew this
    consuming

would be so beautiful? In this country everyone desires royalty
but only you have three hearts—one for here, one
for elsewhere, and one for the world beyond glass
in which you will never be whole.

Sea Otter

(Enhydra lutris)

Fuzzy. Cute. Moving, rolling, swimming, chomping, grooming with energy to
beat the band: Sea Otter. Otter is famed for incredibly dense fur, clever use
of stones as utensils, and a critical role in nearshore ecology. Otter eats slow-
moving fish and invertebrates like Crab, Clam, Mussel, Snail, and importantly,
Urchin, who would otherwise graze down young kelp fronds. In this way Otter
tends and nurtures Cascadia's Kelp forests, their own refuge.

Sea Otter had been long hunted locally by Indigenous people for food and
fur, then when Vitus Bering's ships headed east from Russia in the early 1700s,
fur traders instantly saw rubles. Otter was known as "warm gold" in Europe and
China, where demand for the fur drove colonialization of coastal Cascadia and
exploitation of this being and the people who knew Otter's habits best.

In recent years, Sea Otter has rebounded in Cascadia with the help of Humans
who relocated Otter from healthy Alaskan populations to more southerly locales.

Not all people celebrate this return, though, because in the absence of Otter, commercial fisheries for Crab and Clam have developed. How will Otter and Human find balance in the future? Stay tuned. Part of the balance will be determined by the cleanliness of our waters: Sea Otter, because they keep warm through fur, not fat, is incredibly sensitive to oil pollution.

But let's return to Sea Otter backstroking along, unfurred forepaws held up out of the chilly water, round face peering around. Look closer: Does Otter's nose have scars? If so, you are probably looking at a female, as mating rituals involve violent chomping. Adorable Sea Otter is not sweet—at least not in Human terms. The largest member of the weasel family, Otter has some decidedly feisty traits. Males will bite females on the nose to induce estrus (sometimes they'll even kidnap pups if a female's attention is not keen enough), and Otter will harass other beings for no discernible reason other than amusement. Still, seeing a pup nestled on Mom's chest, both napping as they bob in Bull Kelp fronds, makes even the grouchiest grouch soften and sigh, *Awww*.

KATRINA ROBERTS

That HERACLITEAN SUMMER and a GLIMPSE of GRACE

Ravaged miniature ocean, and you |otters, bobbing like flotsam.
Parched inland, we hardly deserve you. |Lightning strikes its book
of matches. Coyote, deer stepping |from ragged forest hems to find all
aflame. Gunmetal horizon a |box of dust split open, smudged, smoke
blankets, a cloak of ash. Another |year of masks, chokeholds and held

breath, insurrection, collapse. Star-|fish hands pressed to glass, passing
as touch. That anyone's alive at all, |a miracle too easily dismissed.
Elegant sentinels, otters, |you've sniffed extinction. Next? Keystones
in the eco-arch, rich carbon sinks |you balance by existing despite us,
our poisons, our infatuation |with six-pack yokes. Whiskered, lithe, you
fluff silvering cheeks, grin, cradle, |nurse, cuddle, groom. Trust wide sea-
grass fronds wrapped to stave a pup's |drift toward predatory mouths, dive
beside sleek cormorants, bubble |canopies, bladders, blades, to forage, a
favored rock tucked underarm. Braid |understories of golden rope, stipes,
stems, shafts of fin-threaded light. |Snouts lifted, bead eyes toy-bright, tuned
to skies whirling with snowy egrets, |herons, gulls. You lie back into the sea's
breathing, reach for paws of |strangers clutched close on both sides, ride
swells together, your raft salvation |beneath whatever weather comes,
though we'll be long gone. And this |other ocean, wheeling stars, pricked
archer, seven sisters, Orion's |belt, Hydrus, both dippers, Libra's scales,
so cold, far-off, unfathomable, |always, and never ours at all, but yours.

Bigg's Killer Whale

(Orcinus orca)

You see that fin slicing up through the surface—tall, tall, taller—until at last
the body follows and an exhaled plume of breath huffs up? You know you're
in the presence of Killer Whale. Suddenly, the sea around you is enlivened, its
mystery breached by the rise of this sleek, powerful body from the depths. For
Native coastal people of Cascadia, this being—Blackfish, Orca, Killer Whale,
Kéet, Grampus, Ska'ana—has always been an important community member,
never eaten or hunted. Many stories and songs have been written and sung about
Orca, and as you travel the waters of Cascadia, we hope you will seek them from
Elders and storytellers.

If the Blackfish fin is the height of a Human, you're looking at a mature male;
if sickle-curved and about half that height, you have a youngster or a matriarch
before you. Maybe you can even see the saddle patch, a paler, cloudy swoosh
across Orca's back, just along and behind the dorsal fin.

But is this Orca a Resident or Transient (now known as Bigg's)? Fish eater or mammal eater? Or something else (Offshore)? Take a bit more time: look again. How many are in the group, and are they traveling close together or widely spread apart? Maybe you're close enough to evaluate whether the saddle patch is open or closed, terms biologists use to describe the shape. A closed patch, which Bigg's has, is solid, smoky white, with no black inside (Residents can have either open or closed patches). Drop a hydrophone and listen: Are they calling to one another constantly, or are they conspicuously silent? If there's cavorting involved, are the pectoral flippers crazy-large? In all honesty, even such close observation might not bring you certainty.

Three types of Killer Whales traverse the waters of Cascadia, and although for a Human it can take time and careful training to distinguish them, these whales know each other well and easily by language alone. Genetically distinct for thousands of years, these ecotypes have different cultures, food preferences, and habits. It would not be surprising if, in the future, scientists declare them separate species.

Bigg's Killer Whale specializes on marine mammals such as Dall's Porpoise, Harbor Porpoise, Harbor Seal, and Sea Lion (they've been known to take

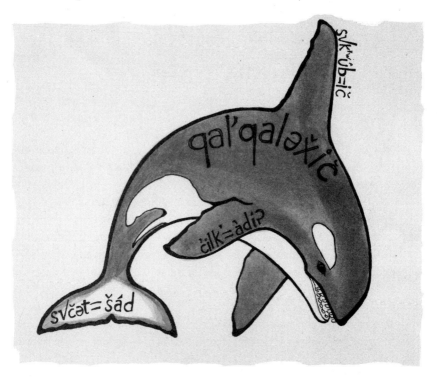

Otter for sport and even, in a coordinated group, an adult Humpback or Gray Whale). The fact that Bigg's Orca feed high up the food chain is, for them, both boon and burden. These whales carry the concentrated pollutants—PCBs and mercury—that all beings they've eaten have eaten. That females pass these contaminants along to their young in their milk is a particularly brutal fact in their matriarchal culture.

If you're lucky and encounter these beings just after a successful hunt, one of them may approach your boat to show you a bit of what's been caught, nosing a chunk of meat up to the surface as if to brag. Bigg's Killer Whale, like all Orcas, travel in matriarchically led family groups; demonstrating success and technique to younger members of the family is an important part of their culture. In that moment, are you part of the pod? It is lovely to imagine so. We have much to learn from the journeys, conversations, cultures, families, and adaptations Orca has shared with us. We are lucky each time we have a chance to greet them.

NORA MARKS KEIXWNÉI DAUENHAUER

Repatriation

for John Feller

A Killer Whale, you bend,
entering the Chilkat robe.
The hands of holders tremble.
The robe ripples
with its multiplying pods
of killer whales.
You dance
to an ancestor's song.
The sea of killer whales
splashes on your back.
We can smell the sea
laced with iodine on beaches
at low tide.

Human
(*Homo sapiens*)

Art by Joe Feddersen

VIVIAN FAITH PRESCOTT

Your Emergence

for Vivian Mork Yéilk'

I floated your tiny body in the ocean
above sea anemones and bull kelp,

a taste of saltwater to your lips. I placed you
on the shore where barnacles scraped

your feet, popweed burst between your toes,
let you eat a fistful of goose tongue.

In the woods we ate spruce tips, dug
licorice roots, peeled salmonberry shoots

and unfolded new ferns. I chewed the land up
in offering to you, a bundle inside your mouth,

set you down and you crawled in dirt,
pulling grass, feeling gummy alder leaves,

licking soil and stones. It's then that I knew
you were ready to surface into this world

tasting the words like the tang on our skins—
wet-sticky-salty-gritty—alive.

Gratitude

This guide is indebted, first, to the land and beings who hold these stories. Without the land, there would be no art, no story, no community. Thank you.

The editors of the other guides created in this spirit—*The Sonoran Desert: A Literary Field Guide* (University of Arizona Press, 2015), edited by Eric Magrane and Christopher Cokinos, and *A Literary Field Guide to Southern Appalachia* (University of Georgia Press, 2019), edited by Rose McLarney, Laura-Gray Street, and L. L. Gaddy—were extremely generous with their time, advice, and insights, and we thank them. Special thanks to Simmons Buntin and Laura-Gray Street for their early encouragement (nagging?) of Derek Sheffield to create this book; you started it. Jacob Valenti, Allison O'Keefe, and Tupelo Press, we are grateful for your early advice and support—you got us going. Bailey Ludwig, whose assistance in the summer of 2021 kept us on track and allowed us to step back from worries about logistics—*thank you*. You were a joy to work with and a gift to the development of this anthology. Lyndsey Nichols, whose help was essential in shaping our vision for the art in this book—*thank you*.

Writers, naturalists, historians, and thinkers from Cascadia and beyond lent their time to help shepherd this book and make sure its facts were both accurate and inclusive—too many to name. Rob Taylor served as a marvelous bridge, making sure that important Canadian voices were present. Special thanks must be extended to Daniel Mathews, Bill Yake, Stephanie Weinstein, Vivian Faith Prescott, Fred Swanson, Tim McNulty, Heather Durham, Robert Michael Pyle, Charlie Crisafulli, Janet Millard, and Dan Stephens, whose keen eyes helped strengthen the stories in these pages. All errors that remain are, of course, our own.

Our own families supported the work of this guide in so many ways—as first readers, critics, cheerleaders, and time-makers (doing dishes and cooking meals so that we could steal a bit more time for this project). Community, in every way, has made this book.

Kate Rogers, Mary Metz, Jennifer Kepler, Jen Grable, and all the team at Mountaineers Books, we are so very grateful that *Cascadia Field Guide* found a home with you. We so appreciate and admire your decades of work in the bioregion and the care you've taken with this book.

Artist Biographies

Jillian Barthold is an artist originally from nowhere, but currently living in Portland, Oregon. Her personal work often centers around her relationship to objects and spaces. Each illustration is a magnifying glass to study the seemingly mundane and force you to take a moment to consider the things and places we interact with daily. Other work includes a wide range of subject matter and clients including, but not limited to, Airbnb, Schmidt's Naturals, Girls Inc., Scout Books, Congressman Earl Blumenauer, Travel Portland, Stella Taco, Flat Brim Wines, Freeland Spirits, the Portland Art Museum, and more. Barthold is the cofounder of the unapologetically silly micro studio Fruit Salad Club and teaches screen printing and book arts at the Independent Publishing Resource Center. Her work is heavily inspired by the Japanese world view or aesthetic of wabi-sabi, travel, and childlike wonder.

Chloey Cavanaugh is an LGBTQ+ indigenous artist. A child of the Was'ineidi Tax'Hit, Eagle Wolf clan in Kake, Alaska, she began her artistic career by turning her grandfather's artwork into graphics as a way to grieve and make sure that he was remembered. Through this process, Cavanaugh started practicing form line through graphic art.

Cori Dantini spends much of her time in her studio in Pullman, Washington, covered in a mosaic of ink stains and glue dabs, bits of wordy paper clinging to her slippers. After earning a BFA in painting from Washington State University and spending a couple decades fiddling with brushes, oils, pencils, markers, and most recently, the mouse attached to her computer, she has discovered an organic process involving layers and language. Any meaning found in her work comes from this process. It is this mysterious, reciprocal quality of art that intrigues her and makes her think of her works as visual poems.

Claire Emery is an interdisciplinary artist and educator who works for community vitality through her woodblock prints, educational workshops, and artist-in-residence programs. Trained as a natural science illustrator, place-based educator, and contemporary artist, Emery sees art as a catalyst that engages people and communities in creating vitality, resilience, and clarity. She has worked as an artist-in-residence in Montana primary and secondary schools for over fifteen years, sponsored by the Montana Arts Council. She has taught at the Missoula Art Museum, Montana Audubon, the Montana Natural History Center, Project WET, the Wilderness Institute, the Watershed Education Network, Montana State Parks, Northwest Connections, and many other venues.

Joe Feddersen grew up in rural central Washington State in Omak. Feddersen was trained at Wenatchee Valley College, the University of Washington, and the University of Wisconsin–Madison. He is an active participant in the contemporary native fine arts movement, exhibiting since the early 1980s internationally and in the Northwest artist community. Pivotal solo shows include the Continuum series for the National Museum of the American Indian in New York. He taught at the Evergreen State College for twenty years and is now retired and living back on the Colville reservation and residing in Omak, the town of his youth.

Erin Fox is a bioregionalist and artist specializing in colored pencils. She received her science degree with a focus on atmospheric science at Seattle Central College and moved into art after research modifying global climate models, earning a certificate in scientific illustration from the University of Washington. Her works showcase the psychedelic beauty of the natural world. She runs her own art business, Psychedelic Lens, out of Seattle.

Raya Friday is a member of the Lummi nation whose tribal lands are situated on the edge of the Salish Sea near Bellingham, Washington. She was born and raised in Seattle where, from an early age, she focused most of her time and energy in the arts. Since 1995, she has worked primarily in glass. Friday earned a bachelor of fine arts from Alfred University in New York and, while there, started working at the renowned Corning Museum of Glass first as a technician and later as an instructor. Friday returned to the Pacific Northwest to be close to the land and community she loved. In 2019, she decided to return to school to pursue a humanities degree in Indigenous studies in the Native Pathways Program at Evergreen State College, where she is currently still a student. The intention of Friday's work is to explore how the unique and haunting vocabulary of glass can amplify and encapsulate both the historical and contemporary issues of her community.

Justin Gibbens is a Central Washington–based artist who creates images of a forgotten natural history, often blending reality and imagination. He utilizes the conventions of both scientific illustration and traditional Chinese fine-line painting within his work. His paintings have been exhibited throughout the Pacific Northwest and beyond. When not in his studio, Gibbens spends his time spotting birds and chasing after reptilian inhabitants of the shrub-steppe.

Rachel Kessler is a writer, cartoonist, and multidisciplinary collaborator and educator who explores landscape and community. As a mother of young children with limited resources, she experimented with boundary-breaking performance art and video, cofounding interactive poetry collaborations Typing Explosion and Vis-à-Vis Society. Her work is deeply rooted in place: she lives and works on Yesler Way, the Seattle street her ancestors immigrated to, worked on, worshipped on, and died on. She is working on a community cartography project called "Profanity Hill: A Tour of Yesler Way." As the artist-in-residence at the public housing project Yesler Terrace (where her great grandparents lived), she and community members activated a vacant apartment slated for demolition with live music, storytelling, potlucks, dancing, and collective murals. She cofounded the collective Wa Na Wari, a residential reclamation project centering Black art and media in Seattle's Central District. Currently, she is working on a children's book about abortion.

Artist **Travis London** teaches art in Spanish at a Title I elementary school in Vancouver, Washington. He combines his passion for the natural world and social justice to create art as a call to action to defend the planet and impacted communities. He works in a variety of mediums, from watercolor illustrations to large-scale public murals. London holds undergraduate degrees in environmental studies from the Evergreen State College and a master's degree in teaching from Concordia University. He has lived nearly four decades along the Washougal River in southwestern Washington.

For **Xena Lunsford**, creating art comes from the desperate need to capture experiences that leave curiosity. She is often surprised by how plants and other beings from the natural world have become the foundation for which she can express human emotions in illustration. She has been lucky enough to live in the forests of Idaho, where she studies under the most profound of teachers: black salamanders and tamarack trees.

Emily Poole was raised in Jackson Hole, Wyoming, and has now put down roots in the mossy hills of Oregon. She received her BFA in illustration from the Rhode Island School of Design in 2016. She has created work for numerous organizations including the National Museum of Wildlife Art, Creature Conserve, Sasquatch Books, and *High Country News*. By making playful and accessible images that foster an emotional connection between the viewer and the subject matter, Poole seeks to engage viewers in learning about what's going on in the natural world and what they can do to protect it.

Carmen Selam is a multidisciplinary artist working in printmaking, painting, and digital art in addition to being a traditional tribal artist in the fields of weaving and beadwork. Selam was born and raised on the Yakama Indian Reservation located in Washington State. She is an enrolled member of the Yakama Nation. Selam is currently pursuing her master's degree in studio arts at the Institute of American Indian Arts.

Sarah Van Sanden is a landscape designer and artist. In her designs and graphic illustrations, she weaves culture, ecology, and materials into a rich sense of place. Van Sanden holds undergraduate degrees in ethnobotany and visual art from the University of Washington and a master of landscape architecture from Harvard University's Graduate School of Design. She is a contributing artist for Broadsided Press and owner and lead designer of SVS Landscape Design in Seattle.

Writer Biographies

Maleea Acker (p. 65) lives in unceded W̲SÁNEĆ territories on Vancouver Island, British Columbia. She is the author of three poetry collections—*Hesitating Once to Feel Glory*, *The Reflecting Pool*, and *Air-Proof Green*—and a nonfiction book, *Gardens Aflame: Garry Oak Meadows of BC's South Coast*. She has lived, worked, and been an arts fellow in Canada, the US, Spain, and Mexico.

Sherman Alexie (p. 208) is a prominent Native American novelist, short story writer, performer, and filmmaker. A Spokane–Coeur d'Alene tribal member, he grew up on the Spokane Indian Reservation and now lives in Seattle, Washington. His book *The Lone Ranger and Tonto Fistfight in Heaven*, a collection of short stories, was adapted as the film *Smoke Signals*, for which he also wrote the screenplay.

Elizabeth (Betsy) Aoki (pp. 195 and 289) came to Seattle for an MFA in poetry at the University of Washington and has been drinking lattes in the rain and writing poetry there ever since. A National Poetry Series finalist, her first book, *Breakpoint*, won the Patricia Bibby First Book Award and is published by Tebot Bach.

Poet, hiker, and gardener **Elizabeth Austen** (p. 172) served as poet laureate of Washington from 2014 to 2016. During her tenure, she led "hike and write" events in state parks. She's the author of *Every Dress a Decision*, two chapbooks, and an audio CD. She grows raspberries and dahlias in her West Seattle garden and provided on-air poetry commentary and interviews for NPR affiliate KUOW for nearly twenty years.

Christianne Balk's (p.225) most recent book is *The Holding Hours*. Honors include awards from the Jack Straw Cultural Center, the Seattle Arts Commission, Purdue University Press (Verna Emery Poetry Book Prize), and the Academy of American Poets (Walt Whitman Award). Her work has appeared in *The Atlantic Monthly*, *Cirque*, *Harper's*, *Nimrod*, *Terrain.org*, and others. She loves hiking in the Cascade Mountains, open water swimming, and the rhythms of everyday street talk.

Rick Barot (p. 216) lives in Tacoma, Washington, and directs the low-residency MFA program at Pacific Lutheran University. His most recent works are a collection of poems, *The Galleons*, and *During the Pandemic*, a chapbook.

After a childhood in the Deep South, **Gabrielle Bates** (p. 272) moved to Seattle, where she is lucky to glimpse Mount Rainier on a regular basis. An employee of Open Books: A Poem Emporium and cohost of the podcast *The Poet Salon*, her poems have appeared in the *New Yorker*, *Ploughshares*, *Poetry Magazine*, and *American Poetry Review*, among other journals. Her first collection is *Judas Goat*.

Linda Bierds (p. 147) has lived in the Puget Sound area since early childhood and is an avid hiker. She is the author of ten books of poetry, and her work has been recognized by numerous organizations including the John D. and Catherine T. MacArthur Foundation. She teaches in the Creative Writing Program at the University of Washington.

Yvonne Blomer (p. 127) lives on the traditional territories of the W̱SÁNEĆ (Saanich), Lkwungen (Songhees), and Wyomilth (Esquimalt) peoples of the Coast Salish Nation. Her most recent book is *The Last Show on Earth*. Yvonne's poetry books also include *As if a Raven* and the anthologies *Refugium: Poems for the Pacific* and *Sweet Water: Poems for the Watersheds*. *Sugar Ride: Cycling from Hanoi to Kuala Lumpur* is her memoir exploring body, time, and travel. Yvonne is the past Poet Laureate of Victoria, British Columbia.

Allen Braden (p. 203) grew up on a farm of over two hundred acres in the Toppenish basin, where Simcoe and Toppenish Creeks run—habitat for rainbow trout, carp, crawdads, magpies, owls, hawks, pheasants, quails, coyotes, beavers, fruit bats, black widows, ticks, sagebrush, willows, teasels, thistles, chokecherries, and rosehips. Author of two collections, he has been anthologized in *The Bedford Introduction to Literature*, *Best New Poets*, *Manifest West*, and *Spreading the Word: Editors on Poetry*.

One of the iconic writers of Cascadia and a cult hero who had much in common with the Beat writers of his time, **Richard Brautigan** (1935–1984, p. 326) was born in Tacoma, Washington, and grew up there and in various other locations throughout the bioregion, including Eugene, Oregon. The poverty that defined his childhood informed much of his writing. He published ten novels, two collections of short stories, and four books of poetry. He is best known for his novels *In Watermelon Sugar*, *The Abortion: An Historical Romance*, and *Trout Fishing in America*.

Robert Bringhurst (p. 256) was born in southcentral Los Angeles but raised in the mountains and mining towns of Utah, Montana, Wyoming, and Alberta. He moved to the British Columbia coast in 1972 and has made his home there ever since, studying Native American languages, tending a small patch of forest, and practicing the typographic arts. His translations from classical Haida, like his poetry and prose, have been widely praised and won many prizes.

National Book Award and Pulitzer Prize nominee **Raymond Carver** (1938–1988, p. 81) was born in Clatskanie, Oregon, and grew up in Yakima, Washington. Often centered on the working class of the Pacific Northwest, Carver published numerous poetry and short story collections, including *Cathedral* and *At Night the Salmon Move*.

Claudia Castro Luna (p. 142) is an Academy of American Poets poet laureate fellow (2019), Washington State poet laureate (2018–2021), and Seattle's inaugural civic poet (2015–2018). She is the author of *Cipota Under the Moon*; *One River, A Thousand Voices*; *Killing Marías*; and the chapbook *This City*. Her most recent nonfiction can be found in *There's a Revolution Outside, My Love: Letters from a Crisis*. Born in El Salvador, she came to the United States in 1981. Living in English and Spanish, Claudia writes and teaches in Seattle on unceded Duwamish lands where she gardens and keeps chickens with her husband and their three children.

Xavier Cavazos (p. 241), a Chicanx from the central Washington desert of Moses Lake, is the author of *Diamond Grove Slave Tree*, which won the inaugural Prairie Seed Poetry Prize from Ice Cube Press, *Barbarian at the Gate*, which was published in the Poetry Society of America's New American Poets Chapbook Series, and *The Devils Workshop* (2023). Cavazos earned an MFA in creative writing and the environment from Iowa State University.

Brittney Corrigan's (p. 140) poetry collections include *Breaking*, *Navigation*, *40 Weeks*, and *Daughters*. She was raised in Colorado and has lived in Portland, Oregon, for the past three decades, where she is an alumna and employee of Reed College. Corrigan enjoys hiking and adventuring in the Columbia River Gorge and on the Oregon coast. She is currently at work on her first short story collection and a series of poems about climate change and the Anthropocene age.

Kevin Craft (p. 93) lives in Seattle and directs the Written Arts Program at Everett Community College. He volunteers as a fire lookout in the North Cascades, where he's well known among the mountain goats and pine martens. His books include *Solar Prominence*, *Vagrants & Accidentals*, and the forthcoming *Traverse*. Editor of *Poetry Northwest* from 2009 to 2016, he now serves as executive editor of Poetry NW Editions.

Laura Da' (p. 133) is a poet and teacher. A lifetime resident of the Pacific Northwest, Da' studied creative writing at the University of Washington and the Institute of American Indian Arts. Da' is Eastern Shawnee. She is the author of *Tributaries*, winner of the American Book Award, and *Instruments of the True Measure*, winner of the Washington State Book Award. Da' lives near Renton, Washington, with her husband and son.

Raised on the East Coast, **John Daniel** (p. 286) washed out of Reed College in the 1960s but hung on in the Northwest, east and west of the Cascades. The most recent of his eleven books are *Gifted*, a novel set in rural western Oregon, and *Lighted Distances: Four Seasons on Goodlow Rim*. He lives in the Coast Range foothills west of Eugene, Oregon, and sometimes in juniper and ponderosa country east of Bonanza, Oregon.

Greg Darms (p. 87) lived within the Cascadia bioregion, from Northern California to coastal British Columbia, for seventy years before recently moving to western Massachusetts. A middle school teacher and publisher of numerous books from Radiolarian Press, he also edited and published the literary magazine *Convolvulus* for fifteen years. His poetry is in such periodicals as *Wild Earth*, *Isotope*, *Volt*, and *High Desert Journal* and his three collections: *Flammable, Inflammable*; *ParaTaxis*; and *in which music*.

Born in Juneau, Alaska, **Nora Marks Keixwnéi Dauenhauer** (1927–2017, p. 359) was a Tlingit writer and scholar. Her works include *Life Woven with Song*, a volume of poetry and prose; grammar book *Beginning Tlingit*; *Haa Shuká, Our Ancestors: Tlingit Oral Narratives*, and others. She won an American Book Award for *Russians in Tlingit America: The Battles of Sitka, 1802 and 1804* and was Alaska's writer laureate from 2012 to 2014.

Noah Davis's (p. 210) manuscript, *Of This River*, was selected by George Ella Lyon for the 2019 Wheelbarrow Emerging Poet Book Prize from Michigan State University's Center for Poetry, and his poems and prose have appeared in *The Sun*, *Southern Humanities Review*, *Best New Poets*, *Orion*, *North American Review*, and *River Teeth*, among others. Davis earned an MFA from Indiana University and lives with his wife, Nikea, in Missoula, Montana.

For over two decades **Chris Dombrowski** (p. 223) has guided anglers on the rivers of western Montana. His books include three collections of poetry, most recently *Ragged Anthem* and the memoir *Body of Water*, a 2016 Bloomberg News Book of the Year. With his family, he lives in Missoula, near where the Blackfoot, Bitterroot, and Clark Fork meet.

Poet, essayist, novelist, and editor **Brian Doyle** (1956–2017, p. 212) was a Catholic writer born in New York City who lived in Oregon. His works include *Mink River* and *Martin Marten*, recipient of the 2016 Oregon Book Award for young adult fiction, among others. His essays have appeared in *The Atlantic Monthly*, *Harper's*, *Orion*, *The Sun*, *Best American Essays*, *Best American Science & Nature Writing*, and *Best American Spiritual Writing* anthologies.

Barbara Drake's (p. 197) newest poetry collection is *The Road to Lilac Hill*. Her nonfiction includes Oregon Book Award finalists *Morning Light* and *Peace at Heart*. She grew up in Coos Bay, Oregon, and has a BA and an MFA from the University of Oregon. Most recently, Drake has edited and published a collection of her father's 20th century aerial photographs of the southern Oregon coast, *Everything Looks Different from the Air*. Retired from Linfield College, she lives with her husband in Oregon's rural Yamhill County.

David James Duncan (p. 206) is the author of the novels *The River Why* and *The Brothers K*; the collections *River Teeth*, *My Story as Told by Water*, and *God Laughs & Plays*; two fast response activist books, *Citizen's Dissent* (with Wendell Berry) and *The Heart of the Monster* (with Rick Bass); and the forthcoming novel *Sun House*. His work has won three Pacific Northwest Booksellers Awards, a National Book Award nomination, and a Lannan fellowship and has appeared in more than fifty anthologies including *Best American Essays* (twice) and *Best American Spiritual Writing* (five times).

Rachel Edelman (p. 347) is a Jewish poet raised in Memphis, Tennessee. Her poems have been published in *The Threepenny Review*, *Wildness*, *Poetry Northwest*, and elsewhere. Edelman earned her MFA in poetry from the University of Washington. She teaches high school English and lives on the unceded Duwamish land known as Seattle.

Charles Finn (p. 183) is the former editor of the literary and fine arts magazine *High Desert Journal* and author of *Wild Delicate Seconds: 29 Wildlife Encounters* and *On a Benediction of Wind: Poems and Photographs from the American West*. A self-taught woodworker, Finn builds custom micro-cabins and furniture using reclaimed lumber and materials. Recently removed from the shores of Puget Sound, Finn lives in Havre, Montana, with his wife, Joyce Mphande-Finn, and their cat, Lutsa.

Kathleen Flenniken (pp. 316 and 349) is the daughter of Oregonians, grew up in the shrub-steppe of eastern Washington along the Columbia and Yakima Rivers, and raised her family in Seattle, walking distance to Lake Washington. She is the author of three poetry collections, most recently *Post Romantic*. Her second book, *Plume*, is a personal examination of the Hanford Nuclear Site and its community. She served as poet laureate of Washington from 2012 to 2014.

Tess Gallagher's (p. 107) tenth volume of poetry, *Is, Is Not*, was published in 2019 by Graywolf Press. Other poetry includes *Midnight Lantern*, *Dear Ghosts*, *Moon Crossing Bridge*, and *Amplitude*. Gallagher's short stories in three volumes are now under contract for film episodes. During her friendship with director Alejandro Inarritu, Gallagher encouraged his work with Raymond Carver's story in the Oscar winning film *Birdman*. She spends time in a cottage on Lough Arrow in County Sligo in the west of Ireland, where many of her new poems are set, and also lives and writes in her hometown of Port Angeles, Washington.

Charles Goodrich (p. 293) writes and gardens near the confluence of the Marys and Willamette Rivers in Corvallis, Oregon. His books include *A Scripture of Crows*, *Going to Seed: Dispatches from the Garden*, *Insects of South Corvallis*, *The Practice of Home*, and *Watering the Rhubarb*. He also coedited *Forest Under Story: Creative Inquiry in an Old-Growth Forest* and *In the Blast Zone: Catastrophe and Renewal on Mount St. Helens*.

Andrew C. Gottlieb (p. 259) has spent many hours in the woods and waters of the Pacific Northwest. He got his MFA at the University of Washington and still thinks of the Cascadia region as home, wherever else he may find himself. His work has appeared in many places including *Best New Poets*, *Denver Quarterly*, and the *Mississippi Review*, and he's done a number of wilderness residencies, including at three national parks. His first full-length collection of poems is *Tales of a Distance*.

James Grabill (p. 170) has lived by choice in the Portland, Oregon, area for fifty years. His poems appear online at *Caliban Online*, *Unlikely Stories*, *Terrain.org*, *The Decadent Review*, and others. Recent books include *Sea-Level Nerve: I & II*, *Branches Shaken by Light*, *Reverberations of the Genome*, and *Eye of the Spiral*. For years, he taught writing and global issues relative to sustainability.

For nearly forty years, Skagit Valley native **Samuel Green** (p. 58) has lived off the grid in a log house he and his wife, Sally, built themselves on remote Waldron Island. His most recent poetry collection is *Disturbing the Light*. Honors include fellowships from the National Endowment for the Arts and Artist Trust, a term as the inaugural poet laureate of Washington, and an honorary doctorate from Seattle University.

Writer **Ursula K. Le Guin** (1929–2018, pp. 166 and 243) was the author of a number of short stories, novels, poems, children's stories, and translations. She was the recipient of numerous awards, including several Hugo Awards and the National Book Award for Young People's Literature.

Raised in the rural northcentral part of Montana, **Tami Haaland** (p. 234) is the author of three poetry collections, most recently *What Does Not Return*. Her work has been featured on *The Slowdown*, *The Writer's Almanac*, *Verse Daily*, and *American Life in Poetry*. A former Montana poet laureate and a recipient of a Governor's Humanities Award, Haaland is a professor of creative writing at Montana State University Billings.

Poet and cofounder of Copper Canyon Press, **Sam Hamill** (1943–2018, p. 85) was the author of numerous books of poetry including *Facing Snow: Visions of Tu Fu*, *Destination Zero*, and *Measured by Stone*, among others. He began a movement called Poets Against War in 2003 in protest of the invasion of Iraq.

Lyanda Fern Lynn Haupt (p. 324) is a naturalist, eco-philosopher, and the author of several books, most recently *Rooted: Life at the Crossroads of Science, Nature, and Spirit*. She is a two-time winner of the Washington State Book Award and a winner of the Sigurd F. Olson Nature Writing Award. Haupt spends her spare time hiking in the Cascadian wilderness, wandering the forest near her home, tending her urban chickens, and knitting magical hats.

Kim Heacox (p. 159) writes opinion-editorials for *The Guardian*, often in celebration and defense of the natural world. His books have earned starred reviews from *Kirkus*, *Publishers Weekly*, *Library Journal*, and *Booklist* and have received several awards. He lives with his wife, Melanie, in the small town of Gustavus, Alaska, next to Glacier Bay National Park, where their home, library, and eighteen acres are part of Tidelines Institute.

An errant southerner, **Sean Hill** (p. 192) has regularly visited Cascadia since the mid-aughts. The author of the poetry collections *Dangerous Goods* and *Blood Ties & Brown Liquor*, Hill's numerous awards include fellowships from the Cave Canem Foundation, Stanford University, and the National Endowment for the Arts. Hill's poems and essays have appeared in journals including *Callaloo*, *Poetry*, *Terrain.org*, and in nearly two dozen anthologies including *Black Nature* and *Villanelles*. Hill lives with his family in southwestern Montana where he is a professor of creative writing at the University of Montana.

Born and raised in Southeast Alaska, homeland of the Tlingit Indians and the Tongass National Forest, **Robert Davis Hoffmann**'s (p. 27) poetry and art reflect his rich Tlingit culture. His writing includes two books of poetry and publications in a number of journals and anthologies. Hoffmann graduated from the historic Sheldon Jackson College in Sitka, Alaska, in 1987 with a BA in elementary education. Now retired from the Sheldon Jackson Museum, Hoffmann and his wife, Kris, live in Sitka. When not tending his wife's garden, Robert loves woodcarving and painting in his Tlingit tradition.

Jackson Holbert (p. 191) was born and raised along the Spokane River in eastern Washington. His work has appeared in *FIELD*, *The Nation*, and *Poetry*. He received an MFA in poetry from the Michener Center for Writers and is currently a Stegner Fellow at Stanford.

Garrett Hongo (p. 153) was born in Volcano, Hawai'i, and grew up on the North Shore of O'ahu and in Los Angeles. His most recent book is *The Perfect Sound: A Memoir in Stereo* (Pantheon). Others include *The Mirror Diary: Selected Essays*. Currently he is at work on *The Ocean of Clouds* (poems). Since 1990, he has taught at the University of Oregon, where he is Distinguished Professor of Arts and Sciences.

Rebecca Hoogs (p. 29) is the author of *Self-Storage*, which was a finalist for the 2013 Washington State Book Award in Poetry, and a chapbook, *Grenade*. She is the associate director for Seattle Arts & Lectures and occasionally codirects and teaches in the Summer Writers in Rome Program for the University of Washington. She lives in Seattle and ferries to San Juan Island whenever she can.

Holly J. Hughes (p. 44) grew up along the shores of the Mississippi River, came west in 1978, and has since migrated between the Salish Sea and Southeast Alaska, where she fished for salmon, skippered a sixty-five-foot schooner, and co-led writing and mindfulness workshops. She's the author of five books, most recently *Hold Fast* and *Passings*, which received an American Book Award. She lives on the Olympic Peninsula where she bikes, swims, and consults as a writing coach.

Aleria Jensen (p. 48) was raised on an island in Southeast Alaska dotted with muskeg, one of her favorite habitats. Her poetry and nonfiction writing have been published in a variety of journals, including *Terrain.org*, *Tidal Echoes*, and *Orion*, as well as in the anthology *Wildbranch: An Anthology of Nature, Environment, and Place-Based Writing*. Jensen makes her home on Douglas Island in Juneau, Alaska, where she lives with her partner, Kevin, and two children between the mountains and the sea.

Jack Johnson (p. 201) was raised in Peshastin, Washington, a small town near the Cascade Range. He received his MA in literature from Southern Illinois University and worked toward his PhD while a teaching fellow at the University of Denver. Upon returning to Washington, he and his wife, Devera Sharp, built their own house and raised two sons there. The field where they built is now a forest made up of the trees they began planting forty years ago, accomplishing their dream of having a small home in the woods. His book of poems, *The Way We Came In*, was published in 2020. He teaches English and Philosophy at Wenatchee Valley College.

Jessica E. Johnson (p. 163), lifelong resident of the Cascadia bioregion, writes poetry, nonfiction, and things in between. She is the author of the poetry collections *In Absolutes We Seek Each Other* and *Metabolics*; and her essays have appeared in *The Harvard Review*, *Entropy*, and *River Teeth*, among others. She studied poetry and science at University of Washington and lives in Portland, Oregon, where she teaches composition, creative writing, and environmental literature at Portland Community College. She is grateful to be a guest on these lands and grateful to their original caretakers.

Jill McCabe Johnson (p. 247) was born in the Cascadia region and cut her teeth on Douglas-fir. She spent her childhood digging clams and geoducks, harvesting red huckleberries, fishing for trout, and reading by dim light. She has two poetry collections, two chapbooks in poetry and nonfiction, plus support from Artist Trust, the National Endowment for the Humanities, Hedgebrook, and more. Her PhD dissertation focuses on ecopoetics and the influence of walking on literature. Johnson is publisher at Wandering Aengus Press.

Ever Jones (p. 244) has wandered between the construction cranes in Seattle and the Fryingpan Glacier on Mount Tahoma for a decade. They are the author of *nightsong* and *Wilderness Lessons*, poetry collections reckoning with queer/trans embodiment, environmental degradation, racism, inheritance, grief, and hope. Jones is a professor at the University of Washington Tacoma and spent quarantine with three adults, one toddler, one cat, and a new puppy.

W. Todd Kaneko (p. 332) is the author of the poetry books *This Is How the Bone Sings* and *The Dead Wrestler Elegies* and coauthor with Amorak Huey of the chapbook *Slash / Slash* and *Poetry: A Writers' Guide and Anthology*. A Kundiman fellow, he is originally from Seattle and now lives with his family in Grand Rapids, Michigan, where he teaches creative writing at Grand Valley State University.

Born in the Palouse and currently residing in the drained bowl of glacial Lake Missoula, **Keetje Kuipers** (p. 296) has spent much of her life migrating throughout Cascadia, including her time earning her MFA at the University of Oregon. Her most recent collection of poems, *All Its Charms*, contains work originally published in the *Best American Poetry* and *Pushcart Prize* anthologies. Keetje is a visiting professor of creative writing at the University of Montana and editor of *Poetry Northwest*.

Vancouver British Columbia's sixth poet laureate, **Fiona Tinwei Lam** (p. 156) is the author of *Odes & Laments*, which celebrates the overlooked wonder and beauty in the everyday while lamenting human incursions on the natural world. She has authored two previous poetry books and a children's book and edited *The Bright Well: Contemporary Canadian Poems on Facing Cancer* and coedited *Love Me True: Writers Reflect on the Ins, Outs, Ups, and Downs of Marriage* with Jane Silcott. Lam won *The New Quarterly*'s Nick Blatchford Prize and was a finalist for the City of Vancouver Book Award. Her work appears in more than forty anthologies, including *The Best Canadian Poetry* and *Forcefield: 77 Women Poets of BC*. Her award-winning poetry videos have screened at festivals locally and internationally. She teaches at Simon Fraser University's Continuing Studies.

Born in Nelson, British Columbia, **Patrick Lane** (1939–2019, p. 318) was a poet, playwright, memoirist, and novelist. His formal education ended after high school, and he worked in the logging industry, cofounded Very Stone House press, and in 2014 was awarded the Order of Canada for his contributions to literature. He taught at the University of Saskatchewan and, later, the University of Victoria.

A 2016 Jack Straw Fellow, Artist Trust Fellow and nominee for a Stranger Genius Award, **Robert Lashley** (p. 53) has had work published in *The Seattle Review of Books*, *NAILED*, *Poetry Northwest*, *McSweeney's*, and *The Cascadia Review*. His poetry was also featured in such anthologies as *Many Trails to the Summit*, *Foot Bridge Above the Falls*, *Get Lit*, *Make It True*, and *It Was Written*. His books include *The Homeboy Songs*, *Up South*, and *The Green River Valley*.

Pulitzer Prize finalist **Dorianne Laux**'s (p. 252) most recent collection is *Only As the Day Is Long: New and Selected*. She is also author of *The Book of Men*, winner of the Paterson Poetry Prize, and *Facts about the Moon*, winner of the Oregon Book Award. She recently published a limited-edition chapbook, *SALT*, from the Field Office Press. Laux teaches poetry at North Carolina State and Pacific University. In 2020, she was elected a chancellor of the Academy of American Poets. She lives with her husband, Joseph Millar, in Richmond, California.

Denise Levertov (1923–1997, p. 67) was born in England and moved to the US after World War II. With Muriel Rukeyser and several other poets, Levertov founded the Writers and Artists Protest against the War in Vietnam. Levertov settled in Seattle in 1989, where she lived and taught until her death. A lauded writer, she is the author of many books of poetry, prose, translations, and more.

Frances McCue (p. 351) is a poet, writer, arts instigator, and professor. She's the cowriter and coproducer of *Where the House Was*, a feature documentary about gentrification and poetry. Her poetry books read as novels, taking us through the life of a stenographer who refuses to take dictation (*The Stenographer's Breakfast*), or the world of Marrakesh where a tragedy ensues (*The Bled*). *Timber Curtain* traces Seattle's Hugo House building into redevelopment. McCue is engaged in a new literary start-up: Pulley Press, a poetry imprint.

After a year living on a farm on an island in British Columbia, **Anne Haven McDonnell** (p. 60) has been making yearly migrations back to the Pacific Northwest during breaks from her teaching at the Institute of American Indian Arts in Santa Fe, New Mexico. Her poetry has appeared in *Orion*, *Terrain.org*, and other journals, and her chapbook *Living With Wolves* is based on wolf encounters and stories from an island in British Columbia. She is the author of the poetry collection *Breath on a Coal*. She has been a writer in residence at the H. J. Andrews Experimental Forest and the Sitka Center for Art and Ecology.

Colleen J. McElroy (p. 100), professor emerita and former editor of *The Seattle Review*, lives in Seattle. She is the winner of the Before Columbus American Book Award for *Queen of the Ebony Isles*. McElroy's recent collections include *Here I Throw Down My Heart* (finalist for the Milt Kessler Book Award, the Walt Whitman Award, the Phyllis Wheatley Award, and the Washington State Governor's Book Award) and *Blood Memory* (finalist for the 2017 Paterson Poetry Prize).

Michael McGriff (p. 334) was born and raised in Coos Bay, Oregon, and writes exclusively about the intersection of class, labor, and landscape. He is the author of several books, most recently the poetry collections *Eternal Sentences* and *Early Hour*. His work has been recognized with a Lannan Foundation literary fellowship, the Levis Reading Prize, and a grant from the National Endowment for the Arts. He teaches creative writing at the University of Idaho and serves as Poetry Editor for the *Northwest Review*.

Joshua McKinney (p. 329) grew up in the mountains and high deserts of Northern California, from the Humboldt coast to the Modoc Plateau and from the Oregon border to Mount Shasta. The author of four books of poetry, he has published widely in national literary magazines. He is the coeditor of *Clade Song*, an online ecopoetry journal. He teaches at California State University, Sacramento, and is a member of the California Lichen Society.

Tim McNulty (p. 135) is a poet, essayist, and natural history writer. He is the author of three poetry collections and eleven books on natural history, including *Olympic National Park: A Natural History*. McNulty has received the Washington State Book Award and the National Outdoor Book Award, among other honors. He's lived most of his life in the foothills of Washington's Olympic Mountains and remains active in Northwest environmental issues.

Kevin Miller (p. 115) lives across the street from Point Defiance Park, the second-largest city park in the United States. Miller's fourth poetry collection, *Vanish*, received the Wandering Aengus Publication Award in 2019. He is most recently author of a chapbook of baseball poems, *Spring Meditation*. Miller taught in the public schools of Washington State for thirty-nine years.

Stacy Boe Miller (p. 261) lives in northern Idaho where she rides her bike on the gravel hills of the Palouse looking for birds and holding poems under her helmet. Some of her work can be found in *Northwest Review*, *Terrain.org*, *Bellingham Review*, *Copper Nickel*, and other journals. She recently won the second annual Terrain.org Editor's Prize. She serves on the board of *High Desert Journal* and currently serves as Poet Laureate of Moscow, Idaho.

Deborah A. Miranda (p. 313) is an enrolled member of the Ohlone-Costanoan Esselen Nation of the Greater Monterey Bay Area in California, with Santa Ynez Chumash ancestry. Her mixed-genre book *Bad Indians: A Tribal Memoir* received the 2015 PEN-Oakland Josephine Miles Literary Award. She is also the author of four poetry collections (*Altar for Broken Things*, *Raised by Humans*, *The Zen of La Llorona*, and *Indian Cartography*) and coeditor of *Sovereign Erotics: A Collection of Two-Spirit Literature*. She was the Thomas H. Broadus Professor of English at Washington and Lee University, where she taught literature of the margins and creative writing, and is now professor emerita, an independent scholar working on projects involving California Mission history and literature.

Donald J. Mitchell (p. 36) lives in Deming, Washington, on land his great-grandfather homesteaded in the 1880s. He's lived there all his life, writing poetry, short essays, and fiction. His essays and poems have been most recently published in *The Far Field*, *Moss Literary Journal*, *The Boiler Journal*, *Animal Literary Journal*, *Four Ties Lit Review*, and *Noisy Water: Poetry from Whatcom County, Washington*.

Living along the Columbia River in a multigenerational commercial fishing community has similarities to the Osage Reservation that **Ruby Hansen Murray** (p. 91) calls home. Years have knit her into the lower river estuary; her prize-winning work can be found in *CutBank*, *Cutthroat*, *High Desert Journal*, *Under the Sun*, *River Mouth Review*, and *South Florida Poetry Journal*. She's an alumna of the low-residency MFA program at the Institute of American Indian Arts.

Shankar Narayan (pp. 321 and 353) explores identity, power, mythology, and technology in a world where the body is flung across borders yet possesses unrivaled power to transcend them. Shankar draws strength from his global upbringing and from his work at the intersection of civil rights and technology. In Seattle, he awakens to the wonders of Cascadia every day, but his heart yearns east to his other hometown, Delhi.

Nick Neely (p. 187) is the author of *Coast Range* and *Alta California*. He lives in La Grande, Oregon, where he teaches at Eastern Oregon University and in the wilderness, ecology, and community concentration of its low-residency MFA program. He is the recipient of the John Burroughs Nature Essay Award, a PEN Northwest Boyden Wilderness Writing Residency, and an AAAS-Kavli Science Journalism Award.

Richard Nelson (1941–2019, p. 69) was an American cultural anthropologist and writer, known for his engagements with northern cultures (*Make Prayers to the Raven*) and the ways humans and animals interact. He was the host to a public radio series called *Encounters*, which offered field recordings of Nelson with Alaskan animals in the wild and ran for ten years. His book *The Island Within* received the John Burroughs Medal, and from 1999 to 2001, he served as writer laureate of Alaska. In 2006, Nelson was awarded the Lifetime Achievement Award from the Alaska Conservation Foundation.

Sierra Nelson (pp. 109 and 344) spent childhood summers in Washington with grandparents from both sides, developing her deep love of tidepooling in Port Angeles and Hood Canal. Nelson earned an MFA from University of Washington, and her books include *The Lachrymose Report* and the collaborative *I Take Back the Sponge Cake*. Her poems accompanying Adam Summers's fish skeleton photographs have appeared at the Seattle Aquarium and Slovenian Natural History Museum. She currently lives in Seattle.

Matthew Nienow (p. 302) is the author of *House of Water*. A former Ruth Lilly Poetry Fellow, he has also received fellowships and support from the National Endowment for the Arts, the Bread Loaf Writers' Conference, the Elizabeth George Foundation, and Artist Trust. Raised in Seattle, he has lived in Port Townsend, Washington, for over a decade with his wife and sons, sharing the land with many of the beings featured in this book.

Emma Noyes (p. 184) citizen of the Confederated Tribes of the Colville Reservation (Sinixt and Colville tribes), has ancestral ties to both sides of the Cascades and both sides of what is now the Canadian border. She is an artist and author transfixed with the geography of story. As a traditional foods gatherer and daughter of an avid storyteller and carver, Noyes is committed to creating a visual and written universe of tribal plateau indigeneity. Her book, *Baby Speaks Salish*, is an illustrated language manual for adults interested in adding more Colville-Okanagan Salish into their daily interactions with children and includes a graphic novel–style story of her family's experience with language loss and language learning. Noyes lives in the traditional territory of the Spokane Tribe under ponderosas and near patches of bitterroot.

David Oates (p. 199) moved to Portland, Oregon, from Southern California thirty years ago. He took a critical look at environmental shibboleths in *Paradise Wild: Reimagining American Nature*, and reconsidered the environmental importance of compact cities in *City Limits: Walking Portland's Boundary*. The award-winning poetry of *The Heron Place* wove personal loss into a vivid sense of natural place. Recent poems have appeared in *Orion*, *Rattle*, and *December*. He is founder and general editor of the small literary press Kelson Books.

Alyssa Ogi (p. 137) received her MFA from the University of Oregon and taught undergraduate creative writing and literature before shifting into book editing for Tin House in Portland, Oregon. A recipient of an Elizabeth George Foundation grant and an Oregon Literary Fellowship, she has been published in *Best New Poets*, *Poetry Northwest*, *They Rise Like a Wave: An Anthology of Asian American Women Poets*, and other journals.

Born on Fidalgo Island in Washington State, **Nancy Pagh**'s (p. 83) first published poem (age twelve) addressed the philosophical question of whether clams are clammy. She is the author of three books of poetry and *At Home Afloat: Women on the Waters of the Pacific Northwest*. Her writer's guide, *Write Moves*, was recently published by Broadview Press. She lives in Bellingham and teaches at Western Washington University.

Oliver de la Paz (p. 103) is the author of five books of poetry. His latest, *The Boy in the Labyrinth*, was a finalist for the Massachusetts Book Award. Raised in eastern Oregon, he grew up by the Snake River where he learned to farm and fish. He teaches at the College of the Holy Cross and in the low-residency MFA program at Pacific Lutheran College.

Raised in the foothills of Mount Rainier, **Jean-Paul Pecqueur** (p. 298) considers the Pacific Northwest his spiritual home. His writings include one full-length poetry collection from Alice James Books, two chapbooks, and numerous poems and reviews published in anthologies and journals. Pecqueur received his MFA from the University of Washington and currently lives in Brooklyn, New York, where he teaches writing to art students at the Pratt Institute.

Lucia Perillo (p. 34) published seven poetry collections, short stories, and essays. Her poetry has appeared in *The New Yorker*, *The Atlantic*, and many other literary magazines. Her work has received numerous awards. *Inseminating The Elephant* was a finalist for the Pulitzer Prize. She was awarded a MacArthur Fellowship in 2000 and summited Mount Rainer twice. She died in 2016.

Jennifer Perrine (p. 263) is the author of four award-winning books of poetry: *Again: The Body Is No Machine*; *In the Human Zoo*; and *No Confession, No Mass*. Their recent short stories and essays appear in *Buckman Journal* and *The Gay & Lesbian Review*. Perrine lives in Portland, Oregon, where they cohost the Incite: Queer Writers Read series and teach creative writing and anti-oppression practices to youth and adults.

A Cascadia native, **Paulann Petersen** (p. 42) was born and raised in Portland, Oregon. Then she lived for three decades near the eastern slopes of the Cascades before returning to Portland in the early 1990s. As Oregon's sixth poet laureate, she traveled over 27,500 miles within Oregon, visiting all of its thirty-six counties to give workshops, readings, and presentations at schools, libraries, and community centers. Her seventh poetry book is *One Small Sun*.

Beth Piatote (p. 311) is a Nez Perce writer enrolled with the Confederated Tribes of the Colville Reservation and has lived much of her life in Idaho and Oregon. She is the author of the mixed-genre collection *The Beadworkers: Stories* and the scholarly text *Domestic Subjects: Gender, Citizenship, and Law in Native American Literature*, as well as numerous stories, poems, plays, and critical essays in journals and anthologies. She is devoted to Nez Perce language and literature and Indigenous language revitalization more broadly and is a founding member of luk'upsíimey/North Star Collective.

Vivian Faith Prescott (pp. 38 and 361) was born and raised in Ḵaachx̱aana.áak'w, Wrangell in Tlingit áani, Southeast Alaska. She lives and writes at her family's fish camp next to Ḵeishangita.aan, the old Red Alder Head Village. Prescott is adopted into her children's clan, T'akdeinaan, Snail House, and she's a member of the Pacific Sámi Searvi. She's the author of nine books. Along with her daughter, Vivian Mork Yéilk', she writes a column for the *Juneau Empire* titled Planet Alaska.

Born Lhaq'temish, **Rena Priest** (p. 40) was raised on the Lummi reservation in the heart of her ancestral homelands, in a house that looked across the bay toward the town of Bellingham, Washington, and the rolling green foothills of the great, shining volcano Kwelshan. She is the author of two collections of poetry with several uncollected poems and articles appearing in literary journals, magazines, and anthologies. She is the incumbent poet laureate of Washington State. She holds an MFA from Sarah Lawrence College.

Robert Michael Pyle (p. 250) studies natural history and writes from an overgrown farmstead on the Lower Columbia. His twenty-five books include the poetry collections *Evolution of the Genus Iris*, *Chinook & Chanterelle*, and *The Tidewater Reach*; *Nature Matrix*, a 2021 finalist for the PEN America Award in the Art of the Essay; the novel *Magdalena Mountain*; and *Butterflies of Cascadia*. *Where Bigfoot Walks*, adapted for the film *The Dark Divide*, is a Cascadian classic.

Born in Cowichan Territory and raised in K'ómoks Territory on present-day Vancouver Island, **Matt Rader** (pp. 129 and 220) now lives with his family on unceded Syilx Territory in the Okanagan Valley. The author of several collections of poetry, stories, and nonfiction, he teaches creative writing at UBC Okanagan.

Laura Read (p. 291) is the author of *But She is Also Jane*, *Dresses from the Old Country*, *Instructions for My Mother's Funeral*, and *The Chewbacca on Hollywood Boulevard Reminds Me of You*. She served as poet laureate for Spokane, Washington, from 2015 to 2017 and teaches at Spokane Falls Community College and Eastern Washington University.

Lois Red Elk (p. 144) is an enrolled member of the Fort Peck Sioux. She is the author of *Why I Return to Makoce*, *Dragonfly Weather*, and *Our Blood Remembers*, which received the Best Nonfiction Award from the Wordcraft Circle of Native Writers and Storytellers. Red Elk has previously worked as an actor and technical adviser for numerous Hollywood film productions. She teaches cultural courses and traditional language classes at Fort Peck Community College in Montana.

Paisley Rekdal (p. 150) is the author of four books of nonfiction and six books of poetry, including *Nightingale* and *Appropriate: A Provocation*. Her work has received the Amy Lowell Poetry Traveling Fellowship, a Guggenheim fellowship, an NEA fellowship, Pushcart Prizes, a Fulbright fellowship, and various state arts council awards. Raised in Seattle, she teaches at the University of Utah and was Utah's poet laureate from 2017 to 2022.

Al Rempel's (p. 237) books of poetry are *Undiscovered Country*, *This Isn't the Apocalypse We Hoped For*, *Understories*, and three chapbooks: *Deerness*, *Four Neat Holes*, and *The Picket Fence Diaries*. *Deerness* records a reconnection to Rempel's place along with the wildlife that cut through Buckhorn, a rural community in central British Columbia. His poems have also appeared in various journals and anthologies. His videopoem collaborations have been screened internationally.

Anastacia-Reneé (she/they, p. 342) is a writer, educator, interdisciplinary artist, TEDx speaker, and podcaster. She is the author of *(v.)*, *Forget It*, and *Side Notes from the Archivist*. Recently she was selected by NBC News as part of the list of "Queer Artists of Color Dominate 2021's Must-See LGBTQ Art Shows." Anastacia-Reneé was former Seattle civic poet (2017–2019), Hugo House poet in residence (2015–2017), and Arc Artist fellow (2020). Her work has been anthologized in *Home Is Where You Queer Your Heart*; *Furious Flower: Seeding the Future of African American Poetry*; *Afrofuturism, Black Comics, and Superhero Poetry*; *Spirited Stone: Lessons from Kubota's Garden*; and *Seismic: Seattle City of Literature*. Anastacia-Reneé has received fellowships and residencies from Cave Canem, Hedgebrook, VONA, Ragdale, Mineral School, and the New Orleans Writers Residency.

On traditional Umatilla and Cayuse homelands, **Katrina Roberts** (p. 356) tends to vines, cloudberries, beargrass, and fairybells on a small horse farm situated between Yellowhawk and Caldwell Creeks. She's published four books and a chapbook of poems, and edited an anthology. *Likeness*, a book of full-color, visual poems, is published by Finishing Line Press.

When not writing or drawing, she teaches and curates the Visiting Writers Reading Series at Whitman College and co-runs Walla Walla Distilling Company.

Deeply influential American poet **Theodore Roethke** (1908–1963, pp. 51 and 124) was the recipient of a Pulitzer Prize and two National Book Awards for poetry. Born and raised in Michigan, he taught poetry at the University of Washington for fifteen years.

Born and raised in Portland and with long stays in Corvallis and McMinnville, **Lex Runciman** (p. 308) has always felt Oregon's Willamette Valley his home. He studied with Madeline DeFrees and Richard Hugo. In 1989, his second book, *The Admirations*, won the Oregon Book Award in poetry. His sixth volume, *Salt Moons: Poems 1981–2016*, was published by Salmon Poetry (Ireland) in 2017. He is father of two and grandfather of four. In 2021, he and his wife celebrated fifty years together. He lives now within easy walking distance of Oaks Bottom Wildlife Refuge, in Portland.

Eva Saulitis (1963–2016, p. 24) was a poet and marine biologist who lived in Alaska and studied orcas. Dissatisfied with the objective language and rigid methodology of science, she later turned to creative writing—poetry and the essay—to develop another language with which to address the natural world. Her published books include the poetry collections *Many Ways to Say It*, *Prayer in Wind*, and *Into Great Silence: A Memoir of Discovery and Loss among Vanishing Orcas*.

Born in the United Kingdom, poet **Robert Service** (1874–1958, p. 270) is best known for his work about the Yukon, informed by his time in Canada. He is the author of a number of books of poetry, autobiographies, and novels.

Prageeta Sharma's (p. 227) recent poetry collection is *Grief Sequence*. She is the founder of Thinking Its Presence, an interdisciplinary conference on race, creative writing, and artistic and aesthetic practices. A recipient of the 2010 Howard Foundation Award and a finalist for the 2020 Four Quartets Prize, she taught at the University of Montana and now teaches at Pomona College.

Sandy Shreve (p. 168) has written, edited, or coedited eight books of poetry and two chapbooks. Her poetry has won or been shortlisted for several awards and is widely anthologized. Shreve founded British Columbia's Poetry in Transit program, was one of the organizers of the first Mayworks festivals in Vancouver, and has served on the West Coast Book Prize Society. She now lives on British Columbia's beautiful S,DÁYES (Pender Island), the unceded traditional territory of the W̱SÁNEĆ peoples.

Martha Silano (p. 189) grew up in suburban New Jersey. In 1981, she spent her first night in Cascadia sleeping under heavy cloud cover at the Oregon Dunes National Recreation Area. Soon after, Silano made Cascadia her permanent home. Her writing includes five collections of poetry, a coedited book of 365 poetry writing prompts, and many reviews and essays. She received her MFA from the University of Washington and lives near Seattle's Seward Park.

Born in Vancouver, **Bren Simmers** (p. 119) spent most of her life living in coastal British Columbia before moving to Prince Edward Island. She is the author of four books, including the wilderness memoir *Pivot Point* and *Hastings-Sunrise*, which was a finalist for the Vancouver Book Award. Her most recent collection of poetry, *If, When*, explores the braided economic and environmental history of Howe Sound, British Columbia.

Sherry Simpson (1960–2020, p. 122), considered one of Alaska's most accomplished essayists, was the author of *The Way Winter Comes: Alaska Stories*, winner of the Chinook Literary

Prize; *The Accidental Explorer: Wayfinding in Alaska*; and *Dominion of Bears: Living with Wildlife in Alaska*, which won the John Burroughs Medal. Born and raised in Juneau, she taught in the Creative Writing and Literary Arts Department at the University of Alaska–Anchorage.

Nancy Slavin (p. 32) lived and worked on the north Oregon coast with her spouse and their daughter for more than two decades, until they all up and moved south of Portland. She's published a novel, *Moorings*, and a poetry collection, *Oregon Pacific*, as well as numerous other writings. She believes storytelling leads to understanding, action, and collective liberation—releasing, spreading, and seeding like fireweed in the most disturbed of grounds.

Kathryn Smith (p. 161) is the author of *Self-Portrait with Cephalopod*, winner of the 2019 Jake Adam York Prize, as well as the collection *Book of Exodus* and the chapbook *Chosen Companions of the Goblin*, winner of the 2018 Open Country Press Chapbook Contest. Born and raised on Washington's Olympic Peninsula, she now lives in Spokane where she makes poems and visual art.

Pulitzer Prize of Poetry and American Book Award winner **Gary Snyder** (p. 219) is a poet, essayist, and lecturer from California. His works include *Turtle Island*, *The Practice of the Wild*, and *Danger on Peaks*, among many others.

Kim Stafford (p. 283) directs the Northwest Writing Institute at Lewis & Clark College and is the author of a dozen books, including *Singer Come from Afar*. He has taught writing in Scotland, Mexico, Italy, and Bhutan. In May 2018, he was named Oregon's ninth poet laureate by Governor Kate Brown for a two-year term.

Poet **William Stafford** (1914–1993, p. 300) was born in Kansas and published many books of poetry and prose, including *West of Your City* and *Traveling through the Dark*, which won the National Book Award for Poetry. In 1958, he settled as faculty at Lewis & Clark College. In 1970, he was named consultant in poetry to the Library of Congress, a position that is now known as poet laureate. From 1975 to 1980, he was poet laureate of Oregon.

Dao Strom (p. 131) is a poet, artist, and songwriter of five books and two song cycles, most recently the poetry collection *Instrument* and its companion album, *Traveler's Ode*. She was born in Vietnam and grew up in the Sierra Nevada of California. Her first Cascadia home was on the southern Oregon coast, on the traditional lands of the Coquille. She now lives in Portland, Oregon.

Rob Taylor (p. 214) is the author of four poetry collections, most recently *Strangers*. He is also the editor of *What the Poets Are Doing: Canadian Poets in Conversation* and the guest editor of *Best Canadian Poetry 2019*. Rob teaches creative writing at Simon Fraser University and lives with his family at the easternmost point of Burrard Inlet (Port Moody, British Columbia) on the unceded territories of the Kwikwetlem, Musqueam, Squamish, and Tsleil-waututh peoples.

Alexandra Teague (p. 281) is the author of three poetry books—*Or What We'll Call Desire*, *The Wise and Foolish Builders*, and *Mortal Geography*—and the novel *The Principles behind Flotation*. She's also the coeditor of *Bullets into Bells: Poets & Citizens Respond to Gun Violence*. Raised in the Arkansas Ozarks, Alexandra now loves living, and frequently hiking, in the Pacific Northwest. For the past decade, she's lived in Moscow, Idaho, where she's a creative writing professor.

Pepper Trail (p. 89) has lived in Ashland, Oregon, at the intersection of the Cascade Range and Siskiyou Mountains, for over twenty-five years. A professional ornithologist, Trail is a frequent contributor of writing on regional environmental issues to Jefferson Public Radio and *High Country News* and was active in the creation and defense of the Cascade-Siskiyou National Monument. His collection of poems about the monument, *Cascade-Siskiyou*, was a finalist for the Oregon Book Award in Poetry.

Born in England, poet and novelist **Peter Trower** (1930–2017, p. 304) moved to Canada at age ten. His works include *Between the Sky and the Splinters*, *The Alders and Others*, and *Grogan's Cafe*, among others. In 1976, Trower was the subject of a CBC documentary titled *Between the Sky and the Splinters*, after his 1974 book of poetry of the same name.

Lena Khalaf Tuffaha (p. 114) is a poet, essayist, and translator. Her first book of poems, *Water & Salt*, won the 2018 Washington State Book Award. She is also the author of two chapbooks, *Arab in Newsland*, winner of the 2016 Two Sylvias Prize, and *Letters from the Interior*, finalist for the 2020 Jean Pedrick Award.

Born and raised in western Washington, **Jeremy Voigt** (p. 74) has always lived surrounded by green trees, low hills, and a large body of water. He currently lives near the ten-mile-long Lake Whatcom in Bellingham, Washington. His poems have appeared in *Terrain.org*, *Prairie Schooner*, *Gulf Coast*, and other magazines. He was runner-up for the 2019 Discovery Poetry Prize, and his manuscript has been a semifinalist or finalist for multiple prizes.

Winner of two Pushcart Prizes, two-time National Book Award nominee, and recipient of an Academy of Arts and Letters Award, **David Wagoner** (1926–2021, p. 111) was the author of ten novels and numerous books of poetry. His works include *Dry Sun, Dry Wind*; *After the Point of No Return*; and *The Hanging Garden*.

Emily Wall (p. 95) is a professor of English at the University of Alaska. She holds an MFA in poetry, and her poems have been published in journals across the US and Canada, most recently in *Prairie Schooner* and *Alaska Quarterly Review*. She has been nominated for multiple Pushcart Prizes and her most recent book, *Flame*, won the Minerva Rising chapbook prize. She is the author of three poetry collections, *Liveaboard*, *Freshly Rooted*, and *Breaking Into Air: Birth Poems*. Emily lives and writes in Douglas, Alaska.

Katharine Whitcomb (p. 174) lives in Ellensburg, Washington, a high plains desert town on the eastern slopes of the Cascade Range. Her family has lived in Washington on and off for three generations. She is the author of four collections of poems, including *The Daughter's Almanac*, chosen by Patricia Smith as the winner of the Backwaters Press Prize. She has had work published in *The Paris Review*, *Bennington Review*, *Poetry Northwest*, *Narrative*, *Kenyon Review*, and many other journals and anthologies.

Joe Wilkins (p. 275) is the author of a novel, *Fall Back Down When I Die*; a memoir, *The Mountain and the Fathers*; and four poetry collections, including *Thieve* and *When We Were Birds*. His awards and honors include the Oregon Book Award, the High Plains Book Award, and a Pushcart Prize. Born and raised on the Big Dry of eastern Montana, he lives with his family in the Yamhill Valley of western Oregon.

Corrie Williamson (p. 239) made her way to the Cascadia region in 2013 when she moved to Montana. She is the author of two books of poems, *The River Where You Forgot My Name*, a finalist for the 2019 Montana Book Award, and *Sweet Husk*. She was the recipient of the PEN Northwest/Boyden Wilderness Writing Residency and spent seven and a half months of 2020 in a remote, off-grid cabin in Oregon's Wild Rogue Wilderness. She works in conservation and is happiest where the bears roam and the grouse drum.

John Willson (p. 55) feels most at home in the two settings where his poem "Morning" unfolds: an island in Puget Sound and a spot in the northeast Olympic mountains. Counting Gary Snyder and Theodore Roethke as primary influences, Willson considers himself a poet of nature whose work reflects lyric and narrative modes. Willson is a Pushcart Prize recipient. His book, *Call This Room a Station*, was published by MoonPath Press in 2020.

Jane Wong (p. 230) is the author of *How to Not Be Afraid of Everything* and *Overpour*. A Kundiman fellow, she is the recipient of a Pushcart Prize and fellowships and residencies from the Woodberry Poetry Room, the US Fulbright Program, Artist Trust, the Fine Arts Work Center, Bread Loaf, Hedgebrook, Willapa Bay, the Jentel Foundation, Mineral School, and others. She is an associate professor at Western Washington University, which occupies the stolen lands of the Lummi and Nooksack peoples.

Robert Wrigley (p. 181, 257) was born in East St. Louis, Illinois, in 1951. He has lived in Montana, Washington, Oregon, and mostly Idaho, for the last forty-four years. He has published twelve books of poems, most recently *The True Account of Myself as a Bird*, and one collection of essays, *Nemerov's Door*. He lives in the woods a few miles north of Moscow, Idaho, with his wife, the writer Kim Barnes.

A poet, naturalist, and scientist, **Bill Yake** (p. 178) was born in the Spokane watershed, passed through the Flathead, Palouse, and Chehalis watersheds, and currently lives on the verge of Green Cove Creek—a salmon stream near Olympia, Washington. His most recent collection, *Way-Making by Moonlight*, gathers poems from fifty years of attention to the wild. These poems have appeared widely in publications serving environmental and literary communities—including *Orion*, *Rattle*, *Cascadia Review*, and NPR's *Krulwich's Wonders*.

A first-generation Hong Kong–Canadian, **Isaac Yuen**'s (p. 96) work has been published in *Gulf Coast*, *Shenandoah*, *Orion*, *The Willowherb Review*, and other publications. A 2019 nature writer in residence at the Jan Michalski Foundation for Literature in Switzerland, he grew up in Vancouver, British Columbia, on the unceded traditional territories of the Coast Salish people.

Maya Jewell Zeller (p. 62) was born in the walk-up apartment above her parents' gas station on the Oregon coast, near Neahkahnie Mountain. Author of the interdisciplinary collaboration (with visual artist Carrie DeBacker) *Alchemy for Cells & Other Beasts*; the chapbook *Yesterday, the Bees*; and the poetry collection *Rust Fish*; she has received honors from the Sustainable Arts Foundation and the H. J. Andrews Experimental Forest for her work.

Jan Zwicky (p. 72) is the author of over twenty books of poetry and prose including *Songs for Relinquishing the Earth*, *The Long Walk*, and most recently, *The Experience of Meaning*. Zwicky grew up in the northwest corner of the Great Central Plains on Treaty 6 territory, was educated at the Universities of Calgary and Toronto, and currently lives in a coastal rainforest succession on Canada's west coast, on unceded territory with a complex history including Coast Salish and Kwakwaka'wakw influences.

Resources

If you'd like to learn more, here are some wonderful resources. We've curated these lists with a mind toward creating a foundational library for your engagements with Cascadia. In each case, these lists only scratch the surface—we invite you to dig deeper.

FIELD GUIDES

A good field guide is invaluable. Maybe it comes with you in your pack. Maybe it stays home on your shelf. But beyond the satisfaction of identification, a field guide helps you focus as you listen, smell, look, and take time to consider what's before you.

The National Audubon Society and Peterson both have guides for birds, trees, mushrooms, butterflies, shells, stars, invertebrates, tracks and sign, and much more; they're all great. In addition to the books listed below, which are particular favorites of the editors, there are many apps you can download to your phone that are wonderful field guides, such as PeakFinder, Merlin Bird ID, iBird Pro Guide to Birds, PlantSnap, Wildflower Search, Sky Guide, and iNaturalist.

Alden, Peter, and Dennis Paulson. *National Audubon Society Field Guide to the Pacific Northwest*. New York: Knopf, 1998. Audubon does a great job of assembling general-interest books for various regions of North America, and if you want a one-book starter kit with plants, animals, and more, this is the resource to have.

Arno, Stephen F., and Ramona P. Hammerly. *Northwest Trees: Identifying and Understanding the Region's Native Trees*. Anniversary edition. Seattle, WA: Mountaineers Books, 2010.

Haggard, Peter, and Judy Haggard. *Insects of the Pacific Northwest*. Portland, OR: Timber Press, 2006.

Keator, Glenn. *Pacific Coast Berry Finder*. Rochester, NY: Nature Study Guild, 1978. This is one guide in an excellent series of hand-sized guides that also has books for fish, ferns, trees, intertidal life, and more.

Mathews, Daniel. *Cascadia Revealed: A Guide to the Plants, Animals, and Geology of the Pacific Northwest Mountains*. Portland, OR: Timber Press, 2021.

Parish, Roberta, et al. *Plants of Southern Interior British Columbia and the Inland Northwest*. Tukwila, WA: Lone Pine Publishing, 2018.

Pojar, Jim, and Andy MacKinnon. *Plants of the Pacific Northwest Coast*. Partners Publishing, 2004.

Walsh, Willow. *Pacific Northwest Edible Plant Foraging: Beginner Foraging Field Guide for Finding, Identifying, Harvesting, and Preparing Edible Wild Food*. Independently published, 2022.

Whitney, Stephen R. and Rob Sandelin. *Field Guide to the Cascades & Olympics*, 2nd ed. Seattle: Mountaineers Books, 2003.

FIRST PEOPLE AND TRADITIONAL ECOLOGICAL KNOWLEDGE

In addition to the books and websites listed below, we recommend exploring the following Indigenous cultural centers: the Jilkaat Kwaan Cultural Heritage Center in Haines, Alaska; U'mista Cultural Centre in Alert Bay, British Columbia; En'owkin Centre in Penticton, British Columbia; Daybreak Star Indian Cultural Center in Seattle, Washington; Tamástslikt Cultural Institute in Pendleton, Oregon; and the Sacajawea Interpretive, Cultural and Educational Center in Salmon, Idaho.

Bohan, Heidi. *The People of Cascadia: Pacific Northwest Native American History*. Independently published, 2018.

Bringhurst, Robert. *A Story as Sharp as a Knife: The Classical Haida Mythtellers and Their World*. Vancouver, BC: Douglas & McIntyre, 2007.

Clark, Ella. *Indian Legends of the Pacific Northwest*. Berkeley: University of California Press, 1953.

Dauenhauer, Nora Marks, and Richard Dauenhauer, eds. *Haa Shuká, Our Ancestors: Tlingit Oral Narratives (Classics of Tlingit Oral Literature)*. Seattle: University of Washington Press, 1987.

Kimmerer, Robin Wall. *Braiding Sweetgrass: Indigenous Wisdom, Scientific Knowledge and the Teachings of Plants*. Minneapolis: Milkweed Editions, 2015.

Native Land Digital, https://native-land.ca.

X̱wi7x̱wa Library, University of British Columbia, https://xwi7xwa.library.ubc.ca.

Younging, Gregory. *Elements of Indigenous Style: A Guide to Writing By and About Indigenous Peoples*. Edmonton, Alberta: Brush Education, 2018.

GENERAL INTEREST NONFICTION

Many books have inspired us over the years, including *all* the books by the writers included in these pages, and we hope you'll seek out their writing. The short list below is particularly resonant for us.

Arno, Stephen, and Carl Fiedler. *Douglas Fir: The Story of the West's Most Remarkable Tree*. Seattle, WA: Mountaineers Books, 2020.

Graves, John. *Goodbye to a River*. New York: Alfred A. Knopf, 1969.

Gumbs, Alexis Pauline. *Undrowned: Black Feminist Lessons from Marine Mammals*. Chico: AK Press, 2020.

Haskell, David George. *The Forest Unseen: A Year's Watch in Nature*. New York: Penguin Books, 2013.

Hogan, Linda. *Dwellings: Reflections on the Natural World*. New York: W. W. Norton, 1995.

LaDuke, Winona. *Recovering the Sacred: The Power of Naming and Claiming*. Chicago: Haymarket Books, 2016.

Lanham, J. Drew. *The Home Place: Memoirs of a Colored Man's Love Affair with Nature*. Minneapolis: Milkweed Editions, 2017.

Lopez, Barry, and Debra Gwartney. *Home Ground: Language for an American Landscape*. San Antonio, TX: Trinity University Press, 2006.

Shepard, Nan. *The Living Mountain*. Edinburgh: Canongate Books, 1977.

Sibley, David Allen. *What It's Like to Be a Bird*. New York: Alfred A. Knopf, 2020.

Simard, Suzanne. *Finding the Mother Tree: Discovering the Wisdom of the Forest*. New York: Alfred A. Knopf, 2021.

Snyder, Gary. *The Practice of the Wild*. Berkeley, CA: Counterpoint, 2020.

Spagna, Ana Maria. *Reclaimers*. Seattle: University of Washington Press, 2015.

ORGANIZATIONS FOR CONSERVATION AND EDUCATION IN CASCADIA AND BEYOND

There is an abundance of riches when it comes to public lands, conservation organizations, and cultural centers in Cascadia. We hope this list inspires you to explore locally.

» Cascadia: Department of Bioregion, www.cascadiabioregion.org

» Cascadia Institute, www.cascadia-institute.org

» Ecological education and conservation centers such as the Pacific Wildlife Research Centre, Sightline Institute, North Cascades Institute, Pacific

Education Institute, the McCall Outdoor Science School, and Montana Outdoor Science School
» Hunting and fishing organizations that advocate for wild spaces and biodiversity, such as Ducks Unlimited and Backcountry Hunters and Anglers
» Land trust organizations or organizations that help the formation of local land trusts or enable and educate people to establish land trusts, such as the Northwest Community Land Trust Coalition, the Land Trust Alliance of British Columbia, and the Land Conservancy of British Columbia
» Literary and arts festivals or organizations such as 49 Writers, the Vancouver Writers Fest, the Victoria Festival of Authors, the Fraser Valley Literary Festival, the Skagit River Poetry Festival, Centrum, Get Lit!, Fishtrap, the Portland Book Festival, the Elk River Writers Workshop, the Freeflow Institute, the Beargrass Writing Retreat, and LiTFUSE
» Long-term ecological research stations and organizations, such as the Spring Creek Project in Corvallis, Oregon, and the H. J. Andrews Experimental Forest in Blue River, Oregon
» Museums with significant natural history and Indigenous culture resources such as the Alaska State Museum, Tamástslikt Cultural Institute, Museum of Anthropology at the University of British Columbia, the Royal BC Museum, the Burke Museum, the High Desert Museum, and the Nez Perce National Historical Park
» Regional Native Plant Societies such as British Columbia Native Plant Society, Native Plant Society of Oregon, and Washington Native Plant Society
» Regional and national parks, monuments, and conservation lands

FOR EDUCATORS

Several educational organizations have reached out to us about using *Cascadia* in their classes. Resources for teachers to use both in classrooms and in the field can be found on our website: www.cascadiaguide.com.

REFERENCES

In addition to many US Forest Service and National Park Service websites, the following books, articles, and websites informed our research.

"Animal Facts." NatureMapping Foundation. Accessed February 28, 2022. http://naturemappingfoundation.org/natmap/facts.

Arno, Stephen F., and Ramona P. Hammerly. *Northwest Trees: Identifying and Understanding the Region's Native Trees.* Anniversary edition. Seattle, WA: Mountaineers Books, 2010.

Blackstock, Michael D., and Rhonda McAllister. "First Nations Perspectives on the Grasslands of the Interior of British Columbia." *Journal of Ecological Anthropology* 8, no. 1 (2004): 24–46.

Bohan, Heidi. *The People of Cascadia: Pacific Northwest Native American History.* Independently published, 2018.

Bringhurst, Robert. *A Story as Sharp as a Knife: The Classical Haida Mythtellers and Their World.* Vancouver, BC: Douglas & McIntyre, 2007.

BugGuide. Accessed March 3, 2022. https://bugguide.net.

Cascadia: Department of Bioregion. Accessed January 13, 2022. https://cascadiabioregion.org.

Cascadia Institute. Accessed March 30, 2022. http://www.cascadia-institute .org/index.html.

Clark, Ella. *Indian Legends of the Pacific Northwest.* Berkeley: University of California Press, 1953.

Cornell Lab of Ornithology. "All About Birds." Accessed March 31, 2022. https://www.allaboutbirds.org.

Dauenhauer, Nora Marks, and Richard Dauenhauer, eds. *Haa Shuká, Our Ancestors: Tlingit Oral Narratives (Classics of Tlingit Oral Literature).* Seattle: University of Washington Press, 1987.

Dawe, Charlotte. "South Okanagan-Similkameen National Park Reserve." Wilderness Committee, March 14, 2019. Accessed March 19, 2022. https://www.wildernesscommittee.org/publications/south-Okanagan -similkameen-national-park-reserve.

Earle, Christopher J., ed. "The Gymnosperm Database." Last modified December 21, 2021. Accessed March 30, 2022. https://www.conifers.org.

Faust, Joan Lee. "In the Garden; Nature's Best Recyclers: The Earthworms." *New York Times,* January 30, 2000. Accessed April 1, 2022. https://www .nytimes.com/2000/01/30/nyregion/in-the-garden-nature-s-best -recyclers-the-earthworms.html.

Fire Effects Information System. Last modified February 10, 2022. https://www.feis-crs.org/feis.

Fryer, Janet L. 2002. *"Pinus albicaulis."* Fire Effects Information System, US Department of Agriculture, Forest Service, Rocky Mountain Research Station, Fire Sciences Laboratory (Producer). Accessed February 2, 2022. https://www.fs.fed.us/database/feis/plants/tree/pinalb/all.html.

Goldberg, Caren S., David S. Pilliod, Robert S. Arkle, and Lisette P. Waits. "Molecular Detection of Vertebrates in Stream Water: A Demonstration Using Rocky Mountain Tailed Frogs and Idaho Giant Salamanders." *PloS One* 6, no. 7 (2011): e22746, https://doi.org/10.1371/journal .pone.0022746.

Haggard, Peter, and Judy Haggard. *Insects of the Pacific Northwest.* Portland, OR: Timber Press, 2006.

Harrington, H. D. *Edible Native Plants of the Rocky Mountains.* Albuquerque: University of New Mexico Press, 1974.

Hibben, T. N. *Dictionary of the Chinook Jargon or Indian Trade Language of the North Pacific Coast.* Victoria, BC: T. N. Hibben, 1889.

Hopkins, Gerard Manley. "Pied Beauty." Poetry Foundation. Accessed March 31, 2022. https://www.poetryfoundation.org/poems/44399/pied-beauty.

Kimmerer, Robin Wall. *Braiding Sweetgrass: Indigenous Wisdom, Scientific Knowledge and the Teachings of Plants.* Minneapolis: Milkweed Editions, 2015.

———. "'The 'Honorable Harvest': Lessons From an Indigenous Tradition of Giving Thanks." *Yes!*, November 26, 2015. Accessed March 30, 2022. https://www.yesmagazine.org/issue/good-health/2015/11/26/the -honorable-harvest-lessons-from-an-indigenous-tradition-of -giving-thanks.

Kovalik, Peter. "AOU-NACC Proposals 2022." Birdforum, November 12, 2021. Accessed March 31, 2022. https://www.birdforum.net/threads /aou-nacc-proposals-2022.416334.

Kozloff, Eugene. *Seashore Life of the Northern Pacific Coast: An Illustrated Guide to Northern California, Oregon, Washington, and British Columbia.* Seattle: University of Washington Press, 1983.

Maclean, Norman. *A River Runs Through It.* Chicago: University of Chicago Press, 2001.

Mathews, Daniel. *Cascadia Revealed: A Guide to the Plants, Animals, and Geology of the Pacific Northwest Mountains.* Portland, OR: Timber Press, 2021.

McCune, Bruce. *Macrolichens of the Pacific Northwest.* Corvallis: Oregon State University Press, 2009.

McKee, Bates. *Cascadia: The Geologic Evolution of the Pacific Northwest.* New York: McGraw Hill, 1972.

McNulty, Tim. *A Natural History Guide: Olympic National Park.* Boston: Houghton Mifflin, 1996.

Moskowitz, David. *Wildlife of the Pacific Northwest.* Portland, OR: Timber Press, 2010.

National Audubon Society. *National Audubon Society Field Guide to North American Wildflowers*. New York: Alfred A. Knopf, 2004.

———. *The Audubon Society Field Guide to North American Trees*. New York: Alfred A. Knopf, 1980.

Native Land Digital. Accessed March 3, 2022. https://native-land.ca.

NatureServe Explorer. 2022. https://explorer.natureserve.org.

One Biota Network. "Ilah and the Giants: Idaho Giant Salamander for State Amphibian." January 1, 2015. Video, 4:04. Accessed February 2, 2022. https://www.youtube.com/watch?v=q7Zg9-fwohk.

Parish, Roberta, et al. *Plants of Southern Interior British Columbia and the Inland Northwest*. Tukwila, WA: Lone Pine Publishing, 2018.

Peattie, David Culross. *A Natural History of Western Trees*. Boston: Houghton Mifflin, 1991.

Petersen, Joseph R., Jonathan J. Scordino, Cole I. Svec, Reginald H. Buttram, Maria R. Gonzalez, and Joe Scordino. "Use of the Traditional Halibut Hook of the Makah Tribe, the čibu.d, Reduces Bycatch in Recreational Halibut Fisheries." *PeerJ* (2020). https://doi.org/10.7717/peerj.9288.

Pojar, Jim, and Andy MacKinnon, eds. *Plants of the Pacific Northwest Coast*. Partners Publishing, 2004.

Pyle, Robert Michael. *The Butterflies of Cascadia*. Seattle: Seattle Audubon Society, 2007.

Rabkin, Richard, and Jacob Rabkin. *Nature in the West: A Handbook of Habitats*. New York: Holt, Rinehart and Winston, 1981.

Ream, Joshua T. "Traditional Tlingit Relationships with Native Alaska Fauna." PhD diss., University of Alaska Fairbanks, 2013.

Scheuerman, Ricard D., ed. *The Wenatchi Indians: Guardians of the Valley*. Fairfield, WA: Ye Galleon Press, 1982.

Seafood Watch. Accessed March 31, 2022. https://www.seafoodwatch.info.

Sibley, David Allen. *What It's Like to Be a Bird*. New York: Alfred A. Knopf, 2020.

Sightline Institute. Accessed February 3, 2022. https://www.sightline.org.

Taylor, Ronald. *Sagebrush Country: A Wildflower Sanctuary*. Missoula, MT: Mountain Press, 1992.

Thomas, Dylan. *A Child's Christmas in Wales*. Norfolk, CT: New Directions, 1954.

Trotter, Patrick. *Cutthroat: Native Trout of the West*. 2nd edition. Berkeley: University of California Press, 2008.

Turner, Nancy. *Ancient Pathways, Ancestral Knowledge: Ethnobotany and Ecological Wisdom of Indigenous Peoples of Northwestern North America*. Montreal: McGill-Queen's Press, 2014.

University of Alaska Museum of the North. "Devil's Club: Tlingit Traditions of Helen Watkins." April 1, 2016, video, 21:53. Accessed March 31, 2022. https://www.youtube.com/watch?v=DyUssKc2TLQ.

Watchable Wildlife. Accessed March 3, 2022. https://watchablewildlife foundation.org.

Whitney, Stephen. *Western Forests*. New York: Alfred A. Knopf, 1994.

Wikipedia, s.v. "Spotted Ratfish." Last modified November 12, 2021. https://en.wikipedia.org/wiki/Spotted_ratfish.

Wustner, Marie. "Knowledge Keepers: A MOA Original Documentary Series." Museum of Anthropology, University of British Columbia, July 7, 2020. Accessed March 31, 2022. https://moa.ubc.ca/2020/07 /knowledge-keepers-a-moa-original-video-series.

X̲wi7x̲wa Library, University of British Columbia. Accessed March 3, 2022. https://xwi7xwa.library.ubc.ca.

Younging, Gregory. *Elements of Indigenous Style: A Guide to Writing By and About Indigenous Peoples*. Edmonton, Alberta: Brush Education, 2018.

Permissions

Every effort was made to reach the copyright holders of the works included in *Cascadia Field Guide* and many of the contributing poets, writers, and artists graciously provided permission to us. Additional permissions were provided to reprint the following works:

Sherman Alexie, "Migration," from *One Stick Song*, Hanging Loose Press, 2000, reprinted with permission of the publisher.

Linda Bierds, "Afterimage," from *The Profile Makers*, Henry Holt & Co, 1997, reprinted with permission.

Yvonne Blomer's "Spotted Owl as Desire" previously appears in *Ravine, Mouse a Bird's Beak*, alongside paintings by Robert Bateman, Nose in Book Publishing, 2018 and subsequently in *The Last Show on Earth*, Caitlin Press, 2022, reprinted with permission.

Elizabeth Bradfield, "Deliquescence," from *Once Removed*, Copyright © 2015 by Elizabeth Bradfield. Reprinted with the permission of Persea Books, Inc (New York), www.perseabooks.com.song

Elizabeth Bradfield, "Succession" from *Interpretive Work*. Copyright © 2008 by Elizabeth Bradfield. Reprinted with the permission of The Permissions Company, LLC on behalf of Arktoi Books, an imprint of Red Hen Press, redhen.org.

Robert Bringhurst, "Song of the Summit" from *Selected Poems*. Copyright © 1982 by Robert Bringhurst. Reprinted with permission of The Permissions Company, LLC on behalf of Copper Canyon Press, www.coppercanyonpress.org.

"Eagles" from *ALL OF US: THE COLLECTED POEMS* by Raymond Carver, copyright © 1996 Tess Gallagher. Used by permission of Alfred A. Knopf, an imprint of the Knopf Doubleday Publishing Group, a division of Penguin Random House LLC. All rights reserved.

Kevin Craft, "Pigeon Guillemots," from *Vagrants and Accidentals* (University of Washington Press, 2017) reprinted with permission.

John Daniel, "To Mt. St. Helens," from *Of Earth*, copyright © 2012, reprinted with permission of Lost Horse Press.

Greg Darms, "In the Last Oak Meadows," appears in *Flammable, Inflammable: Poems, 1991-2006*, Radiolarian Press, 2007, reprinted with permission.

Nora Marks Dauenhauer, "How to Make Good Salmon from the River," from *The Droning Shaman*, The Black Current Press, 1988, reprinted with permission.

Nora Marks Dauenhauer, "Repatriation" previously published in "Alaska Quarterly Review," 2007, reprinted with permission.

Beings Index

About The Editors

Photo: Lisa Sette

Elizabeth Bradfield grew up in Tacoma, Washington, and holds degrees from the University of Washington (undergraduate) and the University of Alaska (MFA). Her years on the Salish Sea and in Southeast Alaska formed her. She is the author of the poetry collections *Once Removed*, *Approaching Ice*, *Interpretive Work*, *Toward Antarctica*, and *Theorem*, a collaboration with artist Antonia Contro. With Miller Oberman and Alexandra Teague, she coedited *Broadsided Press: Celebrating Fifteen Years of Poetic and Artistic Collaboration, 2005–2020*. Her poems have been published in the *New Yorker*, *Atlantic Monthly*, and *Orion*, and her essays have appeared in *National Parks Conservation Magazine* and several anthologies. Bradfield's honors include the Audre Lorde Prize and a Stegner fellowship. She runs Broadsided Press, a monthly publication of original collaborations between writers and artists; works as a naturalist; and teaches creative writing at Brandeis University. Her website is ebradfield.com.

Photo: Mel Ota

CMarie Fuhrman was born and grew up in the shadow of the Rocky Mountains of Colorado. She was introduced to wild places and beings by parents who grew off the land—hunting, fishing, gardening—and passed their knowledge on to their daughters. Fuhrman has lived in west-central Idaho since 2011 and the area, from the Frank Church Wilderness to the deep waters of the Salmon and Snake Rivers, has become more than home, more than character, but intrinsic to all that she is. With an undeniable understanding of the urgency that surrounds protecting these places, both wild and rural, Fuhrman works with organizations that defend beings such as Grizzly, rivers such as the South Fork of the Salmon, and the bodies of Native women—where destruction and erasure is mirrored in humans. Fuhrman is author of *Camped Beneath the Dam: Poems* and coeditor of *Native Voices*. Fuhrman has served as director of IKEEP (Indigenous Knowledge for Effective Education Program) at the University of Idaho and is the Associate Director of the Graduate Program in Creative Writing at Western Colorado University, where she directs the poetry program and teaches nature writing. Fuhrman is a regular columnist for the *Inlander*, translations editor for *Broadsided Press*, and director of the Elk River Writers Workshop. Her website is CMarieFuhrman.com.

Photo: Heidi Swoboda

Derek Sheffield was born in the Willamette Valley of Oregon and grew up there and on the shores of the Salish Sea.

After spending eight years in Seattle and earning an MFA in poetry from the University of Washington, he lived briefly in Oregon's high desert before moving to central Washington, near Leavenworth. Since 2003, he has worked as a professor of English at Wenatchee Valley College, where, in partnership with biologist Dr. Dan Stephens, he teaches Northwest Nature Writing, a learning community that blends the study of field ecology and writing. Sheffield has presented at many conferences throughout Cascadia on the interaction between science and poetry. Thanks to support from the Spring Creek Project, he has been able to work alongside many devoted scientists and artists during field residencies at Loowit–Mount St. Helens and the H. J. Andrews Experimental Forest. His experience of Cascadia is also significantly defined by his identity as hiker, birder, fisher, forest bather, and father. He takes much delight in the fact that his daughters know many of their fellow beings and are often making their own poems and paintings when they aren't assembling twigs, leaves, and grasses into nests and boats for Fairies.

Author of the poetry collections *Through the Second Skin*, finalist for the Washington State Book Award, and *Not for Luck*, selected by Mark Doty for the Wheelbarrow Books Poetry Prize, and coeditor of *Dear America: Letters of Hope, Habitat, Defiance, and Democracy*, he serves as poetry editor of *Terrain.org*, the world's oldest online journal devoted to place-based art and literature. Visit him at dereksheffield.com.

MOUNTAINEERS BOOKS, including its two imprints, Skipstone and Braided River, is a leading publisher of quality outdoor recreation, sustainability, and conservation titles. As a 501(c)(3) nonprofit, we are committed to supporting the environmental and educational goals of our organization by providing expert information on human-powered adventure, sustainable practices at home and on the trail, and preservation of wilderness.

Our publications are made possible through the generosity of donors, and through sales of 700 titles on outdoor recreation, sustainable lifestyle, and conservation. To donate, purchase books, or learn more, visit us online:

MOUNTAINEERS BOOKS

1001 SW Klickitat Way, Suite 201 • Seattle, WA 98134

800-553-4453 • mbooks@mountaineersbooks.org • www.mountaineersbooks.org

An independent nonprofit publisher since 1960

YOU MAY ALSO LIKE

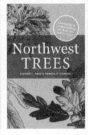